The Patriarch's Wife

DAME ANNE FILMER
Courtesy of James Filmer Wilson

SIR ROBERT FILMER
Courtesy of James Filmer Wilson

The Patriarch's Wife
Literary Evidence and the
History of the Family

M A R G A R E T   J.   M.   E Z E L L

The University of North Carolina Press

Chapel Hill and London

Copyright © 1987 The University of North Carolina Press

All rights reserved

Manufactured in the United States of America

Library of Congress Cataloging-in-Publication Data

Ezell, Margaret J. M.

The patriarch's wife.

Bibliography: p.

Includes index.

1. English literature—Women authors—History and
criticism. 2. English literature—17th century—History
and criticism. 3. Women—England—History—17th century.
4. Family—England—History—17th century. 5. England—
Intellectual life—17th century. 6. Women and literature
—England—History—17th century. I. Title.

PR113.E94   1987   820'.9'9287   86-20720

ISBN 0-8078-1741-4

The author is grateful for permission to reprint part of chapter 5,
which appeared as "Sir Robert Filmer and the English Patriarch," in
Seventeenth-Century News 42 (1984): 60–66.

Contents

Acknowledgments

The first acknowledgment must go to Peter Laslett, whose unfailing generosity and constant enthusiasm for this project kept it alive. His own pioneering research opened up this field for students and his critical readings enhanced my work beyond measure.

Furthermore, without the expertise and generous assistance of the following individuals this book would not have been possible. The late Peter Croft, Jane Irwin, Peter Davidson, Peter Beal, E. E. Duncan-Jones, Susanne Woods, Harrison Meserole, David Vieth, David Souden, David Latt, Suzanne Hull, Katherine O'Keeffe, Malcolm Richardson, John M. Ezell, and Wendy Motooka contributed time, information, and criticism. Joan Skinner, Bruce Filmer, James Filmer Wilson, and Lady Caroline Ogilvy very kindly let me in their homes to view family portraits and made available family genealogies. J. A. Brister assisted me in locating Mary More's painting at the Bodleian and Roy Strong offered advice concerning tracking down her other pictures.

The librarians and staff at numerous institutions made research for this project a pleasure rather than a burden. I am indebted to the following for permission to quote from manuscripts held by them and for general assistance: the Manuscript Division of the British Library; the Royal Society of London; the Friends' Library, London; Dr. Williams' Library, London; the Syndics of Cambridge University Library; Trinity College Library, Cambridge; the Trustees of the Duke of Portland and the Manuscripts Department of the University of Nottingham Library; the Guildhall, London; the Manuscripts Department of the Bodleian Library, Oxford; Christ Church College Library, Oxford; Merton College Library, Oxford; the Henry E. Huntington Library, San Marino, California; Kent County Archive Office, Maidstone; and the Harry Ransome Humanities Research Center, University of Texas.

I am also grateful to the following institutions for providing financial support for my research: the American Council of Learned Societies, Grant-in-Aid; the College of Liberal Arts, Texas A&M University Summer Research Grant and financial assistance for this book's production; and the South Central Modern Languages Association/Huntington Library Fellowship. Special thanks go to Daniel Fallon, College of Liberal Arts, Texas A&M University for his generous encouragement of this project.

Finally, this book is dedicated to my parents, John S. and Jean McLean Ezell. My father has provided a model of scholarly integrity for me to follow in addition to unswerving encouragement, and my mother, whose "Learning, Judgement, Sagacity, and Penetration" would be "very observable" in any age, read and criticized the early drafts; thus together they continued the tradition of parental support for "learned" daughters. I am deeply grateful to them.

The Patriarch's Wife

Introduction

The Queene was brought by water to White-hall,
At every stroake the oares teares let fall:
More clung about the Barge, fish under water
Wept out their eyes of pearle, and swome blinde
    after,
I think the Barge-men might with easier thighes
Have rowed her thither in her peoples eyes,
For how so ere, thus much my thought have scand,
She'd come by water, had she come by land.

Epitaph for Queen Elizabeth, who
ended this transitory life at Richmond
24 March, 1602, the 45 yeare of her
Raigne, and seventy of her age.

—William Camden

With the death of Queen Elizabeth, a new century and a new era began. It
is from this date that scholars have read portents for the changing social
and political patterns of the next hundred years. The seventeenth century

was one of political turmoil in England, interspersed with civil war. Political authority changed hands from monarch to civilian and back again, forced forever into different forms and roles. The social structures of England, historians have suggested, could not have remained unaffected by these conditions. But, it is also asserted, for some sections of the population, the death of Elizabeth did not signal the beginning of new powers and possibilities, but instead the restriction and confinement of existing roles.

The twentieth century's passion for self-analysis has caused it to turn its critical eyes to the past in an attempt to explain the problems of the present. Social and literary historians together with sociologists now ransack areas previously undisturbed by serious academic studies, the lives of the powerless: the poor, the illiterate, women, and children. In particular, the role of women in past western societies is being scrutinized to explain the political and social inferiority of over half of the adult population of Europe and America. Findings suggest that the traditional structure of the family is the historical source of modern inequities. The common conclusion held by social and literary historians is that western European families in the past were in general more authoritarian than today's, with the effective power resting in the hands of the man of the house, and that the family has evolved into a more egalitarian and compassionate "social unit."

This book has two purposes. The first is to explore the current model of domestic patriarchalism from the perspective of a group supposedly heavily under its restrictions, the literate women of the middle and upper classes whose minds and ideals were formed in seventeenth-century England. The second purpose is to assess the methods used to arrive at this impression of seventeenth-century domestic life, our image of "the patriarch's wife," and in particular, the use of literary evidence in creating it.

Seventeenth-century women were excluded from active participation in the institutions where intellectual controversies thrived, the universities, the learned professions, and the church hierarchy. Under the law, seventeenth-century women had few rights; "by the law of God, of nature, of reason and by the Common Law, the will of the wife is subject to the will of the husband," announced Lord Chief Baron Hale in 1663.[1] A husband took life interest in his wife's land and her goods were his absolutely.

Several questions arise from these conditions. How much did this intellectual exclusion and legal restriction limit the intellectual pursuits of the patriarch's wife or daughter and make her passively resigned to a subservient role, not questioning her husband's and father's powers over her? Was the patriarch's wife, unlike her Elizabethan mother or grandmother in our present model of women's history, simply a breeding machine, residing in the provinces and producing legitimate heirs to ensure male succession to property? If so, why did she drop the delights of metaphysical speculation for the intricacies of pickling fruits and recipes for relieving toothaches?

The issue of domestic government in the past carries more than simple historical interest: patriarchalism is very much a political issue in western cultures, and to use this term implies a political consciousness. As expressed by the literary critic Judith Fetterly, the study of women's roles and writings in the past is "a political act whose aim is not simply to interpret the world but to change it by changing the consciousness of those who read and their relation to what they read."[2]

Scholars have used the term "patriarchal" freely to describe any social environment that is perceived as hostile to independent activities of women in spheres other than traditional domestic, nurturing roles. This use of the term is based largely on a notion of how families were governed in the past. This sense of patriarchalism as a historical condition is the backbone of much feminist criticism, a potent force in modern literary and social studies. There is, as Jonathan Culler has noted, a key mode of feminist criticism "based on the presumption of continuity between the reader's experience and a woman's experience."[3] Given this theoretical base, if one is to continue in literary, historical, and social studies defining current situations in terms of the past, if the object is indeed to change the present by understanding the patterns of history, then it becomes essential to have as accurate an impression as possible of those earlier domestic models.

It is important to recognize the extent to which current theories and images of women's lives in seventeenth-century England depend on this one word, "patriarchalism," which is very widely used, but, like the equivalent Marxist term "bourgeois," seldom defined. In its basic sense, patriarchalism refers to the powers of the Old Testament father over his family, to chastise, to sell, and even to kill his wife and children without challenge. Obviously, execution was not a seventeenth-century husband's or father's prerogative, but the impression of absolute unquestioned authority over the most important features in life—education, career, marriage, and property—has remained. The wife's role in this form of family structure is envisioned as that of the loyal, and preferably silent, supporter. Her well-being and scope for independent activity depended on her husband's temper. In the seventeenth century, he did have the legal right (although rarely the literary sanction) to enforce her obedience physically.

Patriarchalism, as it is used in both twentieth-century literary and historical studies to depict family life in the seventeenth century, suggests authoritarianism rather than a sharing of responsibilities, relations between husband and wife expressed "in terms of authority and obedience, not consultation and consent."[4] Certainly, these despotic overtones were detected even by contemporaries in Sir Robert Filmer's best-known political work, *Patriarcha*, written in the 1630s and published in the 1680s. John Locke characterized Filmer's figure of the patriarch as "this strange kind of domineering Phantom, called the *Fatherhood*, which whoever could catch, presently got Empire, and unlimited absolute Power."[5] This type of interpretation of Filmer and domestic authority is the basis of current models in which, in literary, historical, and sociological studies, the husband's and father's authority over his wife and daughters is routinely described as patriarchal. The key text for this approach is Lawrence Stone's influential study *The Family, Sex and Marriage in England 1500–1800*, which labels the family structure in the seventeenth century as "restrictive patriarchalism," where the attitudes held by men effectively limited the activities and status of women in society.

Not only did the patriarchal authority of the husband determine the scope of his female dependents' activities, but, current interpretations strongly insist, it also extended its power over the minds of women as well. In summarizing the domestic situation of the Stuart era, Brian Manning baldly states that "in seventeenth-century English society a wife had to obey her husband, a daughter her father, a maidservant her master: wives, daughters, and maidservants were not expected to have opinions of their own."[6] Felicity Nussbaum finds the family order to have been the source and support of the Restoration period's antifemale satires. She stresses the control over women's thoughts and emotions demanded by this system: "The monarchical privileges of the husband were maintained, and such a patriarchal family unit required a submissive and deferential wife."[7] Likewise, John Wood in his article on William Wycherley's dramas depicts seventeenth-century marriage as bringing the woman under "the total domination of a man and [making] her faithful and obedient. By the end of the seventeenth century, that was what a great many women were becoming."[8] In short, patriarchalism includes as part of its mechanism a devaluation of women's abilities and achievements in deference to those of their fathers or husbands.

Consequently, "patriarchal" has become a loaded, negative adjective in such historical and literary studies. As it is currently used, it connotes physical and emotional restriction and spiritual degradation of one sex by the other. Patriarchalism is depicted as having acted like a blanket of smog, settling poisonously on the past, a universally shared set of attitudes that affected every facet of a woman's life. It is portrayed as a closed system, utterly inescapable. Writing on the women petitioners during the Civil War years, Patricia Higgins defines the context of their endeavors as pervasively hostile: "The society in which these women lived, and the air they breathed, was excessively patriarchal."[9] One could no more escape the negative effects of patriarchalism, it is implied, than one could stop breathing and still live.

In the current model, the arrival on the throne of James I, the son of Mary, Queen of Scots, triggers this decline in the status of women from that enjoyed under Queen Elizabeth. "Whether because [James I] needed to live down his mother, or whether in violent and uneasy response to his own bisexuality," asserts one critic, "his reign discouraged women from enterprise."[10] Nearly thirty years before this pronouncement, Jean Gagen had reached a similar conclusion based on a study of the century's drama, concluding regretfully that "as far as brilliant examples of learned women are concerned, the first half of the century is unusually barren—at least in contrast with the Elizabethan age."[11] Historians unite with literary critics on this point: "With the exception of the middle years of the century, there seems little doubt that the Stuart era was one of the bleaker ones for women. . . certainly it was a decline from that golden age of the Renaissance flowering under the Tudors."[12] Antonia Fraser's helpful compendium of research on seventeenth-century women, a skillful popularization of the common views and standard evidence, also sees that the "graph of female progress, far from ascending in a straight line from the death of Queen Elizabeth to the accession of Queen Anne, rose during the middle decades to drop again with the restoration of the old order in 1660."[13]

According to this interpretation, those women who did attempt to tread in the paths established by the articulate, educated women in Elizabeth's reign did not fare well.

> Did I, my lines intend for public view,
> How many censures, wou'd their faults persue,
> Some wou'd, because such words they do affect,
> Cry they're insipid, empty, uncorrect.
> And many, have attain'd dull and untaughte
> The name of Witt, only by finding fault.
> True judges, might condemn their want of witt,
> And all might say, they're by a Woman writt.
> Alas! a woman that attempts the pen,
> Such an intruder on the rights of men.
> Such a presumptious Creature, is esteem'd
> The fault, can by no vertue be redeem'd.

Current anthologies of women's writings frequently cite these lines (from "The Introduction" to her *Poems*) by Anne Finch, Countess of Winchilsea (1661–1720), often using them as an epigram for women's writings during the period. Because few seventeenth-century women writers are in print in modern editions, it is to such collections and their introductions that most readers, especially students, turn for information as well as poetry. There one receives the impression that the seventeenth century was an intellectual wasteland for women. "Conditioned to a patriarchal culture, women have had serious problems with the subject matter of their poetry as well. Woman's place in literary life, if she survives to write at all," contends Louise Bernikow, "has been a place from which men grant her leave to write about either love or religion." "Everything else," she concludes, echoing Winchilsea, "threatens male turf."[14] Katherine Rogers's anthology presents women writers before the eighteenth century as "exceptions—pressed by the need to express religious experience, like Margery Kempe; or emboldened by high social positions to write academic plays and translations, like Mary Herbert, Countess of Pembroke."[15] Writing "subjected [women] to ridicule and censure," according to the editors of the *Norton Anthology of Literature by Women*, and "literary ladies . . . had to confront the misogynist images of women still prevalent in their culture."[16] The greatest stumbling block for women writers, Joan Goulianos maintains in her anthology, was the patriarchal nature of the culture. Summarizing the common view, she writes that women "depended on men, not only as their critics but as their sources of support and very often as their sources of identity. . . . How many women, I wondered, did not publish because their husbands did not approve? And what of the unmarried women? Were they not as, or even more dependent on men?"[17]

This brief summary obviously does not do justice to the extent of work devoted to the concept of patriarchalism in either literature or life, but the model of domestic patriarchalism outlined here—the decline and fall of the intellectual, independent female—used in literary studies, social histories, and anthologies of women's writings, does highlight the areas in which problems arise. To begin with, this notion of patriarchal power rests on several unspoken assumptions about human behavior. First, it assumes that education leads to the overthrow or the subversion of authority which ignorance unwittingly tends to sustain. It also implies that people, in general, obey written laws. Finally, in order for this model to work, one must assume that literature, admittedly some forms more than others, reflects the values and attitudes shared by its contemporary readers. It is crucial to recognize the role played by literary materials: at the heart of all three assumptions is the unexamined question of the reader's response (both the intended seventeenth-century audience and the modern critic interpreting the original document) to *written* sources, whether laws, instructions, or narratives.

Equally important, the methodologies used to construct this model also contain a number of unspoken assumptions about women, history, and literature. Literary history as a discipline in the past has not directly addressed such issues; early British and American feminist criticism which focused on historical analyses remained tightly allied with a Marxist interpretation of literature, with all its limitations. From Alice Clark's pioneering study, *The Working Life of Women in the Seventeenth Century* (1919), which established this period as a pivotal one in women's history, to Sheila Rowbotham's *Hidden from History: Three Hundred Years of Women's Oppression and the Fight Against It* (1973), this branch of feminist studies emphasizes what Elaine Showalter has categorized as the "oppression" aspect of women's studies.[18] This type of feminism shares with Marxist literary criticism the perception of historical change and of literature as a reflection of the economic base. These feminist scholars also share a basic critical vocabulary with early Marxist critics; Engels's framework of domestic roles under capitalism in *The Origin of the Family, Private Property and the State* (1881) declares that "the modern individual family is founded on the open or concealed domestic slavery of the wife."[19] Engels's presentation also displays a characteristic use of literary evidence; when describing the evolution of sexual love, Engels turns to literary evidence alone as proof of actual practice. Thus, he is able to cite *Gutrun* and the *Nibelungenlied* as "reflections" of the actual practice of the cultures from which they sprang, regardless of matters such as literary conventions, social class, or regional differences.[20] As shall be seen, much of recent social history of the family and feminist criticism also adopts this use of literature as a "reflection" of social attitudes and practices.

Other modes of recent criticism concerned with women's roles and images such as "gynocriticism," which is the study of "the evolution and laws of female literary tradition" as part of the process of "defining the feminine," are involved with literary matters less directly, but no less importantly.[21] As Annette Kolodny has summarized, quoting Lillian Robinson, "feminist criticism very quickly moved beyond merely 'expos[ing]' sexism in one work of literature after another. . . . What was at stake was not so much literature or criticism as such, but the historical, social, and ethical consequences of women's participation or exclusion from either experience."[22]

However, before feminist literary historians can "uncover a lost tradition," the extent and the nature of women's writings in earlier periods must be clearly established.[23] Most of the energy of feminist literary history has been concerned with the idea that "literary history (and with that, the historicity of literature) is a fiction," but the analyses have focused on the aesthetic principles governing what is or is not included in the "canon," what is transmitted as "great literature," through generations. Little attention has been paid to the notion that social history itself is a type of narrative, complete with literary conventions. It has also failed to consider the issues of women's writings in the larger historical contexts of changing attitudes toward authorship, audience, and print during the seventeenth century.

Ultimately, the disturbing question raised by the image of "the patriarch's wife" offered as an explanation for current domestic conditions is how one set of individuals can so thoroughly impose a philosophy that diminishes and restricts another group. What were the historical mechanisms of patriarchal power, how was its theory propagated, and what were women's responses to it? Was seventeenth-century England a society of submissive, deferential, opinionless females whose quietude was ensured by their ignorance and a hostile legal system? Before one can attempt to answer, one must return to the original question of the exact nature of domestic patriarchalism and look just as closely at how modern scholars have arrived at its definition and forms.

Domestic Patriarchalism
The Defining Characteristics

Before examining the images of "the good wife" and the use of literary evidence itself, one must first turn to the framework of domestic government believed to have existed in the seventeenth century as it is determined by other forms of evidence. The characteristic features of domestic patriarchalism as it is presently defined involve two important aspects of human life: education, which shapes one's perceptions of one's self and the world, and marriage, in which social values are confirmed and transmitted to the next generation. Women in a patriarchal system, it is maintained, were educated differently from men and were restricted to studies that did not permit them to challenge masculine authority. Marriage, too, under a patriarchal system, is believed to have been designed to perpetuate the status quo. Supposedly, marriages were arranged by male heads of households to consolidate power and preserve property; the legal authority of a father over his daughter was transferred to her husband. Recent studies in historical sociology and demography, however, are bringing to light new types of evidence concerning women's activities which question the validity of this model.

The first issue to consider when discussing the status of literate seventeenth-century women and their attitudes toward patriarchalism and publication is education. Even though ignorance may result in bliss, it also produces dependence. Based on this logic, one explanation offered for the relative quiescence of seventeenth-century women in the face of the supposed increase in patriarchal authority over their lives is the decline in support for education of girls beyond simple household skills and decorative accomplishments.

The erudition of previous generations is held up as the measuring stick of the seventeenth century's decline. "The prejudice against education for girls—and its dreaded end-product, the learned woman—had derived fresh impetus from the presence of a male sovereign after 1603," announces Fraser, echoing generations of previous critics.[1] Specifically, the education of Queen Elizabeth compared to that of Queen Anne is used as an emblem of the age—Latin and Greek versus singing and dancing. The "learned woman" in Stuart England, instead of being admired as accomplished, was, according to modern interpretations, viewed as a freak and a threat. Nussbaum interprets the evidence as indicating that "earlier in the century the reign of James I had brought an abrupt end to female learning, and both Cavaliers and Puritans later in the century expressed concern about the disturbing effects of women's learning on the family unit and on society at large."[2] J. R. Brink concludes in her study of seventeenth-century women scholars that during this period "it was difficult to justify educating women who were not likely to occupy a throne."[3] Thus, for the majority of women, given the prevalent opinion in their society that females were "weak morally and intellectually," the poor quality of their education set in motion what one critic calls a vicious circle, in which women were criticized for the very behavior that their education had instilled.[4]

Recent interpretations do not deny that an occasional female slipped through the net to acquire a more advanced intellectual education, but the consensus is that her accomplishment was considered by her contemporaries to be a disfiguring, defeminizing mark. "Scorn for the learned lady . . . was one aspect of post-Restoration society [with] which every woman who pretended to achievements beyond purely housewifely . . . had to cope," notes Fraser.[5] As the post-Restoration period is generally considered to have been an improvement over the earlier decades as far as women's education is concerned, this is a serious indictment, especially as Fraser maintains that the derision "generally expressed in cheerful ridicule rather than outright hostility" inhibited other women from even attempting serious studies.

Such interpretations, which make 1603 a crucial moment in women's education, contain some rather disturbing implications about the nature of Elizabethan pedagogy. The notion that after the death of Elizabeth, parents "suddenly" lost interest in educating their daughters implies that girls were only receiving an education in the previous period in imitation of an authority figure, not because of any firm belief in the importance of education for girls or an acceptance of women's equal intellectual abilities. Furthermore, the first part of the seventeenth century is accepted as having been particularly barren of intellectual females. If this is true, then the supposedly more generously educated mothers stopped having their daughters educated. And the sons of these highly educated and admired Elizabethan women refused to permit their female children to pursue scholarly activities. These factors raise the issue of the extent to which one can say that there was a significant decline in the level and quality of education received by women, both within the royal family and for the majority of girls in literate households.

The wives of the Stuart monarchs were not as well educated as Elizabeth, but, on the other hand, neither were they raised in the English tradition. Their daughters fared better, however. The intellectual dry rot attributed to the daughters of James II, who himself would have had little cause to admire English education, having gone into exile in France at age fourteen, did not typify the attention given to earlier English princesses' studies. Contrary to what one might expect, James I took great care of his own daughter's education, which certainly was not restricted to housewifely or decorative crafts. Dorothy Gardiner, in her pioneering study on women's education to which all subsequent works owe a heavy debt, singles out Elizabeth, the future queen of Bohemia, remarking that "the fondness for learning which distinguished the Tudor Princesses appeared afresh, if with a less serious cast of mind" in James I's daughter: "like all of James the First's children, she was most carefully educated, under the supervision of her tutor, Lord Harrington."[6] Likewise, Charles I's daughters appear to have had a rigorous scholarly upbringing, if one believes the enthusiastic testimony of their tutor Bathsua Makin. Commenting on the abilities of her pupil, another Elizabeth, she claimed that at age nine the girl could "write, read, and in some measure understand *Latin, Greek, Hebrew, French*, and *Italian*."[7]

Even on a less exalted level, contradictions exist in the evidence about women's education. Girls were admitted to a few grammar schools in the 1590s, a practice, as Fraser points out, that did not continue in the seventeenth century. However, the Banbury Grammar School, which is used as an example of Elizabethan profeminism, stipulated in its statutes in 1594 (still under the reign of Elizabeth) that girls could stay only until age nine or until they had learned to read in English.[8] This is hardly a high level of education. It seems a drastic oversimplification of both the Tudor and Stuart eras to imply that the actual extent of education available to girls declined from a "golden age" on the basis of the select examples of the daughters of monarchs or in ruling families such as Sir Thomas More's and the practice of grammar schools under Elizabeth.

As Gardiner shows, numerous schools for girls were opened in the seventeenth century. Certainly the best known of these to modern readers is Mrs. Salamon's, which produced both Katherine Philips and Mary Aubrey, but it was not an isolated institution. The first "public" school Gardiner assigned to this period was the Ladies' Hall at Detford, but other schools survive in brief references in diaries and correspondence.[9] "Mrs. Friend" had a school in Stepney, but the majority of the girls' academies were located in Hackney, "which became known as 'The Ladies University of Female Arts'" (p. 211). In 1675, Ralph Josselin mentioned that his daughters were being educated in Hackney; they could have been at any of several schools, including those run by Mrs. Crittendon, Mrs. Margaret Kilvert, or Mr. William Dyer (p. 214). A school that enjoyed considerable reputation in its own day was that of Mrs. Perwich, established in 1643 and educating more than 800 girls in its seventeen-year span (p. 211). Francis North's daughter Anne lived with his sister in Chelsea, "where also was a good school for young ladies of quality which was an advantage."[10]

It was not only the daughters of the aristocracy and the gentry who had access to an education in schools during the seventeenth century. The Quakers in particular were assiduous in seeing to the education of their followers' offspring, both male and female. George Fox established a school specifically for girls at Shacklewell; in 1671, of the fifteen Quaker boarding schools, two at Ramsay and Thornburg were coeducational and two at Warrington and Brighton were for girls only. John Beller continued this tradition by founding in 1696 a "College of Industry" open to both sexes.[11]

One finds references in the biographies of Quaker women to the importance given to their education. Thirteen-year-old Anne Camm was sent to London "to be under the care of her aunt, and have the opportunity to further improvement in learning."[12] The Quaker poet Mary Mollineux, who carried on domestic conversations with her husband in Latin, was educated by her father when it was decided that she had weak eyes and an unusual aptitude for studies.[13] For the lower and middle classes, therefore, due to the efforts of specific religious groups to ensure literacy, girls had a greater chance for education than in the previous century.

What is clear and consistent about education in both centuries is that the majority of women who were considered "learned ladies" were instructed privately, not in schools. Is this an indication of a lower level of achievement, or of a decline in quality?

"I am not a scholar, nor a wit, I thank God," commented the Duchess of Marlborough, who succeeded in life quite nicely without either accomplishment, "an ounce of mother wit is better than a pound of clargy."[14] Interestingly, not all parents believed as she did. As Fraser notes, the most significant factor in whether a girl was educated in this period was her family.[15] This situation, however, is described as being a "fortunate chance." On the other hand, it could also be interpreted as a continuing tradition of educating females privately within the family. Parallel instances have been found in other periods and subjects: a similar idea forms Bell's study of book ownership among medieval women, which postulates "a linear transmission of Christian culture and the development of a mother-daughter or matrilinear literary tradition that may also have influenced later generations." She concludes that the practice "reflects a conscious choice on the part of mothers in shaping their daughters' futures."[16] One can find this same commitment in mothers' arrangements for their daughters' education as well as for their marriages.

When one looks closely at the sources and nature of education received by seventeenth-century women recorded by George Ballard as having been outstanding scholars for their times, one is struck not by the uniqueness of their upbringing but by its conventionality. These women were not, as Lady Mary Wortley Montagu later claimed to be, autodidacts. Their education was provided by their parents, who either taught their children themselves, or procured tutors. The control of the nature and scope of the studies appears to have been not so much patriarchal as parental in nature, with educated mothers taking a lively interest in the intellectual preparation of their daughters.

Brink cites the Countess of Huntingdon, the great patron of the arts, as a solitary example of a "learned noblewoman who insisted upon having her daughters as well as her sons educated in the classical and modern languages."[17] When one moves outside the highest levels of British society, into the gentry, other instances are easily found. Mary Browne Evelyn, who, although she herself publicly repudiated any desire to be considered a learned woman, nevertheless produced daughters of remarkable talents and erudition, who "held in their own day a position in some degree analogous to the More household."[18] Mary Evelyn wrote a spritely satire (*Mundus Muliebris*, 1690), and her sister Susanna is mentioned in her father's diary as having read "most of the Greeks and Roman authors and poets."[19] Likewise, Lucy Hutchinson's parents did not object to educating a daughter so well in the classics that translation became one of her pastimes. Mary Arundell (?–1691) dedicated her translation of "Sayings and Doings of the Emperor Severus" to her father, Sir John Arundell, and was equally proficient in Greek.[20]

The North family, with its strong matriarch Lady Anne, also produced a string of accomplished women scholars. The fourth Lord North himself educated his daughter Mary, who founded a group of "wittified" young ladies whose "symbol was a sun with a circle touching the rays and, upon that in a blue ground were wrote αυτάρκης in the proper Greek characters, which her father suggested."[21] The same Lord North's granddaughter and namesake, Dudleya, "emaciated herself with study, whereby she had made familiar to her, not only the Greek and Latin, but the Oriental languages."[22] When she died, her library, "consisting of a choice collection of Oriental books," was given at her bequest to the parochial library at Rougham, in Norfolk.

Many women scholars in the seventeenth century had the advantage of belonging to academic families. Damaris, Lady Masham, the associate of John Locke, was educated by her father Ralph Cudworth, the Cambridge Platonist. Ann Baynard, the Latinist, was tutored by her father Dr. Edward Baynard. The noted Old English scholar Elizabeth Elstob benefited from the personal tutoring of her Oxford-educated brother William. Some parents even sent their daughters abroad to complete their classical studies: Dr. Denton, the King's Physician, sent his daughter to France to study Hebrew, Greek, and Latin in order that she might assist him in his practice.[23]

It was common, also, for tutors to be hired. Lord Fairfax secured the services of Andrew Marvell for his children; Anne Clifford, Countess of Dorset, Pembroke, and Montgomery, was taught by Samuel Daniels, hired by her mother. Anne Halkett, the autobiographer and religious writer, attributed her education to her widowed mother, who hired tutors for her children. Elizabeth Bland, the Hebraicist, is said by Ralph Thoresby to have been the pupil of Francis von Helmont.[24]

The names of tutors for most of the learned ladies included in Ballard's collection, however, are rarely recorded, usually only when the tutor later became an important literary figure. How many less illustrious teachers were employed in private families to educate daughters is unknown and rarely considered in assessments of women's education during this period. What does remain is the record of the admiration with which the women's accomplishments were viewed. The fulsome praise given to Margaret Cavendish, Duchess of Newcastle, by hungry Oxbridge scholars says more about the condition of academics than the quality of her work and can thus be dismissed. Less suspect in their sincerity are the eulogisms found in funeral sermons and biographies, where, traditionally, universally admired traits, not personal eccentricities, are mentioned.

The early education of Lettice, Countess of Falkland (who later planned to found an academy for women scholars and who did fund charitable education for both sexes), is described with admiration, not reservation, by her biographer John Dunton: "Within a short while, by reading good Authors and by frequent converse with learned men, she improved (by Gods help) her natural talents of understanding and reason, to a great degree of wisdom and knowledge."[25] He continues this style of praise, noting that "she was second to none of her *Sex* and *Age* (I believe) among us, *for perspicacity of understanding and clearness of judgement.*"[26]

Numerous other women were singled out for praise because of their educated minds. In her funeral sermon, Lady Judith Barrington was described by Thomas Goodwin as exceeding "most of her Sexe, and [being] in the very upper Forme of Female Scholars."[27] The seventeenth-century biographer Roger North praised the Countess of Pembroke as a "magnificient and learned lady."[28] He extended the same favor to a "Miss A. Barratt," who "was also addicted to books, and was mistress of French and Italian, as well as to speak as read."[29] Approval was not reserved for dead women scholars, but was also given while the women were young enough to be encouraged by it. Charles Hatton wrote in 1698, "I am very pleased to heare yt not only my nephews but my neices are so good Latin scholars" and there is no indication that he was unusually liberal in his sentiments.[30]

Women are also frequently applauded for the size and nature of their libraries. John Smyth, the steward and later biographer of the Berkeley family, records with admiration that after marrying off her son with great success, the widowed Lady Berkeley retired "amongst her thousands of books, having from the Counsells of those dead brought wisdom and happiness to her widdowhood."[31] Elizabeth Rowe's sister is described as having had "the same extreme passion for books" as her sister the poet, but her interest lay chiefly in medicine, "in which art she arrived to a considerable insight."[32] Martha, Lady Gifford, the sister of William Temple, a remarkably learned lady of any century, had the following suggestion for her niece, Lady Berkeley, in 1698: "I would faine advise about yr reading what I practice myself not to read anything very serious before you goe to bed; that would be a good time to read Virgil in, and let yr Turkish history only goe on a dayes."[33] On her death, Lady Gifford left her French and English books to this niece and her Spanish texts to Lord Berkeley to be housed with his collection in London.

Among the domestic papers preserved of the earls of Bridgewater is a catalogue of the books owned by Lady Frances (Stanley) Egerton, Countess of Bridgewater, in her London house.[34] In 1627, the countess possessed more than 200 volumes on subjects ranging from Turkish history to the sermons of Launcelot Andrewes. Most of her holdings were in English, although there were numerous French works and several Latin authors in translation, including Tacitus, Petrarch, and Boethius. Her main interest appears to have been in theological matters and she owned both church histories and commentaries such as Richard Hooker's *Ecclesiasticall policy* and collections of sermons, prayers, and meditations by authors including John Donne, Bishop Joseph Hall, and Andrewes. Her literary selection shows a discriminating taste, by modern standards; in addition to popular favorites such as Overbury's *Characters* and *A Quip for an Upstart Courtier* (1620), she had the works of Michael Drayton and Ben Jonson, Greville's *The Tragedy of Mustapha* (1609), *The Faerie Queene*, *Don Quixote*, *The History of Lazarillo de Tormes*, and Shakespeare's plays. Interestingly, she also owned copies of Thomas Heywood's *The History of Women* and *The Countess of Montgomeries Urania* by Lady Mary Wroth. This impressive list, it must be remembered, does not include her books at Ashridge, nor does it comprise the family's impressive library.

Based on individual examples such as these, it does not appear that women's education came to a "sudden end" in 1603, or, indeed, that it declined significantly from previous generations either in quality or extent. There were more schools opened for girls than in the previous century, providing more opportunities for girls from a wider social spectrum to achieve literacy in addition to social graces, which admittedly such academies stressed. Higher education, especially the study of the classics, was still primarily a private, family matter. This itself does not necessarily indicate female education was inferior to that experienced by males, as the seventeenth century also saw the intense debate over the benefits of public or institutional education versus private tutoring for boys. This was also the century when educationalists, including Milton and Locke, strongly questioned the role of the classics in male education, urging the inclusion of vernacular and modern languages in the curriculum. So, one cannot even point to the prominence of modern romance languages in female education of this period as a definite sign of discrimination.

Seventeenth-century English domestic patriarchalism was a literary phenomenon—a concept of power derived from a literary source, the Bible, and codified in written documents. Patriarchalism as a practice, rather than as a philosophy, however, was subject to certain demographic factors, a hidden feature of social structures. Statistics, of course, can lie as fluently as any literary source; also, studies on such topics as mortality rates and migration patterns during this period are still incomplete. Nevertheless, the consistency of the patterns found, keeping in mind the difficulties in procuring statistics in this precensus period, does suggest some problems with the image of patriarchalism as an umbrella overshadowing the entire span of a woman's life.

Previous users of demographic studies in reconstructing family life have concentrated exclusively on sex ratios, the number of men compared to women. One theory is that a surplus of available women resulted in a decline in their status; given a glut of marriageable females, English-women could no longer make demands on males, who in turn, apparently taking advantage of the situation, revealed their hostility to independent women.[35] In America, however, where the ratio was reversed and women were a scarce commodity, it is maintained, the laws and the attitudes concerning women were much more favorable, because women were in a better position to "bargain" over their sexual favors.

Although this thesis has some appeal, there are several problems with it as a foundation for a theory of domestic patriarchalism. It implies either that men's attitudes are so flexible they can respond to the slightest shifts in the population, or that men in general were naturally hostile to women and during periods of shortage were forced to suppress, hypocritically, their antagonism in order not to jeopardize the transmission of family property. This theory also does not account for the patterns of the sex ratio imbalances. Typically, surplus females were found in urban centers; this theory would imply, therefore, that country males would have been "nicer" to their women, a notion that certainly has no support in the literature of the period, where country squires are represented as being the most backward and arbitrary of spouses.

This use of demographic evidence seems to raise more questions than it satisfies. Several other demographic factors should be considered in addition to sex ratios. Domestic patriarchalism is a personal authority, deriving its strength from an individual's will and ability to enforce it. Hitherto, a father's disposal of his daughter in an arranged marriage has been considered a classic hallmark of patriarchal power. Speaking of seventeenth-century society in general, Vivien Brodsky Elliott has observed, "In a patriarchal society in which the nuclear family structure was the normal, most commonly occurring form of family structure, fathers were decisive figures in the business of daughters' marriages. . . . Daughters were relatively passive agents in the marriage process."[36] Underlying this observation is the generally accepted premise that an early age at marriage for women strongly indicates an arranged marriage, and arranged marriages are a manifestation of patriarchal strength. The equation fits in happily with the current assessment of social practice based on literary sources. Statistics in Elliott's own study, however, seem to be working against such an interpretation.

Two demographic features that come into play when examining patriarchalism as a practice are suggested in the circumstances and contents of the essays used as case studies in the appendices. The first is the number of women who would have escaped direct patriarchal control because they were left fatherless. Of the women connected with the essays, Mary More's daughter Elizabeth Waller, Robert Whitehall's two sisters, and both Filmer's wife and daughter all lost their fathers before marriage. On closer examination, one finds this to be true in a high proportion of the biographies in George Ballard's encyclopedia of seventeenth-century women, including Lady Halkett, Elizabeth Bury, Elizabeth Elstob, Bathsua Makin, and Anne Finch, Countess of Winchilsea.

In more general terms, 47 percent of the cases Elliott studied of women from all social classes in London in the early seventeenth century had lost their fathers by age twenty. Of those who migrated to London, 64 percent had no fathers when they married.[37] Her findings support earlier ones by Peter Laslett, who summarizes the situation in the seventeenth century. Speaking of patterns of remarriage, he notes, "Many of the brides and bridegrooms had been married before: something like a quarter of them were widowed persons in the seventeenth century. . . . A far higher proportion [of children] had lost their fathers than their mothers, perhaps a third or even as much as half, depending once more on the prevalent mortality."[38] In his study of the Court of Orphans, Charles Carleton suggests that at least one child in three in Tudor and Stuart England lost his or her father before reaching maturity.[39] Because of the late marriage age for men and the age gap between spouses, a child, particularly if it was a third or fourth one, would be more likely to lose his or her father than mother.

In a fatherless family, who arranged the daughters' marriages? In a patriarchal culture, one might expect that the nearest adult male relative would assume the paternal mantle. Studies of individual families suggest otherwise. Dame Anne Filmer's mother Alice Heton drew up her daughters' marriage settlements; a generation later, Filmer left £2,500 to his daughter in his will when she "accomplisheth the age of Eighteen or sooner if shee marry with the consent of her mother."[40] Filmer did not leave discretionary control over his daughter to any of his numerous brothers or his grown sons, but instead to his wife, whom he also named executor of his estates.

Widows such as Dame Anne are traditionally acknowledged by both seventeenth- and twentieth-century commentators to have been more independent in their activities than an unmarried woman or a wife. Not only did widows take the lead in arranging their children's marriages, but also, in the matter of remarriage, widows often suited themselves, disposing of their considerable financial holdings as they pleased. The woman Francis North hoped to marry was the widow of Mr. Edward Palmer, but "never was lady more closely besieged with wooers."

> She had no less than five younger brothers sat down before her at one time; and she held them in hand as they say, giving no definite answer to any one of them till she cut the thread and, after a . . . match with a jolly knight of a good estate, she dropped them all at once and so did herself and them justice.[41]

A document, sent by a possible suitor to a woman of his acquaintance, which claims to be the opinions of Mrs. Mary Ridley on marriage, points out that although parental consent is a primary consideration, "widdowes

. . . have absolute power or themselves in disposing of themselves in marriage in respect of Choyce[,] haueing especiall liberty . . . to marry whom they will."[42]

A second factor to consider, reinforcing the impression of the uncertain tenure of patriarchal authority whether caused by the early loss of the father or the husband, is the acknowledged but undervalued phenomenon of women's migration, also mentioned in Filmer's essay. Laslett again called attention to this practice of leaving one's family to live in another, often as a wage earner, for several years before marriage.

Until recently, attention has focused on the patterns of male migration. But David Souden's investigations suggest that women dominated the migration stream into the cities by the second half of the century.[43] Significantly, it appears that there were more women moving longer distances than during the late Tudor, early Stuart periods. No appreciable differences arise in the patterns of male and female migration, either in age or distance traveled, except that women appear to have been mobile for a longer age span than men, from sixteen years to twenty-five, with a resulting average age at migration in the early twenties.

What do these facts about the mobility of women in seventeenth-century England mean? Elliott finds that migration of women into London had specific effects on marriage patterns, regardless of the woman's social status. Women migrating from the countryside tended to marry several years later than London-born women and "the migrant bride pattern of a later age at first marriage and a small age-difference between partners implies a greater freedom of choice of spouse and a more active role for women in the courtship and marriage process."[44] In short, a woman's migration weakened patriarchal authority in certain important aspects of her life, and the seventeenth century saw an increase, not a decrease, in this activity by women.

This pattern of living away from home during the years of adolescence and early maturity was not confined to lower working-class women. Filmer maintains in his essay that the best way for a girl to learn the fine arts of running a household and servants is by being independent of her own family, if she "be kept in service farre from home" and "be not marri[ed] untill [she] be skilfull in huswifrie." The practice by the gentry and aristocracy of sending their daughters into other people's homes is commented on by both Laslett and Stone and is reflected in Elliott's finding that a third of the London migrant women were from the highest social classes.

Daughters of the gentry went not only to London for this period of their lives, but also to the families of friends and relatives living in distant parts of the country. In Lady Joan Barrington's house, one could find living with her not only her own grandchildren but also "the children of close relatives, and neighboring families of standing." One of these was her niece, the daughter of Richard Whalley, who paid £20 twice a year to keep her there. When he became unable to pay this, "he suggested that she should stay and work for her living, the most important consideration being the increased chance of making a good match which life in a big house could bring to any girl."[45] Unfortunately for parental plans, while living with Lady Joan, Jane Whalley fell in love with a young man of no fortune, a match doomed to failure.

Female mobility at its most exalted level is illustrated in the desire of young women such as the young, fatherless Margaret Lucas to be a maid of honor at court. The future Duchess of Newcastle "wooed and won my Mother to let me go," and then spent two years in the court of Henrietta Maria. However, Margaret Lucas found that once there, "in truth my bashfulness and fears made me repent my going from home to see the World abroad, and much I did desire to return to my Mother again . . . but my Mother advised me there to stay."[46]

The vast majority of young single women did not move into such glamorous positions when they moved into the cities and market towns. The low number of men compared to women in the cities has been used as an explanation for increased patriarchalism. But it also reveals the presence of an army of single women, working as servants, in trades, and in manufacturing. They were not the "activists" of many current studies: they did not publish treatises on women's education or swagger through the streets in male attire scandalizing the bishop of London.[47] Nor were they living at home, being properly disposed of in marriage by either parent. They were supporting themselves independently of their immediate families, a practice that in turn appears to have led to a more active participation in arranging their own marriages.

Factors such as parental deprivation and women's migration open up the question of the nature of women's participation in the supposedly masculine activity of controlling the futures of family fortunes through arranged marriages. The negotiations themselves throw some light on the process involved in arranging a match. The impression left by domestic correspondence is that women were the prime instigators and arrangers, whether they were widowed or not.

Such negotiations are most visible at the upper levels of British society. This is in part because more property was involved in the transaction and more legal assistance was required and also because the family correspondence stands a better chance of being preserved at this level. Letters, therefore, are a limited type of evidence. However, with the trends indicated in studies on women's marriage and migration patterns from other social classes, the importance of women in instigating, investigating, and concluding matches is suggested.

The first difficulty in arranging a marriage was finding a suitable spouse. Networks of helpful friends and relatives were obviously of the greatest help in arranging successful marriages. Women's correspondence with other women during this period displays a keen interest in prospects, whether for one's own child or for friends' children. Dorothy Randolph wrote to Lady Jane Cornwallis in 1629, "I have enquired after matches in other places if this should faile, but can hear of none but some of the nobility, which I harkened not to, becaus I thinke you desire not to match with them."[48] A year later, she was sure she had found the perfect girl for Cornwallis's son: "I heare of a very prety gentillwoman that hath six hundred pounds a year, and her father and mother dead."[49] The only problem with this paragon, she admitted, was the matter of "eighteen hundred pounds to be paid to her grandmother for her wardship," but Dorothy Randolph felt that the sum might be lowered by the old lady. The only masculine contribution to this triangular negotiation was Randolph's report that her husband had seen the girl and "commends her for very hansome, and sixteen years ould."

Mothers, aunts, and interested female friends also consulted male acquaintances for information. They wrote directly to men inquiring about the circumstances of possible suitors, bypassing their husbands and brothers in the process. John Locke, for example, appeared in the unlikely role of Cupid to numerous of his female correspondents' children. Elizabeth Burnet cautiously questioned him about the character of a young man on behalf of the daughter of a friend of hers.

> I think I once named a young Lady to you as very disarving with an intent it should be named to my Lord Ashley . . . she is still uningaged and in my Judgement disarves to be happy in a good Husband; her mother can if she pleases and likes the persone and Estate give her £20,000 down.[50]

Nothing came of this proposal, although the girl was given a glowing recommendation by Mrs. Burnet.

Mrs. Mary Caverley's inquiries on behalf of her daughter were of the same nature. Mrs. Caverley wrote to Locke that she was considering Sir Charles Barrington as a possible candidate, and, having heard that Locke was living in the family of one of Barrington's trustees (the Mashams) and also being informed that "I might know from the trustees if the things were worth my paines," she had decided to pursue the matter through Locke. "I perfectly rely on you," she informed him, "I desire to have your opinion of the young gentleman and his circumstances, etc. . . . pray let this affair be a secrett betwixt you and I."[51]

This injunction to secrecy appears to have been a common feature of marriage arrangements in their early stages. Letters between third party negotiators are often baffling mazes of oblique references for twentieth-century readers. Anne Finch, Lady Nottingham, confided in 1698 her suggestions about an unnamed couple to the Bishop of Norwich. She herself feared

> to pose it where & by the way of my friends is a great step I dare not do, wth out a prospect of succeeding according to my wishes; but if it could be hinted so far to the person concerned in the management of his estate if he be a man of prudence enough for that I should think that would be sufficient to convince him how desireable this is for him who he ought to be concerned for, and perhaps upon his mentioning of it to him he might see his own interest as to offer himself.

Finch, who was perfectly lucid in her other correspondence, revealed the reason for her desire for secrecy at the end. "If it did come to nothing," she concluded, "it would have a better air then if the proposition was rejected on this side."[52]

Although arranged marriages thus appear to have involved a large number of people, not all of whom were related to the children in question, mothers were frequently credited as the determining forces in whether or not the match could be made to succeed. Anne North brought a £4,000 dowry to her marriage, thanks to the prudent management of her mother, Dame Mary Montagu, who also drew up the nuptial agreement.[53] Sometimes, however, even a mother's plans went astray; Lady Russell wrote to her husband in 1680 with a certain amount of amusement that "Mr. Cranford has stole a young woman worth £2000. . . . Her mother had employed him to persuade her against a match she was not willing to consent to, and so he did, most effectually."[54] Mothers could, on the other hand, prove formidable obstacles. John Evelyn gave James Graham little hope of winning Dorothy Howard, "the mother not much favouring it."[55]

Often a mother's tasks were not over with the wedding ceremony, especially when, as in the isolated instances among the upper classes, the bride and groom were underage. Elizabeth (Stanley) Hastings, Countess of Huntingdon, who herself had wed at age thirteen, became responsible for her new daughter-in-law, twelve-year-old Lucy. The girl's parents, the poet and statesman Sir John Davies and the prophetess Lady Eleanor, were concerned about arrangements made for the child's visit to her in-laws. The countess quickly soothed parental fears and defined her own territory. "I perceaue by your last letter and my lords relation that you are much discontented at my daughters coming home without a woman," she began.

If you desire that I should take the charge of your daughter you must give mee leaue to putt such a seruant to waite upon her who I durst trust for her care and diligence and for whose faults I durst be accountable . . . all I stood upon was . . . that if shee brought a woman the woman might take charge of her not I.

The countess added that Lucy's behavior was not the cause of her concern ("in the discreet gouerment and behauiour and in all other things that are comendable shee soe farre exceeds the expectations of her yeeres that I see nothing to reproue"), but Lucy was still so young that "either too violent exercise or too little may impaire her health and one of more yeeres then her selfe can better judge both in this respect and diuers other things."[56]

Although relationships between Lucy and the Hastings family as a whole appear loving and harmonious (the girl is affectionately alluded to in the correspondence of the countess and the earl as well as of her new grandmother-in-law the Dowager Countess of Derby as "our sweet daughter"), matters between the mothers-in-law were strained. The settlement of the marriage terms continued for several years after the actual match. The Countess of Huntingdon wrote to her husband,

I know you will expect a lardge account of my sonnes busyness, butt I haue had to do with such an irisolute woman that 'tis impossible to drawe sartin conclusions from soe fantasticall a cretuer as my Sister Davies; I mayd propositions for a fynall conclusion of all matters betwixt her and my sonn; her answer was that shee had other matters to thinke of.[57]

The final straw was that "I fynd not the parsonall estate to answer expectations." Lady Eleanor, too, had her objections to the countess's handling of the business. She wrote grimly to her daughter that she hoped in the future God would direct Lucy's husband with "more wisdom in the rest of his affaires. I know his Mother bad him: but the time will bee, I hope when hee shall find your advice much the better."[58]

When there were several small children to be provided for, it is not uncommon to find two generations of women working together to further family interests. The widowed Lady Elizabeth Berkeley married her thirteen-year-old son George to nine-year-old Elizabeth Stanhope, the daughter and co-heir of Sir Michael Stanhope. In doing so, Elizabeth Berkeley engaged the assistance of her widowed mother-in-law: "It was the prudent observation of the lady that in the five last descents her Sons family had not received into it the warmth of any other influences, save what their ancestors left to shine upon them."[59] The Countess of Huntingdon participated in a similar female joint effort; she wrote to her husband that "my La: will needs haue Alice brought downe ayrle with me yt my La: Mainwaring and my Cossin may see her." She explained that "if ye match fayle," they intend "to trye my Lo: Darcy agayne; and if all fayle to see if < > Cossin Beaumont wee can gett younge < > for her; my La: sayes shee will giue her three thowsand pownd portion."[60]

Not all parents, however, propelled their children into early matrimony. Francis North, the future Lord Keeper Guilford, tried twice to marry on his own, but each time was turned down for wealthier suitors. He may, therefore, have been secretly relieved when his widowed mother Lady Anne "laid eyes upon the eldest unmarried daughter [Lady Frances Pope] and, when they were gone, turned about and said, 'Upon my life, this lady would make a good wife for my son Frank.'" Lady North pursued the matter and "at the next visit, with his lordship's [Francis North] fair consent she moved it to the countess, who consented that his lordship might make his advances." The countess was uneasy over North's lack of fortune, and had "some qualms and complained she knew not how she could justify what she had done (meaning the marrying of her daughter with no better settlement)."[61] The mothers worked it all out between them, however, and the couple was, from all evidence, very happily married.

The extensive correspondence of the indomitable Lady Russell offers further examples of mothers and their arrangements, not only for their own children but also for those of friends and relatives. This tragic woman, who lost two husbands, stood by her second throughout his trial and execution for treason and never remarried in spite of the urging of her friends. First married at age seventeen to Francis, Lord Vaughan, for fourteen years, the still young widow chose her second husband for herself. She kept Russell in suspense for more than two years. At the beginning of their courtship, her half-sister Lady Percy commented on the persistent Russell, the third son of the Duke of Bedford, as being only one in a pack of eligible suitors: "for [Mr. Russell's] concern, I can say nothing more than that he professes a great desire, which I do not at all doubt, he, and every body else has, to gain one who is so desirable."[62] Russell, however, prevailed over more financially impressive wooers and a letter written in 1680 by Lady Russell, ten years after their marriage, gives some hint why: "My dearest heart, flesh and blood cannot have a truer and greater sense of their own happiness than your poor but honest wife has."[63]

Their fourteen-year marriage produced a son and two daughters. After the execution of her husband, Lady Russell was determined to devote the rest of her life to the education and welfare of their children. In spite of her grief, which she poured out to her friend and spiritual advisor Dr. John Fitzwilliam, she was adamant that her children should have a secure future. "[I] must, as I can, engage in such necessary offices to my children, as I cannot be dispensed from, nor desire to be, since 'tis an eternal obligation upon me, to the memory of a husband, to whom and to his, I have dedicated the few and sad remainder of my dayes."[64] She continued this theme in a later letter. Although she desperately wished for solitude in the country, "I believe to assist my yet helpless children is my business, which makes me take many dinners abroad, and do of that nature many things, the performance of which is hard enough to a heavy and weary mind, but yet I bless God for it."[65]

She had outstanding success in her efforts, marrying her daughters into two of the most powerful families in the country. In spite of the fact that she herself had married for love in her second match, her daughters were married at an early age in carefully negotiated matches. Her daughter Rachel married the son of one of her husband's defenders, Lord Cavendish, later the Earl of Devonshire, when the girl was fourteen and the boy sixteen. Lady Russell did equally well for Catherine, her other daughter. This time the match was proposed by Lady Russell's half-sister Lady Northampton, who suggested John, Lord Roos, later the Duke of Rutland, noted for possessing "the two best fortunes in England." This circumstance alone, however, did not automatically guarantee his success with Lady Russell. "On the other [hand]," she wrote in her reply to the suggestion, "if he had a kingdom with his, I would not agree to put her knowingly in circumstances that I should doubt God's blessing would not go with."[66]

Lady Russell exerted no less control over her son's future. Offers came to her rather than to the child's grandfather, Lord Bedford. She politely refused one from Sir Josiah Child in 1693 to marry her thirteen-year-old son to his granddaughter.[67] Two years later, Sir James Forbes petitioned her to permit the young Lord Tavistock to stand for "knight of the shire for Middlesex," a political move his mother also diplomatically rejected (*Some Account*, pp. 120–21). When he grew older, his mother disagreed with her formidable father-in-law over proper tutors for the boy. As always, she wrote, she wished "ever to take Lord Bedford along in all concerns of the child . . . [yet] I think perhaps to over-come my Lord in that, and assure him [the child] shall not be pressed" (*Some Account*, p. 73). In the end, it was the mother, not the irascible Lord Bedford who selected Mr. Hickes to guide and protect the boy on his European tour (*Some Account*, p. 131). In 1695, when he was fifteen, Lady Russell arranged and concluded his marriage with a wealthy heiress, Elizabeth Howland.

Lady Russell was not alone in her immediate family circle in desiring to see her offspring settled and financially secure at an early age. Her niece, Lady Elizabeth Percy, was twice widowed before she was sixteen. In this child's life, her grandmother, the Dowager Countess of Northumberland, was the determining force. In 1672, when Elizabeth was six, she went to live with her grandmother after extensive negotiations in which Lady Russell played a major part.

> My sister offers to deliver up the child, upon condition [the dowager] will promise, she shall have her on a visit for ten days or a month sometimes, and that [the dowager] will enter into bonds not to marry the child without the mother's consent, nor till she is of years of consent; and, on her part, Mrs. Montague and she will enter into the same bonds, that when [the child] is with them, or at no time, they will marry or contract, any marriage for her, without the grandmother's consent; but [the dowager] was stout yesterday, and would not hear patiently; yet went to Northumberland house, and gave my sister a visit . . . my sister urges, it is hard her child (that if she has no other children must be her heir) should be disposed of without her consent; and in my judgement it is hard. (*Some Account*, p. 172)

The result of this extraordinary matriarchal document, where not a single masculine pronoun intrudes, was the marriage of Lady Elizabeth when she was twelve to Henry Cavendish, Earl of Ogle. Lady Russell wrote to her husband in February 1679 that the grandmother had informed her that as "her grandchild likes the addresses of my Lord Ogle better than any others, she shall accept them" (*Some Account*, p. 203). Not surprisingly, this match provoked the child's mother, who appears to have then quarreled with both the dowager and the young bride. Lady Russell wrote to the preteen Countess of Ogle encouraging her to mend the rift with her mother. "All her advice could have no other aim and end but your being happy; and reasonably concluding the freeness of your choice was likely to make you [the happiest], she could not think your avoiding to see so many [suitors], alike qualified to make their addresses to you, was the way to make you so impartiall in your judgement" (*Some Account*, p. 272). The quarrel was as short-lived as the marriage. Two years later, the girl was married de jure to Mr. Thynne, soon widowed, and remarried in less than a year's time in 1682 to Charles, the sixth Duke of Somerset.

Lady Russell's marriage did not seem to have swayed her in favor of love matches for first marriages, and she expressed no dismay over the youth of the parties engaged. Writing in 1712 to her cousin, the Earl of Galway, and inquiring about her son-in-law's plans to remarry after the death of her daughter Catherine, Lady Russell made a revealing comment on her life and endeavors. She asked in this letter "whether or not the D. of R.—had not fixt a second choice? perhaps as proper to call it the first; for when marriages are so very early, 'tis accepting rather than choosing on either side" (*Letters*, p. 573).

In addition to her own family's marital concerns, Lady Russell was sought after as a skillful negotiator of others' matches.

I have just dated my letter to my Lady Digby, of Coleshill, written in answer to hers, by which she desires me, in pursuance of a dying brother's advice, and her son's inclination, to propose to Lord Gains-borough a marriage between the present Lord, and Lady Jane. I have done it; though I wished she had made choice of any other person than myself, who, desiring to know the world no more, am utterly unfit for the management of any thing in it. (*Letters*, pp. 328–29)

Although there were several adult males in the family who could have been consulted, it was to Lady Russell that the requests were sent and it was she who performed the negotiations.

She was similarly engaged in the unsuccessful attempt to match her sister-in-law, Lady Margaret Russell, with Lord Stafford. The letters pertaining to this affair give some sense of the complexity of the matter and also of Lady Russell's direct involvement with the legal aspects of the negotiations. In 1688, she wrote that although she was under some pressure to see to her own daughter's welfare, she was equally concerned over Lady Margaret's future, "which, by God's grace, I design to do as cordially as to my children" (*Letters*, p. 382). Initially, the procedings appeared to be going well; in March 1688, Russell wrote to Dr. Fitzwilliam, "I have a well bred Lord to deal with, yet inflexible, if the point is not to his advantage. I am to meet him this morning at eleven o'clock at the lawyer's chambers, proposing to give a finishing stroke to the agreement between us, and then the deeds will be drawn in a few more weeks, I hope, and this matter perfected" (*Letters*, p. 390).

She was overly optimistic, however. Lady Margaret's father, Lord Bedford, developed reservations about the match because of conditions in Ireland. Sometime in 1689, Lady Russell apologized to the Earl of Stafford: "I am so very sensible of that great civility your Lordshp chooses still to preserve toward me, who have been no fortunate instrument and perhaps sometimes a faulty one thro' ignorance, in this so long depending treaty" (*Letters*, p. 449). After all her meetings and concerns, however, nothing came of this particular match.

Inquiries on a less grand scale were also under way for her male relatives. On 9 February 1687, the Reverend John Howe wrote to Lady Russell to ask about the character of her brother-in-law, the eldest son of Lord Bedford, Lord Edward Russell, as a possible match for a widowed Englishwoman residing in Utrecht. Howe was particularly concerned to discover whether or not the gentleman in question maintained "strict sobriety." Does he, Howe demanded, have "seriousness in religion, without being addicted (to the degree of bigotry) unto any of the distinguishing modes of it used among sober-minded Protestants; and (which is a great essential) [has he] that goodness of temper, wherein is a composition of prudence and kindness, that shall neither incline to a fond levity, nor too morose sourness?" (*Some Account*, p. 278).

Lady Russell replied obliquely.

> I would for no advantage to myself, or friend, deceive any; especially by false acts, be an instrument to lead one eminently confident into error, and so desparate a one, out of which there is no recovery. But where there is great honour, truth, courage, and great good-nature, what supposition can there be that, when joined with a prudent and virtuous woman they should not feel the felicity of the happiest state of life? (*Some Account*, p. 281)

For Lady Russell, the arrangement of marriages was no frivolous pastime, despite the number of dinners it required one to attend. It was also a legal matter involving as many meetings with lawyers as dowagers, requiring a skilled arbitrator to manage the desires and fears of both families. Nevertheless, for Lady Russell (perhaps with her own second match in mind), marriage remained an institution whose goal was human happiness.

Elements of the matches depicted in the preceding examples were not typical of seventeenth-century marriage arrangements in general. Certainly, the early age at marriage exhibited in Lady Berkeley's and Lady Russell's arrangements was not typical of the practice of the population as a whole during the period. Laslett has suggested the common age at marriage during this era was twenty-six and a half for men and twenty-three and a half for women, with the husband's life expectancy some four years less than his wife's.[68] Child marriages such as Lady Berkeley's son's, therefore, can be assumed to have been extraordinary; the practice would seem to have been confined to families with extensive property interests to protect. The examples provided by the Russells and Berkeleys also suggest the theory that single-parent families may have adopted this practice more frequently than others.

Not all arrangements, of course, were as happy as the Norths' and the Russells'. The unpublished diary and meditations of Elizabeth Levingstone Delaval (1648–?) give some impression of how it felt to be the object of such negotiations when the heart was otherwise engaged. She is used by Lawrence Stone as an example of repressive, patriarchal marriage manipulations; however, Stone's selections from her diary ignore the role played by her aunt, grandmother, and female cousins in the decisions that formed her life.[69]

Lady Betty, as she was called at court, was the only daughter of Sir James Levingstone, later Earl of Newburgh, and Catherine Howard, who died when the child was two. Betty was raised by her father's sister, Lady Stanhope, and from her diary she appears to have had little direct contact with her father, although she did maintain an affectionate correspondence with her half-brother Charles Stuart, Duke of Richmond. Betty grew up with the prospects of a brilliant future. After escaping the early snares of Presbyterianism set by a childhood companion, she lived quite happily at Nocton, presenting lavish theatricals involving the estate servants (although they understood their parts no better than if the play had been in Hebrew, she noted with indignation), and occasionally visiting her widowed grandmother, Lady Gorge, in London.[70] When she was fourteen, her aunt settled an allowance of £100 a year for the girl to spend as she pleased and her half-brother secured her a place in court as "First Maide of the Preuy Chamber to the Queen" (pp. 23, 26).

Her diary gives the impression of a vivacious spirit attempting to maintain a suitably serious and sober view of life and not always succeeding. Constantly, she reproved herself for enjoying frivolous conversations and priding herself on her reputation as a wit. As she admits in the beginning of her account, however, "there is so much fier in my natural temper, that where I either loue or hate, tis with the greatest Violence imagenable, and most unhappy haue I been in the beginning of my life by misplacing of my heart" (p. 8). It was a misplaced heart that turned a future of sparkling romance into a life of pensive resignation.

Having passed her early years absorbed in fairy stories and the adventures of "the Grand Cyrus, Cleopatra and Astrea," Betty found the court much to her liking (p. 15). When she was eighteen or nineteen, a dashing foreigner, the "Conte Dona," began paying his addresses to her. Although she seems to have been intrigued and flattered by his attention, she nevertheless preserved a prudent perspective on the process, displaying a mature awareness of the mechanics of arranged marriages. "I resolve neuer more," she declared firmly,

> to hear a young man Talke of Loue to me (though I keep that unrully passion out of my own heart) unlesse he is aproved on by my Parents and is also at liberty to dispose of himselfe. for when I listen to discourses of that nature from one that is in the power of others, I giue them incouragement to Sin by offering me a heart that is not there own to giue away and may iustly hereafter be reproach'd by him when he finds a hopeless loue increase whilst all the while I men nothing but harmlesse mirth; finding a Deuertion to hear him talke like one of the Louers I have red in Romances. (p. 227)

Betty recorded that Conte Dona's uncle sent the unfortunate younger son home and, although he "continuously writ me letters full of passion and respect," Betty found herself drawn to Lord Annesley, the son of Lord Anglesey, the Keeper of the Privy Seal. His attentions, she believed, "wou'd have been most agreable both to his Parents and mine, nothing being more suteable then both our Birth, and fortunes were and our Age also" (p. 241).

More than practical considerations were involved in her interest in Annesley.

> Though vertuous Loue in a Vergins heart, is no crime: yet this new guest which is now come to mine, I find by Experience is infinitely dangerous to be entertained; since that passion when once admitted dos so increase that it soon banishes all other thoughts, but those only which it is ready to present us with. Thus what euer company I am in, what eyer busyness I am about, the obiect that I best like seems allways before my eyes. Euen at the time of my prayers is my Head filled with thoughts of him. (pp. 158–59)

As the match even had the blessing of Betty's father, Lord Anglesey and his wife confidently approached Lady Stanhope to present their son's suit. But, to the amazement of all, noted Betty, Lady Stanhope "coldly answer'd she had resolved not to medell with the disposing of me." Her response was taken as an insult by Anglesey, who was "courted euery day, with great offers for my Lord Annesley" (p. 164).

The reason for her aunt's refusal to consider the match is unclear, but Betty strongly believed that "because I once disobey'd my Aunt in not giuing my selfe to a young Man that she had chose for me (who was indeed both hansome, Rich, and great, yet one who being off a Contrary Relighon to mine, My Consience wou'd not suffer to be ty'd to) she crosses me now out of pevinge" (p. 163). Her "tears and many prayers" to her aunt and father had ended that proposed match, but her aunt had then decided on her near neighbor, the not yet divorced Earl of Rutland (whose son married Catherine Russell), as the next most promising candidate (pp. 163, 244).

For several years, the unhappy lovers attempted to reconcile irate family members and overcome objections to their marriage. Annesley repeatedly asked Betty to marry him secretly, but she refused, even though her own father urged her "not to refuse a maryage so advantageous to me, and so agreable to my own heart" (p. 245). It was her aunt's permission, not her father's, that was the deciding factor in Betty's actions.

Meanwhile, the Earl of Rutland, impatiently waiting in the wings for his divorce, consulted with Lady Stanhope "how they might keep me till that time unmary'd. for they extreamly dreaded I shou'd dispose of My selfe" (p. 244). Rutland hit upon the happy idea of involving his mother in the proceedings. He went to consult her, "whom he had all along trusted with the secret of his passion for me, to beg that she wou'd imploy a Friend of hers (who had interest with the Earl of Anglesey) to make a maryage betweixt one of her Daughters and Lord Anesley" (p. 245). According to Betty, Rutland's mother promptly dangled the prospect of marriage to her daughter Lady Elizabeth Manners and £10,000 pounds in front of Annesley's father. Anglesey, in turn, invited his son to consider how his life would change if he were disinherited (p. 250). Annesley capitulated. Ironically, just before this series of events, Betty had decided, after the urging of her cousin Essex Griffin and her husband who themselves had successfully eloped and been forgiven, to marry Annesley clandestinely.

In his letter breaking off their relationship, Annesley protested that "he had done all that was possible to haue the hapynesse of being euer mine, without absolute ruine to us both," and begged her to release him from any vows (p. 250). "Tis impossible," Betty recorded, "for me to express the surprise I was in upon the reading of this letter, nor the Rage I felt. . . . I did not balance one moment but imediately writ him word that since he was capable to write me such a letter I fre'd him with great willingnesse and scorn" (p. 250). She did not return to court, nor was she forced into the country by her father as Stone implies—her diary shows that she fled to Nocton, seeking the comfort of her aunt.

By this time, it seems that her father had indeed lost patience with the unsuccessful arrangements of his womenfolk. The title of Betty's next meditation too plainly reveals the results of this unhappy business: "Upon Continuall Mellancholy for severall Weeks. Mr. Delaval being then at Nocton My Father haueing promis'd that I should be his Wife." From this point on in the diary, she wrote little about her private emotions or the negotiations going on about her, concentrating instead on meditations and prayers for humility and patience. The twenty-year-old seldom mentioned her former love after declaring him "Alltogether unworthy of my heart, since the threat's of a Couetious Father had power to change his [mind to marry a woman] he has yet neuer seen. which some time or other I am sure he will smart for" (p. 5). Nevertheless, it is evident that he was not so easily dismissed from her heart as she could wish. On 10 May 1670, she entitled her meditation "Upon my Fathers Anger that I refused to marry Mr. Delaval and his threatening to send for me away from Nocton" (p. 279).

She married Delaval in October 1670. Perhaps, after the unhappy experience of her own management of affairs of the heart, she simply resigned herself to the direction of others; "God haueing in his prouidence," she observed bitterly before her marriage, "so order'd my Fate, that when I thought my selfe wise, I shou'd become a fole" (p. 280). The marriage did not begin happily. She describes her husband as a "very sickly young man," who drank and hunted with a "sort of Deboach'd Crew" that associated with her former suitor, the Earl of Rutland (p. 320). Betty found marriage bewildering rather than stabilizing: "I am as it were amazed in a new world, and haueing quited my Beloved Virgin state of life, I scarce yet know where I am" (p. 313). She soon discovered that married life was not as carefree as courtship and required more diplomacy than her experiences as a sought-after heiress had led her to believe.

> I was so folish at that time of my Life as to believe t'was in my power to change any Costume [Delaval] had that I did not like; and to be very much disobliged when I found my selfe mistaken, so that this beginning of a maryed life was very disagreable to me but I knew there was no remedy. (p. 320)

This tone of controlled resentment runs through the short remainder of the diary, which ends with no mention of Elizabeth Levingstone Delaval's former love or her future.[71]

The real significance of this example and those cited earlier is not the fate of the young lovers. It is the extent to which women participated in arranging and concluding matches in which considerable power and property were at stake. To say that women were deeply involved in the process of arranging marriages is not to deny that these were marriages founded primarily on economics. The Dowager Countess of Derby bluntly told her widowed son-in-law that it would give her great pleasure to hear that "your Lordship were towards the marriage of a good and rich wife."[72] These were, no doubt, the sentiments of many concerned mothers and aunts.

As Laslett notes, marriage at any level during this period was a significant public event. The first marriage, in particular, "was an act of profound importance to the social structure."[73] Thus, for women to be so directly involved in the process of determining the age at marriage and the spouses of their offspring implies a much greater real power over the nature and structure of the domestic unit than the current theory of patriarchalism suggests.

These examples also remind one that women had control over the lives of their sons as well as their daughters. Too often arranged marriages are discussed only as an imposition on women's lives. The third Lord North, himself forced into an unwanted marriage, commented on behalf of all young men such as Annesley, declaring, "Grossely hee erres, who thinkes that words or law / Can sympathy of heart and love persuade."[74] Parents, he asserted, ought to "leave their Children full freedome with their consent in so important a case."[75] All of his children selected their own spouses, although, as seen, his son's wife Ann was a firm believer in exerting matriarchal authority in her children's lives.

Women's active participation in these important social as well as private transactions also highlights the presence of matriarchs within the system. Lady Stanhope obviously had as much if not more power over Elizabeth

Delaval's life as her father, as did the Countess of Northumberland over her granddaughter. Likewise, Lady North, who also handled estate matters for her husband, was a direct and significant force to be reckoned with in the lives of her adult sons and daughters. The widowed Lady Joan Barrington is described by her twentieth-century editor as "the focal point of the extended family, the dowager and respected matriarch on a recognisable early seventeenth-century pattern."[76] In a different manner, Elizabeth, Viscountess of Falkland, controlled her children's futures, to the fury of her husband and her son Lucius Cary. "Her religious convictions not only caused her to defy her husband's authority but also deeply affected the lives of her children, six of whom accepted the Roman Catholic faith."[77] There is also Vita Sackville-West's memorable characterization of Anne Clifford, Countess of Pembroke:

> She was born to rule over houses and households, to tyrannise over her dependents, to have an enormous number of grandchildren and great grandchildren . . . to fuss after their alliances, to give advice— and woe betide those who did not take it—to govern from the midst of a little court of her own, and to receive the homage of those who were summoned to visit her.[78]

Any model of seventeenth-century domestic patriarchalism that does not take into consideration the power wielded by women in arranging marriages and the existence of what one editor has called a "recognisable" pattern of matriarchy during the century overlooks an important aspect of women's activities.

Finally, when evaluating the effectiveness of patriarchal power as reflected in marriage arrangements, in addition to considering the number of women whose marriages were arranged by their mothers or who had lost their fathers, one must also consider those couples who simply avoided parental management entirely. Had Annesley held firm, Betty Delaval would have been one of these, like her cousins. In 1640, Anna Mackenzie married Alexander Lindsay over her guardian uncle's vehement objections. Her new husband attempted to mend fences afterward, for without her uncle's consent, Anna could not have "that portion which her father left her; but I protest to your Lordship . . . that my affection leads me beyond any consideration of that kind, for (God knows) it was not her means made me intend it."

> Therefore, my Lord, since both by the law of God and man marriage should be free, and that she whom it concerns most nearly is pleased to think me worthy of her love, I am confident that your Lordship, who is in stead of a father to her, will not continue in your averseness from it, but even look to that which she, who has greatest interest,

thinks to be for her weal; for none but one's self can be judge of their own happiness.[79]

This same independent attitude was expressed by Margaret Kennedy, the first wife of Bishop Gilbert Burnet. Burnet recorded that after many years of friendship with her "she was much concerned [when I began courtship] for as she had no mind to lose my company she had as little mind to marry me . . . she saw marriage on such an inequality would much lessen her."[80] Likewise, his second wife, Mary Scott, expressed a view found frequently in literature written by women; she "continued unmarried till she was twenty-seven years old resolving not to marry till she saw a person that she could like."[81]

The majority of marriages that figure in domestic correspondence, however, were based on parental approval if not actual arrangement. Most children, not unreasonably, felt the need for the approbation of those who had raised them, even if they did not express the sentiments attributed to Dr. Basore found in a manuscript commonplace book that "there is nothing more hurtfull to ye Commonwealth then former Contracts without the Consent of Parents . . . the Inconveniences that follow are not Sufferable."[82] And, not surprisingly, domestic correspondence reveals that this desire for the blessings of one's mother or father did not stop with marriage. When arranging her own daughter "Jug's" marriage, Lady Elizabeth Masham wrote in 1629 to her mother Lady Joan Barrington soliciting approval for the arrangements concerning the distribution of land, for "we desire to do nothing withowt your advise."[83]

In summarizing the available evidence other than literary sources, too little statistical reconstruction of the part played by women in arranged marriages has been done to allow much more than speculation. But the early demise of the patriarchal figure and transference of his authority to his widow, even if his place was later taken by a stepfather, sharply undercuts the image of seventeenth-century patriarchalism as an unbroken reign of male dominance passed from father to husband. Women's migration patterns also imply a greater flexibility in their life choices. In the higher social classes, the active role taken by women in arranging marriages, even when a capable male head of the family was available, suggests that women traditionally were involved in this important social process, creating by their matches the social structure of the next generation. Given such factors as these, there appears to be a good case for replacing the "patriarchal," with all its connotations, with a notion of "parental" authority in seventeenth-century family models.

In view of the evidence found in letters and diaries in addition to statistical reconstruction of marriage and migration patterns, the current model of domestic patriarchalism as a pervasive, restrictive blanket of strictly male control over women's education and marriage seems to be overstated. The theory, however, is pervasive and emotionally appealing—from whence does it derive its form and persuasive power? It is the image of women in the literature of the century, not family reconstitution as practiced by historical sociologists, that is the most emotionally compelling evidence offered in support of the model. Specifically, it is the century's concept of the Good Wife and its satiric portraits of the Learned Lady that are claimed to reveal the century's attitudes toward women.

The Patriarch's Perspective
The Good Wife

Books about women written by men abound during the seventeenth century and from them the present age has derived much of its picture of the lot of the patriarch's wife. From elegant, erudite treatises to crude, lewd chapbooks, writings about women made up a large part of the entertainment available to English readers from the court to the village. Excluding romantic petitions, these literary outpourings, many of which continue well-established Elizabethan literary forms, fall into four categories: celebrations of the virtues of the Good Wife, histories of famous women, satires on the general nature of women, and defenses refuting the satires.

Filmer's essay praising the virtuous wife was composed in a literary environment described by some modern critics as "misogynistic," where the "vast majority of writings . . . [on] 'women' are either misogynist or semipornographic, or both."[1] Even books praising feminine virtues are interpreted as sending messages to readers about the limited capacities of women which had "lasting and devastating effect," especially on female readers. Hull writes, "Women were told over and over and over that they were inferior, that they had lesser minds, that they were unable to handle their own affairs. Reading their [women's] books and instructions today, it appears to be power by 'put-down' and propaganda, not unlike the situation in a modern totalitarian society."[2] These critics, including the feminist school of "phallogocentrism," see all seventeenth-century litera-ture, not just the satires, as reflecting repressive patriarchal ideology, mir-roring the popular attitudes of the readership.

If satiric tone is thus to be accepted as a significant indication of social attitudes, then the popularity of the character of the Good Wife and of the female eulogists suggests that women did not move seventeenth-century essayists and poets only to misogynistic venom. "The houses where no wemē were, ought to bee esteemed as vast Deserts, or untilled lands," declared Anthony Gibson in his early translation of *A Womans Woorth* (1599), and this opinion did not change throughout the seventeenth cen-tury.[3] "There is neither religion nor goodnes in that man, that loueth not an honest and a loyall wife," avowed Barnaby Rich.[4] During the seven-teenth century, the joys of marriage to the Good Wife were extolled in a variety of ways, aimed at a variety of readers. Her virtues were celebrated in pious conduct books, witty character books, plays, funeral sermons, and proverbs. Her qualities and conduct can be found chiseled on tomb-stones, painted on roundels, posted as broadsides, and even carved into the bedstead at Crathes Castle. All emphasize that "nature it selfe, is the foundation of coniugall friendship . . . it is pleasure, that tyes the indisolu-ble knot of true friendship; delight begins it, honestie confirmes it"—not to love a good wife is to be unnatural and joyless.[5]

Patrick Hannay provides a typical characterization in his preface to *The Happy Husband* (1622).

> To keep him good, his wife must be
> Obedient, mild, her huswifery
> Within doors she must tend; her charge
> Is that at home; his that at large;
> She must be careful: idle wives
> Vice works on, and to some ill drives:
> Not toying, fond, nor yet unkind,
> Not of a weak dejected mind,
> Nor yet insensible of loss,
> Which doth with care her Husband cross:
> Nor jealous, but deserving well,
> Not gadding, news to know, or tell;
> Her conversation with the best,
> In Husband's heart her thought must rest:
> Thus if she choose, thus use her mate,
> He promiseth her happy state.[6]

There is no proof, of course, that this literary convention mirrored reality any more than any other, that seventeenth-century women were indeed any more chaste, silent, and meek than their Elizabethan grandmothers. As one seventeenth-century author notes of literary evidence,

> is there any will fashion himselfe by the model of a person that never was? . . . women never dresse themselves by the pattern and example of puppets, and follow the phantasies of Painters in attiring themselves as personages in pictures . . . they take not for example the Minions of love-pamphlets and Poets, nor live like Nymphs of the metamorphosis.[7]

The character of the Good Wife did not originate during the seventeenth century, but nevertheless was popular during it.[8] The character indicates conventional assumptions about the ideal marriage for seventeenth-century authors and readers, whether or not their own marriages bore any resemblance to it or not. It also establishes the framework for the arguments about the nature of marriage carried on between the satirists and women's defenders.

In general, the character of the Good Wife represents a conservative force, whose appeal is to tradition, not innovation. Her virtues are frequently associated with a country setting rather than the city. The life of the "country Dame," writes Wye Saltonstall approvingly in his book of characters, "is nothing but a continuall stirring about business and huswifery, till shee be laid in her grave, and then she rests from her labour."[9] The "Fine Dame," on the other hand, is depicted as feeble in both intellect and activity. Her day's labor consists in being ornamental and consuming the money her husband brings home, for "to drinke choyse Wines, eate Banquetting stuffe, and play with a Parret, is the onely employment of her houres."[10]

Seventeenth-century writers consistently stress the importance of the Good Wife's labor in the family. She is no "gadder abroad," but confines her industry to the home, which includes overseeing children and servants. In the anonymous manuscript "Properties of a Good Wife," the author declares that unlike city women, the Good Wife "hateth the doore & the windowe . . . [and] careth not for feastes & banquets, nor for Dancing." Instead, she spends her time profitably employed and "laboureth truly to provide for her family."[11] Like Filmer, the majority of those writing about this character find their model in Proverbs, which praises the woman whose skills support her family and household.

In this characterization, the Good Wife's labor is presented as different in kind from her husband's, but not less valued. There is no indication that her function in the household is seen as less valuable than her husband's, or that the domestic realm is "inferior" to the world of commerce. In an "agreeing match," "yee may obserue a heauen of gouerment, the husband intent on his business, the wife imploied in her house, the chil-

dren brought up religiously, their attendants, their seruants, euery one . . .
busied in his place."[12] The bishop of Carlisle in his funeral sermon on
Anne, Countess of Pembroke, speaks of domestic government as

> an equal Duty (where the Family is complete and mixt of man and
> wife) belonging to the Man as well as to the Woman, yet in regard
> to the Man's imployment is commonly more abroad, and without
> doores, the well ordering of the House seems to be more particularly
> the Woman's Office; who therefore in our *English* is properly called
> the House-wife.[13]

Milton, in his figure of the Good Wife, has Eve working side by side with
Adam; as Barbara Lewalski points out, "fully shared work in and responsibility for the human world is . . . central to Milton's rendering of the
Edenic life."[14] After the Fall, the division of labor between home and
abroad makes the husband and wife mutually dependent on each other's
good performance. The husband cannot take over the wife's duties. The
mistress of the family, according to John Brinsley in *A Looking-Glasse for
Good Women* (1645), is supposed "to rule over her *Children* and *Servants*.
This the Woman may do, as much as God hath made them subject to
her."[15] The notion that women cannot work with men, or that their efforts
and duties are of an inferior nature, is nowhere found in this characterization.[16]

Men are repeatedly warned against marrying a woman who cannot or
will not govern her household. Unlike the seduction lyrics that focus on
lily hands and ruby lips, the portraits of the Good Wife emphasize looking
past a woman's physical charms. "Sr He yt an apple chusseth by ye skin /
And Woman by no other / May haue a rotten bit ith on / And a French
core ith other."[17] Money is as poor a criterion as beauty. "It is the fashion
much in use in these times to choose wiues as Chapmen sell their wares,
with *Quantum dabitis*? what is the most you will give?" comments Alexander Niccholes disapprovingly.[18] "And if their parents, or guardians shall
reply there vertues are their portions, and other haue they none . . . [they]
shall be nothing valued." In the opinion of this self-declared bachelor, the
Good Wife is the one who brings her husband not wealth, but a *"merry-
age*, [where] thou not onely unitest unto thy selfe a friend, and comfort
for society, but also a companion for pleasure, and in some sort a seruant
for profite too."[19] The Good Wife is not merely an ornamental accessory,
she is a profitable fellow laborer, too.

Unlike the love lyrics and ballads, youth is not necessarily an element in
these portraits. In fact, marrying a girl rather than a woman able to command a household is frequently condemned as a mercenary rather than a
prudent match. John Wing in *The Crown Conjugall* (1620) rebukes the
parents "with the *severest reprehension*" for making a daughter *"a Wife*

before she well understands what it is to be *a Childe*."²⁰ The seventeenth-century ideal was not the charming, dependent child bride found in many later literary representations.

The Good Wife, then, represents the happy medium—neither too young nor too old to be both a companion and a fellow laborer with her husband. The emphasis in the characterization is on her skills, shrewdness, and love for her family. In a charming poem, an anonymous poet defends his choice of a "Gentlewomen more vertuous yn fayre," illustrating in the process that the virtues desired in a Good Wife are not the same demanded of a romantic mistress, but instead the more hardy and enduring qualities of the mind.

> . . . I search farther & do find
> A richer treasure in her Mind
> Where something is so lasting Fayre
> That Art, or Age cannot impaire
> Hadst you but a prospectiue so cleere
> That you couldst view my obiect there
> Then you her vertue shalt espie
> Then wonder thy & thinke that I
> Had cause to like her, & thinke thence
> To Loue by Iudgment & not sense.²¹

In the portraits of the Good Wife, she manages to be both the partner and the reflection of her husband. She maintains the "right ordering" of her family by pleasing him, its head. A good wife, writes Sir Thomas Overbury, "frames her nature unto his howsoever: the *Hiacinth* followes not the *Sun* more willing."²² Likewise, Patrick Hannay instructs the wife, "Nay, thou must be a mirror, to reflect / Thy husband's minde: for as is his aspect, / So should be thine."²³ The point of these examples is adaptability; it is not that the wife has no mind of her own, but that she deliberately alters it if necessary to conform with her husband's situation. He, of course, being the Good Husband, attempts likewise to oblige her. "The good Wife commandeth her Husband in equall Matter," insists John Shirley in *The Illustrious History of Women* (1686), but she does not demand that her personality or opinion take precedence over his. "She never Crosses him, in the height of his Anger," Shirley explains, "but patiently waits till it is abated, and then she mildly argues the Matter with him, not so much to condemn him, as to acquit her self."²⁴ Shirley is not pretending that the Good Wife never differs with her husband, but in their differences, she never challenges his role.

Companionship in labor and love is a consistent element in these portraits: "She shares of thy grievances and lessens the burden: shee participates in thy pleasure and augments the ioy: in matters of doubt shee is thy counseller; in case of distresse thy comforter: shee is a co-partner with thee in al the accidents of life."[25] Overbury declares that she "is more than a friend, lesse than trouble: an equall with him in the yoake."[26] To be a Good Wife, of course, she must also have as her yokefellow a Good Husband, a character discussed in the next chapter.

By the end of the century, the Good Wife and her spouse appear in the same roles, but in settings different from the earlier domestic spheres of the countryside. In George Powell's comedy, *A Very Good Wife* (1693), he presents a "modern" marriage in which husband and wife are openly affectionate, using pet names for each other. Courtwit and his wife Annabella must scheme together to save the mortgage that Widow Lacy is about to foreclose.

> ANNABELLA: Give me thy hand then, *Phill*, I have a trick without the help of Law, or fear of Gibbits, to over reach this Widow, get thy Mortgage, and make thee out of the Court Fashion.
>
> COURTWIT: Get my Mortgage from the Widow, Chymeras and Impossibilities.
>
> ANNABELLA: Impossibilities! Why is there any thing impossible to a Woman's Wit? never despair, by this hand I'll get thee thy Lands releas'd; I tell thee, *Phill*, this angry Widow shall be so Chuckled, and so wheedled out of her little Senses; . . . but thou shalt have thy Mortgage given up.

Annabella explains that she had attended a masquerade in men's clothes and that the widow had conveniently fallen madly in love with her. Her husband does not find this in the least peculiar, but urges her on, having decided on a separate little scheme of his own to work on his friends. "One Kiss for good luck then," declares the plucky Annabella, "and let us part / You to your Project, *Phill*, and I to mine."[27] Although the Good Wife in this piece is a witty and fashionable courtier's wife, she preserves the same identifying characteristics as the earlier figure: the willingness to labor on behalf of her family, the complete identification of her interests with those of her husband, and the sense of a working camaraderie in their marriage, where although their plans are different, they have the same goal.

Thus, although the character of the Good Wife in seventeenth-century representations stresses her duty to her husband and her devotion to furthering his fortunes, it does not represent her as feeble, incapable, or servile. The characterization does not devalue women's work in the domestic sphere, nor does it exclude them on the grounds of incapacity from acting in the public, commercial sphere. As her husband's partner, she is expected to be able to take over his work when the occasion arises: "in her

Husbands absence, she Officiates his place, in regarding and takeing care of his Affairs."[28] Although she is portrayed as being perfectly capable of performing his tasks, she does not infringe on his sphere any more than he does on hers. The ideal represented by the Good Wife is an able companion who maintains harmony by maintaining order.

Seventeenth-century readers, male and female, also had plentiful opportunities to become acquainted with the stories of women who excelled not as Good Wives but in masculine spheres. The enthusiasm for female eulogy and history reached a peak during the seventeenth century, with numerous male authors recounting the deeds of illustrious women and praising the virtues of the sex in general. Some even went so far as to attempt to prove the superiority of the female over the male.

Six histories of notable women appeared in English during the century, written by Richard Ferrers, Thomas Heywood, Charles Gerbier, Pierre LeMoyne (translated by the Marquise of Winchester), and John Shirley. Their books are significant for several reasons. They provide a female mythology and confirm women as part of the all-important classical tradition, they offer precedents for female accomplishments, and they spread the fame of admired women on the Continent. In addition, such books must have provided a marketable and profitable topic for professional writers such as Heywood, who saw it to his advantage to write two histories and offer a revised edition.

The earliest of these histories, Richard Ferrers's *The Worth of Women* (1622), is less of a history than a brief verse compendium of notable females. It does list many of the women who would become the subject of longer discussions by later writers. Ferrers begins with Eve and mentions the memorable women in the Bible, such as Deborah, Sarah, Ruth, and the Virgin Mary. He also details the activities of the female prophets, Anna, Susanna, Tabitha, and Priscilla, characters who would become the proof for Quaker writers in the mid-century that the Bible sanctioned women's teaching and preaching the Gospel. Finally, Ferrers, to avoid the label of a Bible-thumping poet and to appease the learned, concludes with women mentioned in the classics. He concentrates on Daphne and Penelope and briskly rattles off a list of other female characters.

Thomas Heywood's first history, Γυναικειον: Or, Nine Books of Various History Concerning Women (1624), later reissued as *The Generall Historie of Women* (1657), goes into much more detail. The nine chapters are organized under the names of the muses, but the contents strain at these labels. The first chapter is devoted to goddesses, the second to muses, sybils, and prophetesses. The third concerns illustrious queens and famous mothers; the fourth depicts their opposites, "incestuous women, Adulteresses, and such as haue come by strange deaths." The Amazons absorb the fifth chapter along with other women known for their valor.[29] Six and seven describe chaste, wanton, and pious females. The eighth, which produces in the table of contents the intriguing coupling of "poetesses and Witches," is concerned with women who excelled in learning of all types, secular, spiritual, and arcane. Finally, the ninth chapter discourses on women in general and the rewards of the virtuous compared with those of the wicked. The work is a massive collection of miscellaneous learning derived from the classics, the Bible, popular literature, and folklore. It provides a multitude of images of women as harlots and rulers, pious matrons and ruthless Amazons, chronicling female activity in the home, the church, the academy, and on the battlefield.

Heywood's other enterprise is on a much smaller scale. In *The Exemplary Lives and Memorable Acts of Nine of the Most Worthy Women of the World* (1640), he uses three Jewish women, three "Gentiles," and three Christians to illustrate various aspects of feminine character. In his epistle, Heywood addresses "the most generous of both Sexes . . . of what qualitie or condition soever." Speaking of these women, he asserts, "whether we take them nationall or singular, we shall finde them to parallell men, as well in the liberall arts, as in such Facinorous Acts."[30]

Heywood chooses Deborah, Judith, and Esther to represent women in the Old Testament; Boadicia, Penthesilea, (queen of the Amazons), and Artemisia (wife of King Mausolus of Caria) as his gentile or pagan women. For his Christian women, he singles out three Englishwomen— Elphelda (wife of Etheldredus, Duke of Mercia), Margaret (wife of Henry I), and Queen Elizabeth. In making his selections, Heywood picks women of political importance as well as notable virtue. He does not choose models of domestic piety, but Amazons, warriors, and queens, each of whom is allotted a full-page engraving showing her garbed for war or sovereignty.

Charles Gerbier, the son of the hapless courtier Sir Balthazar Gerbier, divides his *Elogium Heroinum* (1651) by the nature of the talent displayed. His tone is by far the most unctuous of any of the female eulogists—"it is *woman*, the miracle of the world and marvel of marvels"—and from the numerous dedications and commendatory verses, this volume appears the most blatantly commercial venture of the histories.[31] His first dedication is to Princess Elizabeth of Bohemia, then to the Countess Dowager of Claire ("the Patroness of all Vertue and Learning"), and finally to "the Vertuous Accomplish't Lady Anne Hudson." At this point the printer interjects his apologies for cutting out several commendatory verses and the frontispiece of Princess Elizabeth. When Gerbier finally arrives at the main body of his work, he opens with a strong account of learned women, not pious maidens or long-suffering queens. He runs through the by now standard list of women in the classics, but then goes on to discuss the current state of women's scholarship. In addition to Lady Jane Grey, a popular figure in these histories, he also includes Christian de Pisa and Olympia Fulvia Morata of Italy who "writ many learned and elaborate works." He is also familiar with the accomplishments of "Helisian of Crennes" and Duena Ligua, a maid of honor to the sister of the king of Portugal who "was wonderfully verst in five sundry Languages, viz. the Hebrew, Greek, Latine, Chaldean, and Arabian."[32] He mentions Isabella Rosera's commentaries on Richard Lescot and the unspecified achievements of "Dona Margarita de Noronha, a Lady of Portingal." Queen Elizabeth, Margaret of Vallois, and Princess Elizabeth of Bohemia are grouped as monarchs noted for their scholarly activities. His final European example is Anna Maria van Schurman, who reigns as the model for the learned lady in Europe throughout the latter part of the century.

Gerbier is emphatic that intellectual attainments are not restricted to foreign climates or queens. "There have been likewise many Ladies and Gentlewomen of our Nation, whose learning and Knowledge may wel be parallel'd with the before-named."[33] Sir Anthony Cooke's daughters—Lady Burleigh, Lady Russel, Lady Bacon, and Mrs. Killigrew—are cited, as in other histories, but Gerbier also includes the Countess of Pembroke.

Gerbier makes little attempt to argue women's virtues or superiorities—he simply praises lavishly. The French Jesuit Pierre LeMoyne, on the other hand, in his work *The Gallery of Heroick Women* (1652), translated by the heroic royalist the Marquise of Winchester, uses the stories of individual women to pose philosophic questions about the sex in general. Winchester explains in his preface that by "heroic" is meant all women of strong virtue. As in Heywood's book, the work is divided by nationality—Jewish, barbarian, Roman, and Christian. LeMoyne's list overlaps with Heywood's, but not too surprisingly, this Catholic text substitutes Joan of Arc and Mary, Queen of Scots, for Queen Elizabeth.

The moral question posed by the life of Deborah in LeMoyne and Winchester's text is whether women are capable of government. "I know very well," the text begins, "that there be Politicians who are against the government of Women, but I know also, that these Politicians are no Evangelists, and that there is no Creed as yet made of their Opinion." Deborah is offered as proof that women can and should govern. Women are as naturally capable of government as men; states are governed by "the strength of wit, and with the vigour and activity of reason: and Wit may be as strong and Reason as vigorous in the Head of a woman, as in that of a Man." "It is not from the bulk the instruction is formed; it is not the strength of the nerves which produces good Counsels," he concludes tartly. "If wit and prudence were so meanly derived, the Law-makers and Wise men of *Greece* would have been Wrastlers."[34]

Using the example of Paulina to answer the question of whether or not women "be capable of true Philosophy," LeMoyne announces "there is nothing, which the Understanding of Women may not attain; nothing which is above their reach." In agreement with the other profemale writers, he asserts that the differences between men and women are merely superficial and "all things then are equal between Men and Women, in respect of the soul, which is the Intelligent part, and makes Learned men and Philosophers."[35] This treatise obviously must have struck seventeenth-century readers as quite radical, especially coming from a native of France where Salic Law prohibited female succession to the throne; Winchester preserves all of LeMoyne's examples and his acerbic tone.

The other female history written during this century is only slightly less radical in its assertions but no less laudatory of women's accomplishments. In John Shirley's *The Illustrious History of Women* the examples are drawn from "Authentique Histories." The author states he can hardly undertake the task, for "what Volume can contain them in their proper Lustre, or set them forth at large? what Rhetorick can Paint them to the life, and not be found therein deficient?"[36] His divisions are by virtues, among which he includes (apart from the standard citations for piety, chastity, and modesty) "courage and conduct in war," learning, and skills in painting and weaving. "Virtue" in all of these histories has a much larger definition than in modern terms and is not restricted to spiritual matters. Of the abilities of women "in Relation to Learning, Arts, and Sciences," he concludes, "though Men may boast of their Wonderfull Abilities, yet certain it is, the Fair Sex, may boast the like, especially a Capacity of performing as much, seeing the Soul proceeds from one and the same Fountain of Life."[37] Shirley closes his histories with the characters of the Good Wife and the Vertuous Widow and "Reasons why Mans Happiness is not compleat on Earth without the Charming Creature Woman."

These female histories as a group run the gamut from enormous dictionaries to elegant exemplary lives. Rather than being content with Barnaby Rich's graceful evasion concerning women's accomplishments—he cannot possibly detail all the women renowned for their abilities in the arts and sciences or else "I might heape together a greater volume then euery mans leasure would serue to peruse"—these writers seek to offer specific examples of famous (and infamous) women as examples to their readers of feminine achievements.[38] With formats ranging from modest verse endeavors to fancy commercial enterprises and the handsome equivalents of seventeenth-century coffee-table books, the female histories were directed at a variety of readers, not just wealthy ladies. From the dedications and prefaces we know that the authors expected women to read these volumes, but it is also clear that they anticipated men's interest in the topic as well. All of these volumes, regardless of form, exhibit women excelling in roles other than that of the domestic model of the Good Wife, although their authors also emphasize the "heroic" nature of virtue itself.

The most widely studied type of literature written by men about women apart from love poetry, however, constitutes a small but potent genre—the antifemale satires. Perhaps as a backlash to hearing women's praises sung so lavishly, some men were moved to ask,

> Oh heavenly Powers why did you bring to light
> A Thing calld Woman[,] Natures ouersight.
>
> . . . .
>
> . . . this is shee
> That first pluckt fruit fro ye forbidden tree
> From wch shee yn accurst began to fall
> From bad to worse from worse to worst of all
> Wee therefore thus define a Woman
> A spightfull creature—true to noe man.[39]

Antifemale satires and sentiment had flourished under Elizabeth for the obvious reasons of the questions over her right to the throne, but even earlier, one finds poets such as C. Pyrrye declaring women to be "most proude, seruile / cruell without measure: / Reason and lawe she doth exile, / to haue her wicked pleasure."[40] Antifemale satire was not an invention of the Stuart writers, nor does it appear to have noticeably increased in vehemence or quantity, to judge from the defenses of women against the satires produced in the sixteenth century, such as that by Jane Anger.[41]

In the Stuart era, the most notorious of the antifemale satires and the one most frequently cited to support the interpretation that the literature of the time became more misogynist is Joseph Swetnam's *Arraignment of Lewd, Idle, Froward and Inconstant Women* (1615). The numerous reprints—ten editions in its first twenty-eight years—of this "savage anti-feminist piece of polemic" is considered to be "highly significant of popular attitudes" and typical of the "sharpening acrimony against women in general."[42] Certainly, passages from it do not lead to high expectations of blissful relations between the sexes:

> betwixt their [women's] breasts is the vale of destruction, and in their beds is hell, sorrow & repentance. Eagles eat not men till they are dead, but women deuoure them alive: for a woman will pick thy pocket, and empty thy purse, and laugh in thy face and cut thy throat. . . .[43]

Even though Swetnam protests that "I wrote this booke with my hand, but not with my heart," and carefully points out his praise of virtuous women at its end, the work as a whole leaves a very unpleasant aftertaste. He does not dismiss women as the passive, obedient creatures extolled in conduct books, but sees them as an active, independent menace, obviously not the least cowed or controlled by patriarchal authority. After this vivid portrait of seventeenth-century femininity, one is skeptical about the sincerity of Swetnam's closing observation that "there is no ioy nor pleasure in the world which may bee compared to marriage."[44]

The significance of this unpleasant work, however, as an indicator of either popular attitudes or practices is less clear. His satire is presented as part of the content of a jest-book composed of witty paradoxes and proverbs: "if thou marriest without respect, but only for bare loue, then thou wilt afterwards with sorrow say, that there is more belongs to housekeeping then foure bare legges in a bed."[45] Such sound advice is intermixed with lurid invectives such as the one quoted earlier; the ribald tone of many of Swetnam's comments, and of many of the other antifeminist satirists, makes one question whether Swetnam's popularity was due so much to his conformity to popular opinion or his sensational flouting of it.

As significant, perhaps, as his tone is Swetnam's observance of certain literary conventions governing the subject matter of his piece. He obviously feels obliged by literary, if not social, constraints to present his attacks in the form of paradoxes and jokes. Furthermore, even after his invectives, Swetnam closes with a conventional salute to the joys of marriage which is very near an apology. From such conventions, it appears that an open, unabashed piece of misogyny was not considered prudent or saleable.

One finds this practice of apologizing for previous satires or offering concluding conciliatory praises in other antifemale satires. The anonymous author of a poem with the alarming opening "Servill proud, cruell, kind of womankind / nor law, nor rule, nor reason well obserued / squirminge att what is right with hatefull mind" apparently did not receive the reception he had hoped for, at least not from his female readers. Therefore, he also offered "A Recantation and Excrie for the precedent Inuectiues against women" to excuse his churlishness.

> Pardon, though I to your faire viewe present
> this monstrous Brood of my disturbed Braine
> to Sicknes, Waywardness is incident
> Suche was I when I caught this raylinge paine
> Sweete, then let sickness and not me be shent
> and though I once theis errors did mainetaine
> yet now by Truth made sound, by Time made wise
> I utterlie recant such [l]ies.[46]

Whether one accepts his ingenious plea as genuine, the poet is bowing to a custom as well established as being rude about women's constancy; he

ends by disavowing his aspersions as the product of "sick" humor, implying that no sober, right-minded individual would condone such statements.

Derogatory slurs once cast, in any language, however, leave behind
them damage no recantation can totally repair. "Mockery is nothing else,
but a Artificall injury," observes one contemporary of such antifemale
pieces, "we must confesse that to jest is tollerable, but to doe harme by
jesting is insufferable."[47] Satirists' apologies were, with justification, often
viewed as insufficient; Swetnam's example also raises the question of the
extent to which antifemale satires generated responses by male writers.

In addition to the problems posed by the convention of the satirist's
recantation and how contemporary readers would interpret it, one is left
with the problem of the number of antifemale satires and their replies
which were translations from Latin, French, and Italian pieces—do they
reflect native English attitudes? Swetnam was a home-grown product, but
the most challenged *Discourse of Women Shewing their Imperfections Alphabetically* (1673) was originally a French piece attributed to "T. Martine."
Juvenal and Martial, too, were favorite sources of invectives, especially in
epigrams; in pieces such as Robert Whitehall's verses to Mary More, the
question is whether the antifemale bias comes from Whitehall's attempt to
ridicule women or to copy Martial.

Even minor pieces such as epigrams and anagrams drew specific retorts
when their objects were women. The anagram of "WIFE," published during the Restoration in William Ramsey's *Conjugium Conjurium* (1675) and
frequently found in commonplace books, is often paired with an alternative poem.

> Of a Wife
> The W is double Woe
> The I is nought but Iealousie
> The F a fawning Flattering Foe
> The E wt else but enmity
> > If in ye Name there be such strife
> > The Gods defend mee from a Wife.

> The Answer to yt on a Wife
> The W is double Wealth
> The I is euerlasting Ioy
> The F a Friend in Greife & Health
> The E an End of all annoy
> > Therefore Good L. grant this to mee
> > That I may once well-marryed bee.[48]

One finds this pattern of satire and response in other pieces. Richard Ames, who himself wrote an antifemale satire, *The Folly of Love* (1691), also wrote *Sylvia's Revenge, Or a Satyr Against Man; in Answer to the Satyr Against Women* (1688), a defense against Robert Gould's *Love Given O're* (1682), and the two were published together as a set in 1709.[49] The abusive poem "Against Marriage," once thought to be by the Earl of Rochester, drew forth the less skillful but equally determined reply, perhaps by Robert Whitehall, "The Wives Gasping Reputation Revived: A Reply to an Inconsiderate Pen Satyrizing Against Marriage." The unknown poet implies that the satirist's motives are personal and his outlook diseased: "What canker'd Lungs & Poyson'd Pen conspire / To patron, raise, & blow unruly Fire?" He closes his rebuttal by transforming the satirist's ending, turning abuse into panegyric, "A Wife! Devils be gone! spite of Hell & Fate, / *She Saves Soul, Body, Credit, and Estate.*"[50]

Antifemale writers such as Swetnam, Taylor, Gould, and Ames did not print unchallenged nor did they receive universal applause. Their productions are best viewed in context with the responses they drew, as part of a continuing satiric dialogue which had been going on in print since Elizabethan times and no doubt long before that. For each single piece printed by the satirists, several profemale rebuttals were printed, the majority of which were by men, but some, which will be discussed later, by women writers.[51] The conventions of the replies to the satirists are as well defined as the satires themselves.

Swetnam's book provoked three direct replies by women, which will be discussed in a later chapter, as well as masculine retorts. He ended by becoming a literary convention himself, "Swetnam the Woman-hater," a buffoon villain in a play of that title, his name having become synonymous with mean-spirited misogyny. John Taylor, "The Water Poet" whose verse was admired by James I, had a similar fate. He produced two small volumes of nagging speeches by virago wives, *A Iuniper Tree Lecture* (1635) and *Divers Crabtree Lectures* (1639), which manage to insult almost everyone. Typically in these vignettes, a merchant's or farmer's wife launches a tirade against her wimpish spouse who has slunk home drunk from the pub.

> What, good man Clowne, doe you thinke to make me still your drudge to sit up late and rise thus early every day, to worke like a horse, and you to ride a hunting, gentleman like every morning, and none but I left at home to look after your horses in the stable, your kine in the field, your swine in the yard . . . you a Husband? you a Coxecombe; a meere Lubby, a Moone-Calfe, one that hath more haire than wit. . . .[52]

The volumes provide a handy dictionary of domestic invectives; what the wives lack in deference to their husbands' patriarchal position, they more than make up in verbal dexterity. In fact, the books could be seen as celebrations of the power of insults, although they paint a daunting picture of wives as bullying, whining gabblemongers.

"Mary Tattlewell" and "Ioane Hit-Him-Home" chose to regard it in the latter light. In their response, *The Womens Sharpe Revenge* (1640), they address their espistle to the "Mal-Gender" announcing that since men "suffer us to be reviled, and railed at, taunted & terrified, undervalu'd, and even vilified," the authors will deal with Taylor, whom they christen "Sir Seldom Sober," themselves. From their male readers they ask only a fair comparison of the merits of the two works. Given only their pseudonyms and the label of spinsters, it is impossible to declare with certainty the gender of these writers or writer, although the pseudonyms are sufficiently reductive to make one query whether women would use them; the work is, however, consistent with the pattern of satiric response by other male writers and its content typifies the nature of the exchanges between the satirists and women's defenders.

The Womens Sharpe Revenge opens with an acknowledgment of this pattern, a long literary tradition of "railing, bitter invective Pasquills and Scurrilous Libels . . . all of them made and forg'd on purpose to callumniate, revile, despight, jeere, and flount women." Like the unjust attacks in the past, they declare, "one or two sonnes of Ignorance" have taken it upon themselves "(out of the most deepe shallownesse of the Authors aboundant want of Wisedom)" to lay "most false aspersions upon all women generally."[53]

The first tactic employed in replying to any satire is to assert that the criticisms are unjust and unwarranted. The second is to attack the attacker. Typically, the antifemale satirist is depicted as a not very bright young man attempting to be clever. In 1534, in the earliest English translation of Henry Cornelius Agrippa's *A Treatise of the Nobilitie and Excellencye of Woman Kynde*, David Clapam characterizes the satirist as a "base *Fopp*" who on "poor Womens Judge doth sit / Who thinks Railing at them proves him a Wit," a view shared by seventeenth-century respondents.[54]

The satirist is inevitably accused of having personal motives. It is implied that the "foppish" author had not gotten as far with the ladies as he hoped and was being spiteful as a result. "Perhaps some one did thee displease, / in earnest game or iest: / And thou thy furie to appease, / doth rayle at all the rest," observed C. Pyrrye, who combined both forms of satire and rebuttal in one piece in *The Praise and Dispraise of Women* (1569).[55] A century later, the scenerio had not changed; Henry Care recreates the same situation of passion scorned as the motive behind antifemale satires in *The Female Secretary* (1671). Care (who also translated Agrippa's text as *Female Pre-eminence* in which he casts similar aspersions at a contemporary French satirist) uses a set of letters between two women. One writes to her friend, sending a copy of verses, explaining that her lover had written them in a fit of the sullens: "he grew so peevish on a suddain, as to threaten a Revenge on all our Sex."[56] She is sending them to her friend as a joke; Care gets in a reference to Taylor as she explains that she intends her friend "to laugh at [them]; the simple *Water-Poet* making us sometimes as merry as the worthily admired Dryden." Her friend responds in the proper spirit of amusement; the women regard the antifemale, antimatrimony verses as they would a tantrum of a not particularly attractive child. The final exchange contains a copy of the repentant poet's apology for his first efforts: "I here *Recant*, what I before have writ, / And *damn* that spawn of too luxuriant wit."[57]

Amused scorn for the unsuccessful wit is frequently joined with indignation that the satirist should turn on the sex that gave him life and nurtured him, the conclusion being that he must be in some way unbalanced or diseased. Pyrrye exclaims indignantly, "I thinke he was not of mans seede, / that this did take in hand" and seventeenth-century writers saw no reason to disagree. "Jane Anger" had likewise declared in 1589 that men who write antifemale satires have let their wits escape them: "their mindes are so carried away with the manner, as no care at all is had of the matter: they run so into Rhetorick, as often times they ouerrun the boundes of their own wits, and goe they knowe not whether."[58] This image of the satirist as slightly crazed is echoed in *The Womens Sharpe Revenge* which denounces the satires as the "superfluity of a chankered heart, overcome with Choler."[59] The desire for revenge on the woman or women who have slighted him, unable to have direct expression, corrupts the heart and wit of the satirist and "discovereth it selfe by [its] lewd tongue, and those that speake evill of Women, are held no better than Monsters amongst good men."[60]

Viewed in their literary context, the satirists offer a more complicated statement of seventeenth-century attitudes and interests than a simple hostility toward or fear of women. The conventions surrounding the form—the numerous Elizabethan precedents, the borrowings from continental authors, the practice of presenting the material in the guise of jokes, paradoxes, or comic dialogues, and the author's recantation, and, in the Restoration, the practice of using actresses or court mistresses as the specific targets of the satire (characters with whom few women readers would identify)—as well as the number and type of responses they provoked call into question how far one can use them as simple reflections of popular misogyny.[61] Indeed, one of their most interesting side effects is that they provided profemale writers with the perfect platform from which systematically to attack the central tenets of patriarchal ideology, the primacy of the male and the subjection of the wife to her husband.

One of the most striking characters of the paired groups of satires and responses is the differing degree of intensity in them. Conventionally, the satires emphasize wit in their attack, no matter how lewd or malicious; the responses, on the other hand, often do not stop in merely responding in kind, but also go on to examine the source of the vices and follies attributed to women. Often the tone in the denunciations of the conditions that created the satires is as vehement as the charges against women; the countercharges against men are equally likely to be exaggerated. The authors are unanimous in laying the blame for women's faults at the feet of men and the ways in which women are educated.

When the authors of *The Womens Sharpe Revenge* declared that "it hath been the policy of all parents, even from the beginning to curbe us of that benefit [education], by striving to keep us under, and to make us mens meere Vassailes even unto all posterity" they were not expressing a new idea, nor was it one that would be silenced by the Restoration satirists.[62] The charge made by the male defenders of the female sex throughout the century is that the women's weaknesses decried by the satirists are not so much the product of feminine nature as masculine nurture.

"*Generosos animos Otium corrumpit*," writes the Oxford-trained divine Christopher Newstead in *An Apology for Women* (1620). "Want of imployment, corrupts the brauest spirits; the fountain of their vertue, corrupts by standing. Want of use, causeth disabilitie; but custome, perfection."[63] The stagnation of feminine talents, rather than the lack of them, because of a limited education is explicitly stated to be for male benefit in *The Womens Sharpe Revenge*. "We are set only to the Needle, to pricke our fingers: or else to the Wheele to spinne a faire thread for our own undoings . . . if . . . wee be brought up to Musick, to singing, and to dancing, it is not for any benefit that thereby wee can ingrosse unto our selves, but for their own particular ends, the better to please and content their licentious appetites, when we come to our maturity and ripeness."[64] Prefiguring the same argument made by Mary Wollstonecraft at the end of the eighteenth century, the authors assert that women are being educated to be ornaments and toys for men, not rational, virtuous companions. "Thus if we be weake by Nature," they conclude, "they strive to make us more weake by our Nurture. And if in degree of place low, they strive by their policy to keepe us more under."[65]

This same argument was carried on throughout the century in the repeated translations of Jacques Du Bosc's *L'Honnete femme*. Part I of this work appeared three times, translated anonymously as *The Compleat Woman* (1639), in an abridged version by Walter Montague as *The Accom-*

plish'd Woman (1656), and by Theophilus Dorrington, who also translated Part II as *The Excellent Woman* (1691–92). Each edition offered the translator the opportunity to insert his own personal observations and to make references to contemporary works he wished to refute; thus, although all are based on the same text, each is an individual response.

The original text expresses its disapproval of the education of women in uncommonly strong terms and the English translators do not attempt to tone it down. "Women who are so trained up in seruitude, can do nothing with a freeness and liberty . . . their thoughts are alwaies base, and how good soever their inclination, yet, shame and ignorance, hinders them much so to come off well in their enterprises."[66] In the strongest of the three versions, Dorrington amplifies the points made in the original source. In his dedication to Lady Mary Walcot, he declares that whatever vices and follies have been attributed to women by satirists, "we may justly blame Men for; who take upon them to govern all Things, and condemn the women to such an Education, as can render them but very little useful, and leaves them apt to be only mischievous and hurtful to the world." Dorrington's imagery recalls that found in John Locke's *An Essay Concerning Human Understanding* (1690) as he then makes his point that confining women to trivial pursuits only undermines the moral strength of society in general, forcing women to "the Moulding up of Wax, when they should be forming of their Minds, by the Laws of Vertue and Wisedom." Such studies as women typically follow cannot "hinder the growth of Vice and Folly, from the Seeds of them that are in our corrupted Nature."[67]

Continuing their attacks on the inadequacy of women's education, male defenders are quick to make the connections between the position of women in the family and society and the interests of society at large. Like Locke in his later treatise on education, Dorrington views education as a socializing force, permitting social norms to be established and preserved. Ignorance, on the other hand, permits vice to flourish and thus undermines the general fabric of society, rendering the ignorant person "useless" if not actively harmful to society. To neglect this important cultivation of half the population, the half that oversees the early training of the next generation, is for Dorrington an invitation for social discord.

Still other male writers, as well as the female ones discussed later, see the issues raised in the satires in abstract political terms—freedom and liberty versus tyranny. Part of this stems from the earlier debates over the fitness of women to govern begun during Elizabeth's reign, but the ideas are enlarged and developed by radical thinkers during the Civil War years. "I.G." opens his *Apologie for Womenkinde* (1605) with an appeal to the muses to guide his trembling hand while he writes of "The sacred honours of your fellowe Sexe, / Which mens unlawfull tirannye doth vexe."[68] Though it is universally agreed among seventeenth-century writers that "males predominate in all animals," the degree and nature of this domination experienced in human couples is a matter of complex and lively controversy throughout the period. The degree of "lawful" dominion of a man over his wife drew the sharpest answers from the female defenders and the most intricate arguments from those attempting to establish the boundaries of personal power. During the seventeenth century, the patriarch's powers, according to these writers, are neither clearly defined nor secure.

Much of the most strident patriarchal or misogynistic writing cited outside of the jest-books and satires is found in popular theological works. As Kathleen Davies shows in her essay, many of these, like the satires, were reissues of Tudor works such as Dod's *A Plaine and Familiar Exposition of the Ten Commandments* and many of the views expressed in the so-called Puritan manuals of the later century also were continuations of those found in Renaissance texts.[69] Therefore, when considering these manuals as evidence of popular belief and practice, in addition to these factors, one must recall Dod's rueful acknowledgment that these are books of advice. "So much for the duties of the husband and wife: which I doe not so speake of, as though it were in the power or nature of any man or woman, to performe them: nay, by nature, we are all inclined to the contrary."[70]

It is widely agreed in literary representations of marriage that a husband who is tyrannized by his wife is a poor creature. "Beware (*my Sonne*)," warns the royalist gentleman and popular writer Richard Brathwaite, "that thou shalt be tide to her / Which servitude (though it is too to common) / Disvalues man that's subiect to a woman."[71] There are such women, admonishes Great Yarmouth preacher John Brinsley in a sermon on the occasion of numerous of his female flock deserting his ministry for the "refined Error of Separation," who are of "such *high* and imperious spirits . . . as if they were made only to *Rule*, not at all to *obey*."[72] The spirits of such wives "will not stopp to any kinde of *subiection*, specially to their Husbands. . . . If their *Husbands* wear the Crown, yet they will sway the *Scepter*. If their Husbands be in places of *Authority*, they will *Rule* with them, if not over them."[73] This, according to Brinsley, is plainly unacceptable according to Paul and Peter, and he hopes he never has to preach on it again.

Ballad writers have a tendency to be more direct in their observations concerning tyrannical women. The husband in "The Cruell Shrew" obviously was not successful in impressing his wife with his authority.

> She neuere linnes her bauling,
> her tongue it is so loud,

But alwaies shee'le be railing,
and will not be contrould;
For shee the Britches still will weare,
Although it breedes my strife—
If I were now a Batchelor,
I'd neuer haue a Wife.[74]

The Shrew, however, is hardly a seventeenth-century invention and although she appears frequently in jest-books, her character stands outside the limits of what patriarchal authority can impose in the household itself.

According to the writers of domestic conduct books and manuals of practical piety, the Good Wife, unlike the Shrew, is obedient to her husband in the same way she is to God: "the husband is by Gods ordinance the wiues head . . . so must the wife also submit and apply her selfe to the discretion and will of her husband."[75] Even though some women may be "wiser and more discreet" than their spouses, admits this writer, "yet still a great part of the discretion of such women shall rest in acknowledging their husbands to be their heads."[76] The necessity for this is to exercise the grace given to them by God and to ensure that their husbands are "honoured, not contemned."

"Thy desire shall be to thy Husband and he shall rule over thee" is accepted as a statement of fact by most seventeenth-century writers, apart from Locke's contention that it is unclear whether "desire" could be binding. But the issue does not stop there—where the province of the husband terminates, admits Mary More's antagonist Robert Whitehall, is "rightly questionable." He warns his readers that "he must be as famous in metaphysicks as those 7000 Archers, who could direct an Arrow to a hairs bredth . . . who can exactly determine this Controversy, and prescribe ye Limits of ye Husbands oeconomy."

There was no shortage of writers in the seventeenth century willing to try. Genesis is at the heart of the dispute as it is of patriarchal theory. The issue was felt to be sufficiently complex that a return to Eden was deemed necessary in order to establish a framework for discussing the behavior of contemporary women. Such an approach necessitates their grappling with "the rib question," and the intricate implications of Eve's creation.

The fact that Eve was created from a rib rather than the head or foot has potential for both sides. Brathwaite comments on the two views taken and decides on a middle ground:

Yea, but the *Matter* shee was made of, fore-told what shee would bee. Shee was made of a *Crookt* Subject, a Rib: and out of her crooked disposition (will some say, who stand ill-affected to the Salique state) shee will not stick to tyrannize over a sheepish husband, and give him *rib-roast*. A poore Objection! An equall and ingenous exposition rather frame this conclusion: that the *Subject* whereof she was made, begot not in her *crookedness*, but *pliableness* of nature: ever ready to *bend* her will, and apply her affections to the mould of Man.[77]

This debate over the sequence and substance of Eve's creation did not originate in the Stuart era but had flourished during the Elizabethan as well. In the sixteenth century, Anthony Gibson had explained that man "must say, himselfe is made but of slime and dung, whereas woman was formed of a matter otherwise prepared, finished in a happy and wel ordered substance, with al qualities being a most perfect creation."[78] This was not a view confined to rarified theological circles: the soldier-turned-author Barnaby Rich likewise declares in *The Excellency of Good Women* (1613) that the creation of Eve was *"the last and therefore perfectest hand worke of the Creator,"* a sentiment repeated throughout the century by the female apologists.[79] William Austin summarizes their position in *Haec Homo* (1637), arguing that Eve was "the last and most perfect creation" since she had been a refinement of a refined substance.[80]

Honors are generally even between disputants over Eve's creation, but with the first sin, those defending women come up against several immovable objections. The principal impediment to arguing women's equal status is that Eve ate the apple and gave one to Adam. But was woman thus responsible for the mortality of mankind? Seventeenth-century writers are by no means unanimous in condemning Eve. Many support Milton's Michael who rebukes Adam, supposedly the stronger of the two: when our fallen father whines, "I see the tenor of Man's woe / Holds on the same, from Woman to begin," the angel rebukes him sharply, "From Man's effeminate slackness it begins . . . who should better hold his place," and many male writers agreed.[81]

Seventeenth-century supporters point out in Eve's favor that she was deceived into eating the apple and the Serpent had to argue to win her over. "At first she did well shun his sleights," states *An Apologie for Womenkinde*, "yet at length he catch'd her by his baites. / Well what did Adam? he did not deny, / But eat the fruite forbidden readily."[82] Echoing these sentiments, Brathwaite later points out that "Shee expostulated the cause with the *Serpent*, e're shee consente: Whereas hee, without any more adoe weakly received, what she so unhappily offered."[83] Heale similarly concludes, "I see no reason then, but in this cause Man was more in fault to bee so suddainlie deceived, then woman who was more hardly drawne thereunto."[84]

The political significance of this biblical excursion is made clear in *The Womens Sharpe Revenge*. "Man might consider," the authors warn, that "women were not created to be their slaves and vassalls, for as they had

not their Originall out of his head (thereby to command him;) so it was
not out of his foote to be trod upon, but in a *medium* out of his side to be
his fellowfeeler, his equal & companion."[85] If men do not recognize and
respect this middle state and attempt to raise themselves above women,
the writers have no hesitation in calling it unjust and unlawful tyranny.

Moving outside plain biblical exegesis and taking an even more provocative stance was one of the most prominent and prolific of the profemale writers (although neither an Englishman nor a contemporary),
Henry Cornelius Agrippa (1486–1535). He wrote *De nobilitate et praecell-
entia feminei sexus* shortly before he died; it was translated into English
under three titles with several editions of each during the sixteenth and
seventeenth centuries—David Clapam's *A Treatise of the Nobilitie and Excellencye of Woman Kynde* (1534, 1542); Edward Fleetwood's *The Glory of
Women* (1651), and Henry Care's *Female Pre-eminence* (1670, 1683). Agrippa's major premise is that "the true distinction of the Sexes, consists
meerly in the different site of those parts of the body, wherein Generation
necessarily requires a Diversity."[86] Women, by nature, are not incapable of
"managing the most arduous or difficult affairs," nor, "in primitive and
more innocent Ages" were they prevented from doing so. It is the "*tyranny* of men [which has] usurpt the dispose of all business, and *Unjust
Laws, foolish Customs*, and an *ill mode* of education" which has "*retrencht*
their liberties." Men are not represented in a flattering light in any of the
editions. By "unworthy, *partial* means" women have been "forced to give
place to Men, and like wretched Captives overcome in war, submit to
their *insulting* conquerors, not out of any natural or divine reasons, or
necessity, but only by the prevalency of Custome, Education, Chance, or
some tyrannical occasion."[87]

Foreshadowing *The Womens Sharpe Revenge* and Wollstonecraft's passionate denunciation of women's inadequate education, Agrippa condemns raising a woman "as if she were only the passtime of Mens idle
hours, or a thing made meerly for *trifling* Courtiers to throw away their
non-sensical Compliments on."[88] Agrippa's tone in all the editions is rendered sharp-edged, indignant, and uncompromising. The unjust usurpation of power and the preservation of tyranny through ignorance draws
forth Agrippa's and his English translators' most acerbic attacks on their
own sex.

Several other seventeenth-century English writers followed in Agrippa's
path, declaring the superiority of women. Usually, as in Gerbier's book,
women demonstrate their spiritual superiority in the absence of vice
rather than by the performance of virtue. Speaking of women governors,
Gerbier concludes, "It clearly appears that they have therein excelled most
men, and therefore God never appeared to them in his wrath armed with
thunders as a revenger of crimes, but with crowns in his hand, as a dealer

of rewards: for this Sexe hath never been infected with such Monsters as Vitellious, Nero, Heliogabalus, Caligula. . . ."[89] Others, however, are more adventurous in their arguments. William Page (1580–1663), a royalist divine, left two unpublished treatises, one on the duties of widows and the other entitled "Woman's Worth, or a Treatise proving by sundry Reasons that Women doe excel Men." Beginning with Eve, Page laboriously works through the several areas in which women surpass men: they are less sinful, more chaste, more pious, wiser, more valiant, and more charitable. Even women's "badness," concludes Page, is less culpable than men's goodness.[90]

Daniel Tuvill had argued as early as 1616 in *Assylum Veneris* that women's supposed weaknesses are "onely shadows" of men's and that the principal reason for men's complaints about women is their own inability to select a wife for the proper reasons. He cites Plutarch as his precedent to attack the notion that women should not be "superior" in any fashion over their spouses. "Nothing, say our opposites, [is] more swelling and imperious than a Woman, that seeth shee hath the superiority and start of her Husband in any thing."[91] Yet Tuvill points out, refuting Dod, if the woman possesses the better mind, then she should lead her husband, rather than let the family suffer.

> He that is depriued of his bodily sight, is content to bee led, though by a childe: and shall hee, that is blinde in his understanding, disdaine to be directed by her, who by the ordinance of God, and the rules of sacred Wedlocke, is alotted him a fellow-helper in all his business?

The husband and wife are "the eyes of a Familie," he concludes, "if the right one bee so bleared, that it cannot well discerne; the guiding of the Houshold must of necessity be left unto the left, or on a sudden all will go to wracke."[92]

An Apologie for Womenkinde by "I.G." uses only the skeleton of this argument but preserves the forceful terms of liberty versus tyranny in a much lighter presentation. When God punished Eve, He "tooke the rule out of the womans handes, / Making her thrall unto subiections bandes."[93] However, the author continues, this does not mean that women were declared inferior to men.

> Yet did he not her cast in slauery,
> Nor any baser soule seruilitye.
> But left her guidance to her husbands will,
> Onely for order yeilding to him still.
> So Abell was subiected unto Cain,
> Yet Cadets Iudge th'authoritie is vaine.
>
> .   .   .   .

Therefore wise men that choose in veritie
Wiues, *amore, more, ore, et re*
Ought them as equals in each point t'esteeme,
And but for order them inferiours deeme.[94]

The same concept of hierarchy by which the elder brother is "above" the younger, not inferiority of substance, places women "under" men, a concept explored by Mary More in her essay. For men to abuse this ordering turns proper ranking to slavery, a perversion of the divine order.

John Wing uses the metaphor of the wife as her husband's crown to explore the nature of marriage in *The Crown Conjugall; Or The Spouse Royall* (1620). This image, he believes, epitomizes the multifaceted role of the wife in the family. His prime contention is that marriage is "to *joyne hart to hart*, and to *glew* the Husband and Wife, in good affection together."[95] If this be the case, then, "the Wife being the Husbands crowne must be much *respected* by her Husband, in his cohabitation with her." But, Wing continues, some may object that "the Wife is the *inferior*, and must the *superior* honour the *inferior?*" Wing's argument, like I.G.'s, is that although, of the two, the wife is in the inferior position, her husband's superiority is not such that he can withhold due respect from her.

> . . . indeed this inferiority is not so much, as most men doe (*customarily*) conceiue it to be . . . it will yet fall short of that which too many would haue it to be: who *imperiously* presse, that the *Husband is the head*, let it be; yet is not she *the foote*: he is the superior, true; yet she is not the *slaue*; the disparity is not so extraordinary, that she being to call him *Lord*, she must thereupon be counted his *vassall*.[96]

There is no attempt to deny that Eve was placed under Adam's will, but the issue of the nature of this dominance was obviously one of contention, not certainty, for readers and writers throughout the century.

John Shirley, the historian of feminine accomplishments, is almost as aggressive as Agrippa in linking the abuse of hierarchy with the poor state of women's education. He explains that the motive behind his history was to reveal how both men and women "have been imposed upon by the haters and contemners of the Beautious Sex, and consequently induced to harbour a mean Esteem of Female virtue."[97] Having established the base of his argument as the equality of male and female souls, Shirley asserts that men "having attain'd the upperhand in Rule and Power, claiming it by Birth-right as first Created, as much as in him lyes strive to keep that station as his prerogative, by endeavouring to keep the *Softer Sex* in Ignorance."[98] He compares this male effort with the refusal of the Turkish emperor to permit printing in his country, "least the greatest part of whom he through Ignorance, holds as in a Chain of Slavery, Reading the

Histories of other Lands, should find how much they are Abus'd," and also the practice of the Spanish toward conquered Indian nations enslaved to work the mines.[99] In this self-proclaimed liberating document, Shirley is making explicit connections between physical conquest and slavery and the domestic abuse of subordination imposed by enforced ignorance rather than by inferiority.

Finally, at the end of the century, Theophilus Dorrington offers a middle course, not accusing men quite so violently of a deliberate effort to enslave women, but still using the rib question as the key to his argument on the nature of a wife's obedience. Marriage is a bond, he declares, held together by *mutual* duties between husband and wife, "as it is necessary for the making a Knot that the two Ribbons be folded together." If the duties are not reciprocal, the union is "Imperfect and Unjust." The clincher for Dorrington, as it had been for past generations, was that "the manner of creating the first Woman sufficiently shews this; she was not taken from the Feet, nor from the Head, but from the Side, to shew that she ought not be either Slave or Mistress, but a Companion."[100]

Obviously, the manner of Eve's creation did not show *anything* sufficiently clearly to settle the controversy over the extent of patriarchal authority in the seventeenth century. The theory that Eve was made subject to her husband after the Fall was agreed on, but the practical application for contemporary marriages was not. As *The Emblem of a Virtuous Woman* (1650) remarks in commenting on 1 Esdras 14–18, "Here in this Chapter you apparent see / That women very strong, and mighty be: / For though man be her head, why yet I wist, / She'll rule her head and body as she list."[101]

Tyranny by either sex was strongly censured, as was the notion that women because they were "subject" were to be "servile." "Servilitie," states Heale, "is only to be imposed on such as are servile; and therefore not on wiues."[102] Relations between husband and wife are part of the larger questions in the seventeenth century on the nature of political authority and individual liberty. It is also part of the same argument made between Milton's Satan and Abdiel over the nature of obedience to a superior; for Satan, any form of submission is slavery, whereas for Abdiel, "Orders and Degrees / Jar not with liberty, but well consist."[103] Although universal sovereignty is claimed for Adam, for contemporary husbands and wives, "neither is the one so predominant, nor the other so servile, as that from them should proceede any other fruits but of a roial protection, and a loial subiection."[104] Even the authors of the very conservative *A Godly Forme of Household Government* observe that those husbands who "use them not as wiues, but as their servants,"

. . . surely they are but very fooles, that iudge and thinke matrimony to be a dominion. For such as would be feared, do afterwards piteously lament and complaine, that they can find no loue in their wiues, whose loue and amitie through their owne crueltie and hard dealing, they have turned into hatred.[105]

The theory of patriarchal authority underwent intense scrutiny and debate during the seventeenth century by the very sex it supposedly benefited. Its principal tenet, the unquestionable authority of the male head of the house, was severely criticized from within the ranks of male writers as part of the larger issues of power and governance. At no time during the century does one find authoritarian, rigidly patriarchal, or misogynistic opinions in theological or satirical writings left unchallenged. Instead, one finds a lively dialogue, where the male defenders of the female sex are actively engaged in sawing through the very supports of domestic patriarchal authority.

Women Writers

Patterns of Manuscript Circulation and Publication

At the heart of the current interpretation that women experienced a decline in status and increasing restriction of their activities is the apparent lack of articulate, intellectually aggressive women in the seventeenth century who had the respect of both male and female contemporaries. Scholars seek the equivalent of an erudite public figure such as Queen Elizabeth or Lady Jane Grey behind whom all rallied to praise their wit and learning. In comparison with these women, that apparently rare creature, the seventeenth-century female writer, seems timid, preferring to hide behind a pseudonym or to let her works remain hidden, in manuscript. Literature by and for women, it is maintained, did not exist in any significant amount during this period. It is, therefore, the absence of literary evidence that is being interpreted as a further indication of a repressive social structure.

Current studies, however, focus on the extraordinary individual instead of surveying the general pattern of women's participation in the intellectual life of the century. The result is a picture of literary women as isolated eccentrics protected by their husbands' ranks, such as the Duchess of

Newcastle and the Countess of Winchilsea, or persecuted victims of popular prejudice, such as Katherine Philips and Aphra Behn, standing in the stock of public opinion while critics and satirists ridiculed them. This limited selection presents a narrow base for analysis. Therefore, before analyzing the content of women's writings during the seventeenth century and considering the patriarch's wife's perspective, it is necessary first to examine the nature and extent of their participation in the intellectual life of their times.

Modern studies have concentrated on the very top layer of women writers, usually singling out the poets and dramatists for discussion rather than the controversialists and writers of devotional literature. Were the women who achieved the most acclaim (for better or worse), however, actually a fair representation of women's activities? This concentration unfortunately blocks our sense of the importance of female coterie poets and neglects the fact that women hack writers existed. In order to answer the question, one must first attempt to reestablish the intellectual context in which women wrote, and then to examine women writers by groups according to the subject matter on which they wrote.

One also needs to consider current interpretations of the reasons for the scarcity of women writers. Intuitively, one feels that being denied the benefits of association with the traditional sources of academic training and credibility, the public schools and the universities, must have placed intellectual females at a disadvantage. In recent years, this disparity in training has been studied by those interested in uncovering a "female poetic" in the different rhetorical styles of men and women.[1]

"Social pressures" are most frequently cited as the prime reason women did not engage in public controversies. In a biography of a successful seventeenth-century author, Aphra Behn, one critic contends that the majority of Behn's female contemporaries were successfully inhibited from writing and publishing, intimidated by popular sentiments that "wit belonged to the masculine province" and by women's "fear of violating feminine 'modesty.'"[2] Goreau states, "It is not surprising that a good deal of the earliest writing by women should have taken the form of letters, diaries, or autobiographies. They are entirely private forms of writing, not destined for publication and dealing only with what limited experience might come within the circumference of a lady's life."[3] As another commentator summarizes, before the 1800s "women knew quite well that if one woman signed her work with her own name, she opened herself to moral and social abuse."[4]

Such interpretations insist that seventeenth-century society's definition of femininity had sufficient force to control the extent of female participation in the intellectual world and the forms in which women could "safely" write. According to this view, society uses the threat of sexual libel to control women, explicitly linking intellectual and sexual aggression. Seventeenth-century satirists, in one critic's view, saw intellectual women as being in "rebellion against all aspects of patriarchal order and authority." Nussbaum maintains that "society easily accepts a satire against the things it most fears, especially if those things are created by the object of the satirist's attack. As that object, women become a metaphor for all that is threatening and offensive to the society at large."[5]

These readings of the intellectual environment of the seventeenth century are now widely accepted. But how much do they reveal about the actual extent of women's participation in literary and philosophical circles where issues conerning the status and nature of women might be raised? The problem with this interpretation is that it obscures several important distinctions between the twentieth and seventeenth centuries' attitudes toward literature. It is based largely on the careers of women dramatists and poets and pays scant attention to the activities of women in other disciplines. The divisions between different intellectual and artistic pursuits are blurred by the failure to consider whether a seventeenth-century professional woman dramatist faced different responses to her activities than did a woman who wrote plays for coterie productions, or the woman who was interested in theology or Old English verbs.

Furthermore, this theory of sexual intimidation fails to take into account adequately the seventeenth century's attitudes toward the act of printing itself, and toward those who derived an income from writing, whether male or female. The modern emphasis on publication as the measure of feminine accomplishment discredits any method of intellectual exchange that does not conform to twentieth-century practices as refuges for the intellectually repressed or second-rate. Although valuable groundbreaking work is being done in constructing bibliographies of women's works printed during the last two decades, the very criterion of such lists badly distorts the literary context in which women writers worked and undermines any conclusions drawn about the general status and situation of literate women.[6] If all that is known is a list of women who published their works, we do not really know who the women writers of the seventeenth century were or how and why they wrote.

Manuscript Circulation and Correspondence Networks

The seventeenth century was a turning point in the history of print. The slow acceptance of publication as a respectable activity is well documented among male writers at the beginning of the century. John Donne saw no need to publish his secular verse and Ben Jonson was ridiculed for doing so. This attitude was not extinct by the end of the century. The court satirists took little or no care to publish their works. Commenting on the difficulties of producing the definitive text of Rochester's poems, Vieth notes that many of the Restoration poets' works "came to be printed only by sheer accident."[7] There is good evidence that writers in the country were equally oblivious to the charms of seeing one's name in print. In 1677, John North wrote to his mother to thank her for the copy of his father's verses she had sent; he had shown them to friends in his college and hoped that Lord North could be persuaded to publish them—they finally appeared in print in 1984.[8] Reluctance to commit one's words or name to print, therefore, cannot be seen as a peculiarly female trait, but a manifestation of a much more general, and much older, attitude about writing, printing, and readership.

The writings of Grace Carrie of Bristol provide some insight into this mentality. She had been encouraged by friends to publish her treatise of prophecies. The subject matter of "Englands fore-warning or: A relation of true, strange and wonderfull visions and propheticall reuelations, concerning these tragicall, sinnfull, and dismall times shewed foure yeeres since to Mrs. Grace Carrie of Bristoll. 1639" had caused her to "humblie and Zealousye solicite his maiestie wth great trauell and expence." However, she announces in the preface, "upon more serious consideration and zealous praiers to god; for direction, with aduice of gods people," she decided to circulate the piece in copies, even though it had been "an intent by some to haue it publisht." She deliberately refused this offer, not on the grounds of "modesty," but because she felt it was "very unfitt, that such diuine & miracalous truth should be made common in these times wherin so manie falasies and false printed papers are set fourth." Print, for Grace Carrie, was no guarantee of quality or significance. Furthermore, she feared that "coming to the View of the meaner sort, of voulgar people, bye scandallous mouthes, it might somewhat eclipse the truth hereof."[9]

Carrie's concerns, therefore, are less with herself than with control over her writings. Print is seen by her as the medium of "falasies." She fears that her thoughts might be perverted by "voulgar" readers; her objections concern the lack of quality in published treatises and the loss of control over her readership and their applications of her writings. She did not remain "silent," however: she prepared manuscript copies, two of which are known to have survived.

For women writers in general, three forms of manuscript exchanges were available. They could produce manuscript books, circulate individual items in loose sheets which might also be preserved in commonplace books and manuscript miscellanies, or they could engage in correspondence. Obviously, these three modes are related—a poem or essay could begin in a letter, be copied and circulated, and finally end up either in a printed text or in a manuscript volume. Moreover, for some of these manuscript items, using one of these forms was a prelude to printing it. Others, however, were intended only for manuscript circulation.

Of these three forms, manuscript books survive in the smallest numbers. These are bound volumes of complete texts, which have the appearance of a printed book. They have title pages, prefaces or dedications, and are usually dated. Some also have page numbers, tag words at the foot of the page, and, like their medieval predecessors, intricate border ornaments and designs at the beginnings and ends of sections. These volumes range from plain and workmanlike to delicate and fantastic. Some of them were prepared by professional scribes such as "Jacobo Smitho scriptore" who produced Elizabeth and William Elstob's *Excerpta. e. Textu Roffensi.*[10] Other books are the result of painstaking labor by the authors or perhaps family members.

In much the same way that male writers such as Sir Robert Filmer did with *Patriarcha*, women writers had these elaborate texts transcribed as gifts for friends or patrons. "M.A." collected her poems, some of which had previously been circulated in separate sheets, to create a volume of verse for her benefactor William Sancroft, the archbishop of Canterbury. *A Collection of Poems humbley presented and Dedicated to the most Reverend Father in God* WILLIAM *by Divine Providence Lord Archbishop of* CAN-TERBURY *1689* contains ninety-seven pages of contemplative verse, none of which has ever been printed. In the preface, the author explains that she hopes her verses, "these mean productions which a little reading, a small experience, and smaller fancy, has made shift to bring forth," will make some modest return for the "condiscention and Candor, with which your Grace was pleased to receive a poor unknown, who hath no place to fly unto and none that careth for her Soul, when even my Kinsfolk had failed, and my familiar Friends had forgotten me."[11] The first poem is dated "made June 8, 1683," so that the volume represents M.A.'s poetic output over several years.

Another example of a work intended for circulation outside the immediate family circle is a beautiful text, *The Death, and Passion of our Lord* JESUS CHRIST, *As it was Acted by the Bloodye Jewes and Registred by the Blessed Evangelists* (c. 1637) by Elizabeth Middleton.[12] This vellum book of twenty-five pages has an elegant title page bordered with leaves and flowers; the dedicatory anagram to Mrs. Sara Edmondes and the poem itself have elaborate calligraphic ornaments and use two colors of ink for effect. In addition to the 172 six-line stanza poem, the book contains part of the text of William Austin's *Ecce Homo*. The pairing of these complementary pieces by the compiler suggests a wider readership was intended than simply Middleton's family.

Other texts were designed specifically for the entertainment of family and friends rather than for presentation to a patron. In these books, later generations sometimes added material to the original text, so it is not unusual to find more than one handwriting in the volume (this type of book apparently was passed down through the women in the family, for one often finds recipes and remedies added in different hands on the blank pages). Anna Cromwell Williams compiled *A Booke of Several Devotions collected from good men by the worst of Sinners* dated 1656 and 1660.[13] An inscription explains that it was a New Year's gift between sisters. In addition to verses by Donne, Williams included her own. There are also poems dealing with the deaths of relatives, such as that on Bettina Cromwell, which are in a different handwriting from the body of the text. Books such as this one were kept in the family and appear to have been women's legacies or gifts to each other, each generation of women contributing to it.

Charles Hutton, on the other hand, did the complete transcription of *My Lady Carey's Meditations & Poetry from ye first to ye 222 Page* in 1681.[14] Mary Carey dedicates the book to her "honest loving, and dearly beloved Husband, George Payler Esq" and the contents of her meditations concern the deaths of their children, a pathetic string of tragedies from 1650 to 1657. The titles of the other poems, such as "A Dialogue Betwixt the Soule and the Body," indicate both Lady Carey's familiarity with poetic conventions as well as her reflective turn of mind. Although her subject matter, like Anna Cromwell Williams's, was domestic in nature, the power of her verses appealed to a wider audience, a universal lament transmitted through scribal copies.

On a lighter note, the daughters of William Cavendish, Duke of Newcastle, and his first wife, Elizabeth Howard, produced a charming collection of their literary efforts designed strictly to entertain. Before their marriages, Lady Elizabeth Brackley, the Countess of Bridgewater (?–1663) and her sister, Lady Jane Cheney (1621–69), compiled *Poems, Songs, a Pastorall and Play* which is sometimes referred to by the play's title alone, *Concealed Fancyes.*[15] The types of items found in this collection are comparable in nature to the amateur verse and dramas composed by other lively young wits such as Henry King and Dudley, Lord North. Lady Elizabeth continued her literary pursuits after she became the Countess of Bridgewater, but her tastes shifted from pastorals to more serious matters. She left behind an enormous volume of *Meditations on the Several Chapters of the Holy Bible* in the Bridgewater library.[16] There is no textual evidence that either of these books was meant to be read by those outside a circle of friends and relatives, yet the books' contents demonstrate that these young women, as much as the young men, were actively engaged in literary activities, exploring the literary conventions and forms of their day, and believing that their final productions were worth preservation in formal, bound copies so that in the future others might read them.

Poetry was not the only literary area explored in such manuscript volumes. Translation was a popular pastime among seventeenth-century writers of both sexes. Jonathan Swift was occasionally employed by Sir William Temple's sister, Lady Gifford, to transcribe her translations, of which all that survive are "several scraps" in her papers.[17] Elizabeth Cary, Viscountess of Falkland (1585–1639), to whom *The Tragedie of Mariam* (1613) has been attributed, left manuscript translations of Cardinal Peron's works. Lucy Hutchinson chose to dedicate her translation of Lucretius to Lord Anglesey in a manuscript volume; he inscribed the gift "Given me June 11, 1675 by the worthye author Mrs. Lucie Hutchinson."[18] This presentation copy, as explained in her dedication, is a corrected version of an earlier piece which "by misfortune *got* out of my hands in one lost copie." Catherine Howard, an unknown author, prepared her own formal copy of her translation *A Methode to Converse with God Written in French* in 1683; there is no evidence to show for whom it was intended.[19] The best-known female translator in her own day and to historians is Elizabeth Elstob (1683–1756), whose studies of Old English won her respect and repute, but not, unfortunately, financial security. The British Library owns five of the manuscript editions prepared by her and her brother William at the beginning of the eighteenth century.

Theological and philosophical topics were also suitable materials for manuscript volumes. In addition to Grace Carrie's "Fore-warning," several religious manuscripts by Jane Lead (1623–1704), the founder of the Philadelphian Society, and her associates have been preserved. Lead also published numerous titles, which will be discussed later, and on her death, her son-in-law wrote to the German branch of the society to suggest they publish the remaining manuscript treatises "for the nourishment of the faithfull."[20] Lead's lieutenant in the society, Anne Bathurst, also compiled her own "Works" in a fair copy, some of which is taken from her diary. It contains a brief autobiography and lengthy accounts of "a Transportation or Manifestations made to Me, whither in the Body or out of the Body . . . I cannot tell" for the edification of the faithful, with helpful marginal glosses for the confused.[21]

Manuscript volumes such as these indicate that it was not essential to publish one's long or collected pieces to ensure their survival. These books are intended to preserve and present the poems, meditations, translations, and essays in an impressive, substantial form, making their content available and attractive for future generations of readers and perhaps attracting patronage for the author. They were first and foremost presentation pieces, not closet productions. They were "private" only in the sense that the author, not the bookseller, had control of the manuscript.

More common than these elaborate, lengthy presentation volumes, however, were the single items that survive in loose sheets or as entries in commonplace books and manuscript miscellanies. This was the form in which most of the writings of Katherine Philips and the Countess of Winchilsea were originally read. It also appealed to the obscure and probably untraceable women writers such as "Mrs. Taylor," "Mrs. H.," "Lady L.," and "Mrs. B.P."

Many of the editions of women's writings that were published posthumously had previously been circulated in manuscript. The religious devotions of Gertrude More (1606–33), an English nun who helped to found the convent at Cambray, were published posthumously as *The Holy Practices of a Divine Lover* (1657) and *The Spiritual Exercises* (1658). Her seventeenth-century biographer recounts how More while at Cambray, to settle herself in her religious vocation, "read over . . . all the books that were in the house, or that she could get from abroad, printed and manuscript, and read them seriously."²² She began writing her responses to these other authors and also composing her own prayers and meditations. "Some others in the house liked them so well, that they copied them out, and in time a great store of these amorous affections of her collection, or framing, were to be found scattered here and there in divers books and papers."²³ After her death, these separate pieces were assembled by the head of the house at Cambray, Father Augustine Baker, to form the second and third sections of a book he unfortunately subtitled *The Ideot's Devotions*.

Although she was born at the other end of the century and held religious beliefs at the opposite end of the spectrum, the Quaker poet Mary Mollineux shared More's attitudes toward writing and readers. Mollineux (1661–95) permitted her verses to be read by fellow Quakers. Tryall Ryder recalls in the preface to Mollineux's posthumous book *Fruits of Retirement* (1702) that on reading "some Copies of her Verses, which she gave me, I felt such Unity of Spirit with them, that I said, I thought they might be of Service, if made Publick in Print." But Mollineux refused, "not seeking Praise amongst Men" with her poems, but "to communicate the Exercise of peculiar Gifts amongst her near Friends and Acquaintance."²⁴ Like Grace Carrie of Bristol, Mollineux had no qualms about sharing her "peculiar Gifts," but she wished to control with whom she shared them.

The posthumous publication of Mary Monck's (d. 1715) verses in *Marinda* (1716) reveals similar manuscript transmission practices. Her father, the Viscount Molesworth, dedicated the volume to the Princess of Wales. After a lengthy preface decrying the practice of writing excessive, flattering prefaces, he introduces the verses in a few paragraphs, describing the contents as "the Product of the leisure Hours of a Young Gentlewoman lately Dead . . . as we found most of them in her Scrittore after her Death, written in her own Hand, little expecting, and as little desiring the Publick shou'd have any Opportunity either of Applauding or Condemning them."²⁵ Although she may have cared little for the applause of the multitudes, internal textual evidence and surviving single sheet copies of her verse in the Bodleian Library suggest that she did seek the approval and response of a circle of poets. *Marinda* contains, in addition to several superb translations of Spanish and Italian poets, a series of verse exchanges, such as "Upon an Impromptu of Marinda's, in answer to a Copy of Verses." It is evident from the content of several of the "epistles" that "Marinda" was engaged in a "poetic" correspondence like that Katherine Philips had enjoyed with her friends.

The female poet most celebrated by her contemporaries and who never published during her lifetime was Anne Killigrew (1660–85), the subject of John Dryden's famous ode. In an epitaph she wrote for herself, she reveals that she believed her reputation as a poet would survive: "When I am Dead, few Friends attend my Hearse, / And for a Monument, I leave my VERSE."[26] The volume published shortly after her death includes poems by other unidentified writers which were found among her papers; their presence suggests that not only was Anne Killigrew reading and copying the poems of her friends, but they were also doing likewise with hers. Moreover, she proved indirectly her participation in a manuscript exchange circle when in another poem she refutes angrily the charge that she is not the author of a certain piece.[27]

Killigrew's career also raises the issue of the extent to which manuscript circulation was intended to be a "private" affair to shield the author's "modesty." Manuscript circulation did not prevent one from having a reputation as a poet or philosopher. There are numerous examples of male writers for whom this was true—Sir Philip Sidney and John Donne are the most obvious—and women writers such as Killigrew, Philips, Anne Wharton, and the Countess of Winchilsea had public reputations long before their verses were printed. Anne Bradstreet is another example of a writer whose reputation was built on circulated manuscripts; her first volume was read in manuscript copies in both America and Britain for several years before it finally appeared in print.

Elizabeth Singer Rowe (1674–1737) at the end of the century provides an example of a woman who declared her preference for manuscript over print and had a popular reputation as a poet, although she professed complete disdain for it. Rowe, whose verses were admired by Matthew Prior, had attracted the patronage of Lord Weymouth in 1694 by "a little copy of verses of hers." Her name became more widely known with her "paraphrase of the thirty-eighth chapter of Job [which] was written at the request of Bishop Kenn . . . and gained her a great deal of reputation."[28] Even so, her biographer declares, "she could not be persuaded to publish her works by subscription or even to accept the advantageous terms offered by the booksellers, if she would permit her scattered pieces to be collected and published together."[29] The reason was not feminine modesty so much as spiritual disdain for the follies of the world: "she wrote verses through inclination, and rather as an amusement, than as a study and profession, to excel in which she should make the business of her life."[30]

Other women were either less spiritual or more tolerant of the plight of booksellers, because manuscript miscellanies such as *The Muses Magazine* frequently contained verses by women. Even after printed editions of their poems appeared, Aphra Behn and Katherine Philips enjoyed the attentions of these commercial manuscript collectors. This form also has preserved several other now lost and forgotten women poets in addition to the well-known ones. Numerous copies of Anne Howard, Duchess of Arundel's poem "The Death of Prince Henry" (c. 1612) survive in collections such as *Miscentur seria iocis, Elegies, Exequies, Epitaphs, Epigrams, Songs, and Satires and Other Poems. 1647.*[31] "Mrs. Elizabeth Linseys Song" also proved popular with compilers, no doubt for its rebuke of masculine indifference as well as its clever rhymes: "Why should you bee so full of spight / To man or woeman-kinde / To say when they are out of sight / Theire allso out of minde?"[32] Catherine Crofts's reply to the frequently copied verse "When Aurelia first I courted" ("When my Charles he first adored me") was picked up by two collections, one containing mostly poems with a play by Charles D'Avenant dated 1670 and the other in an unrelated small book which heads the poem "Carolus 2d in Barbara Countess of Castle" in reference to the royal mistress.[33] "Mrs. B.P.'s" archly humorous "To a Friende of Hers in Love" likewise found a place in two volumes, although nothing else of hers seems to have survived.[34] Sufficient copies of these verses must have been in circulation for booksellers and scribes to lay hands on them. They also must have been considered sufficiently attractive to be saleable merchandise.

Some women writers survive only in one copy of one poem. "Mrs. H's" pretty lyric "Shall I thus dying in despaire" found a home in a commonplace book, along with "My Lady L's" more daring "Phylis on ye new made hay / in wanton postures Lay."[35] There was an anonymous "Young Lady of Quality" whose contemplation of King James's picture, "What Briton can survey that Heavenly Face," earned a place in *The Muses Magazine or Poeticall Miscellanies in Two Parts* (1705) along with verses by Katherine Philips, William Congreve, Dryden, Rochester, and Abraham Cowley.[36] "Mrs. Taylor," who may or may not have been the same one published by Aphra Behn in her *Miscellany, Being a Collection of Poems by Several Hands* (1685), surfaces with a lone poem, "Of the Duchess," in a commonplace book.[37] "Mrs. M.R." makes one brief appearance in *Old Songs & Verses* with her doleful complaint, "How can the feeble sorte but yeelde att last?"[38]

Manuscript miscellanies compiled by booksellers were the most visible commercial record of individual women poets, but the commonplace books compiled by amateurs are much more typical of the literary practices of the seventeenth century. Through stray copies, these private amateur circles in many cases provided the materials for the professionals. The piracies caused cries of outrage from disgruntled writers, male and female, including Sir Thomas Browne and Francis Quarles in addition to Katherine Philips.

Outside the circle of Katherine Philips and her friends, the Tixall papers present the most complete picture of the practices of a group of dedicated amateur authors. At the heart of this circle was the Aston family, whose poems and correspondence were edited as the Tixall papers during the Regency period. The numerous brood of Sir Walter Aston (1584–1639), the patron of Michael Drayton, were engaged in literary pursuits of various types with enthusiasm and some skill, but their writings were not published until the early nineteenth century.[39] The youngest daughter, Constance Aston Fowler, assiduously collected and copied verses for her commonplace book. Along with pieces by Sidney Godolphin, Ben Jonson, Henry King, Thomas Randolph, and Aurelian Townshend, she gathered many poems by her brother Henry, her sister Gertrude, and friends such as Sir Richard Fanshawe and Lady Dorothy Shirley. "Send me some verses," is her constant plea to her brother, "I want some good ones to put in my booke."[40]

The difficulties of this form of manuscript transmission become apparent in her correspondence.

> You writt me word in your letter by Mr. Fanshawe, that heretofore you sent me verses which begun (Whilst here eclipsed,) this letter I did never receave, nor verses, which I am most truely afflicted att; and if you doe truely love me, do not denye me, but send them me againe; for you know not how much I suffer that they are lost.[41]

In another letter to her brother Herbert who was in Spain on a diplomatic mission, Constance finds fault not with the transport, but with the sender, rebuking him with mock seriousness: "I have not received yet those three copyes of verses you promised me for sending your box to Mr. Henry Thimelby . . . [I have] beged of you most pittyfully that you would send mee some verses of your own making." This seems particularly unfair, she points out, since "I have sent you all the verses that I could gett perpetually, never omieting the sending of any that I could get that wer good ones."[42]

Less precarious than these international exchanges was the collection of verses by her sister Gertrude Aston Thimelby and her friends Lady Dorothy Shirley and Katherine Thimelby, whose marriage to her brother Herbert Constance gleefully arranged. Many of the verses are companion pieces, written in response to other poems. "Lett not thy grones force echo from her caue," in which an unidentified young man urges his friend to stop moping over a lost love, draws forth the "Answer to these uerses Made by Mrs. K.T." which sets the fickle male writer straight.[43] Other poems comment on more common daily occurrences, such as "Upon the L D saying K T could be sad in her company," which necessitated the reply "Deare Cosen pardon me if I mistawke / I thought thy face had bin the truest booke."[44]

The Tixall papers give a picture of a lively network of friends and relations all interested in "modern" poetry. Through Sir Richard Fanshawe and Herbert Aston, European literary influences were added to native English ones. The group was primarily interested in collecting the efforts of contemporary writers, although the content of Constance's commonplace book and references to "Dr. Dunne" in Katherine Thimelby Aston's letters suggest that these women had a wider acquaintance with English verse. It is clear, too, from the correspondence, that the members of this circle enjoyed reading each other's poems and having friends read them, whether male or female.

The final avenue through which Stuart women enjoyed intellectual activities has, like the manuscript circles, been dealt with in a preemptory fashion as being a "private" literary form. Correspondence networks, however, provided educated women as well as men with opportunities for intellectual engagements and insights which their circumstances, excluded from universities and learned societies, might not immediately suggest.

There is an obvious distinction between domestic letters concerned with a family's health and happiness and an "epistle" or essay in letter form on an intellectual or literary topic which was directed outside the immediate family circle. It is not surprising that women were prolific correspondents of the first sort, witness the enormous collections of letters by Lady Brilliana Harvey, Dorothy Osborne, and the women of the Hastings, North, Barrington, and Finch families. What has received little or no attention in assessments of women writers during the seventeenth century is the extent of female participation in the second type of correspondence and how such activity was perceived by their male contemporaries.

An interesting feature of this period's correspondence is the quantity that has been preserved, not only in the original letters, but also in letter books and in transcribed copies. Such practices argue that correspondence of a certain type was viewed not as a discreet communication between two people only, but a formal composition to be preserved and perused by others as well. An indirect indication of this aspect of transcription can be found in the titles of many seventeenth-century publications. A popular format of printed treatises was to publish an exchange of letters on a controversial topic or a lengthy epistle refuting or defending another author, typified by John Locke's *Letter on Toleration* and George Hickes's *A Second Collection of Controversial Letters Relating to the Church of England and the Church of Rome* (1710).

Hickes's book is an exchange of letters between him and a "lady of quality" (identified in a letter to his wife as "Lady Carew of Haccombe in Devon, near Exeter") concerning her conversion from Catholicism.[45] The appendix of this volume is a long letter by a friend of Hickes's, Susanna Hopton (1627–1709), written to Father Tuberville about a similar occasion some twenty years earlier. Hopton "let me copy her Letter fourteen Years ago at her own House," Hickes writes, "and as soon as I had thoughts of printing it with my own, I sent her Notice of it, and asked her Consent, with Liberty to revise it: Both of which she gave me."[46] These revisions, explains Hickes, consisted of altering "several old, and now unfashionable Words, and Expressions, taken out of Authors before that time: These I took the Liberty to change for others, more in present use."[47] Not only had Hickes carefully preserved his own correspondence, he had also held on to Hopton's, which was not actually addressed to him at all, but merely a copy from her copy.

Usually, the first step in establishing a philosophical exchange such as that between Hickes and Lady Carew was to write to a published author with questions, compliments, or elegant criticisms of his or her work. As Hester Chapone comments to George Ballard in a letter in the early eighteenth century about this practice, "unity of opinion is generally f[ound] to be as strong a tye as that of Blod, and therin a liberty often taken with eminent authors."[48] Mary Astell's letter to Henry Dodwell on his *Case in View* concerning schismatical "erectors of Second Altars in the Dioces of Norwich" manages to criticize and compliment at the same time. "These hints, on wch I might easily have enlarged," she concludes her letter, "and which are but inartificially put together, I submitt to yr candid consideration not doubting that a person of yr great sagacity and blessed Peacemaking Temper will improve them all that may be, in order to ye happy Re-Union of which you appear so desirous."[49] In a postscript she adds, "If you think me worthy of an answer, be pleas'd to direct it to be left at Mr. Wilkins at ye Kingshead in St. Pauls Church yard." Dodwell was more than willing to accept the invitation to correspond, being "glad that Providence has given me this happy opportunity of being known to you, though not unaquainted formerly with your excellent and ingenious writings." Their exchange was of such interest that copies of the letters were circulated, one ending up in the commonplace book of an Oxford scholar, John Leak.[50]

Women were frequently the initiators of such epistolary exchanges, but they were not always in the position of having to solicit the attention of famous men. Both Ralph Thoresby and Sir Hans Sloane cultivated the acquaintance of Mary Astell, and John Locke sought out Catherine Trotter Cockburn after the publication of her defense of him. Cockburn's fame as a controversialist was strengthened by her participation throughout the latter part of her career in epistolary exchanges such as this. Her biographer records that "the worthy and learned Dr. *Sharpe* Archdeacon of *Northumberland*, who had read [her] *Remarks* in manuscript, and encouraged the publication of them, being convinced by them, that no person was better qualified for a thorough examination of the grounds of morality, entered into a correspondence with her upon that subject." Unfortunately, Cockburn's health did not permit her to continue this exchange, a situation much regretted by her biographer who concludes a bit sanguinely that "a discussion carried on with so much sagacity and candour on both sides would, in all probability, have left little difficulty remaining on the question."[51]

The best known of these epistolary exchanges was that between Astell and John Norris, eventually published as *Letters Concerning the Love of God* (1695). Astell again opened the correspondence by writing to Norris, and, with her usual tact, pointed out his weak links.

Reading the other day the Third Volume of your excellent Discourses, as I do every thing you Write with great Pleasure and no less Advantage; yet taking the liberty that I use with other Books . . . to raise all the Objections that ever I can, and to make them undergo the severest Test my Thought can put'em to before they pass for current, a difficulty arose which without your assistance I know not how to solve.[52]

After several letters in which Norris and Astell worked through their difficulties, the epistles became, by mutual consent, wider ranging. "The sincere Love you seem to have for the Truth, and the great Progress you have made in it," wrote Norris to Astell, "together with that singular Aptness of Genius that appears to be in you for further Attainments, makes me not only willing to enter into a Correspondence with you, but even to congratulate my self the Opportunity of so uncommon a Happiness."[53] He desired that their future letters

may be continually imployed upon serious and important Subjects, such as may deserve the Time, and reward the Pains that shall be bestowed on them, and may occasion such Thoughts and Reflections to pass between us as may serve to give true Perfection and Inlargement to the Rational, and right Movements and Relishes to the Moral Part of our Natures.[54]

Obviously, neither Norris nor Astell looked upon their correspondence as a trivial pursuit, nor, by the preservation and publication of the exchange, did they apparently consider it private speculation.

A correspondence exchange such as this one, or that of Anne, Lady Conway, with Dr. Henry More, the Cambridge Platonist, offered women who were isolated by either geography or temperament to participate actively in the intellectual controversies of their day and sometimes provided the testing ground for material that was eventually to be published. Lady Conway's disputes and discussions with More are reflected in several of More's treatises and in his "Heroic Pupil's" book *The Principles of the Most Ancient and Modern Philosophies* (1690).[55] A similar situation existed between Damaris, Lady Masham, the daughter of another Cambridge Platonist Ralph Cudworth, and John Locke. In addition to exchanging verses, their correspondence argued matters of theology and expressed a personal attachment; it led in part to Lady Masham's publication of *A Discourse Concerning the Love of God* (1696) and *Occasional Thoughts in Reference to a Vertuous or Christian Life* (1705).[56]

Women's involvement in epistolary networks is also documented in the posthumous publication of their papers and from pirated editions. Quite often, however, such practices resulted in general confusion over authorship. The mistakes made over Susanna Hopton's writings illustrate the difficulties encountered when discussing attribution and publication during this period. Her circle of friends included her future editor Nathaniel Spinckes and her spiritual advisor Thomas Traherne. One notable tangle that still troubles editors occurred in the eighteenth century when Traherne's meditations were attributed to Hopton because her reputation as a writer of devotional literature was greater than his during that period. Concerning another work that Hopton did write, Hickes declares that the

> excellent Book of Devotion without her Name, Entitled, *Daily Devotions, Consisting of Thanksgivings* etc. *By an Humble Penitent*, was her collection and composition, of which she communicated some few Copies in manuscript, by which means, I suppose, it came to be printed at London for *Jonathan Edwin*, 1673.[57]

Yet thirty years later the same piece appeared with a different title, attributed to a different person, *The Humble Penitent, or Dailey Devotions with The Sacrifice of a Devout Christian, or Preparations to the Worthy Receiving of the Blessed Sacrament. By a late Reverend Divine of the Church of England.* Hickes insists that Hopton knew nothing about this new edition: "the True Author of the Book told me it was not of her making, nor did she know by what Hand it was done." The practice of sending out copies of her writings provides Hickes with the answer and he deduces that the second book was "printed from a manuscript of a venerable deceased

Clergy-man of Herefordshire, with whom she had intimate Correspondence," and after his death, the confusion over the authorship arose.[58] Commenting on Hopton's practice of circulating copies, Hickes explains that in his own library, "I have two more manuscripts of her Composition, both Books of Devotion; one in her own Hand, the other an English *Hexameron*, transcribed fair, and ready for Press, Entitled, *Meditations Upon God's Works in the Creation of the World.*" Hopton's editor, Spinckes, supports Hickes's theory about the confusion over her first book, stressing again Hopton's practice of copying and circulating "some few Copies in manuscript."[59]

Some of the pieces by women devotional writers have survived only in manuscript copies. Dionysia Fitzherbert (1608–?), for example, was so anxious to ensure the preservation of her meditations and diary for future readers that she deposited two copies with Dr. John Rouse, the Keeper of the Bodleian.[60] A more widely known writer who exchanged thoughts with numerous leading intellectual lights of her time was Lady Dorothy Pakington (d. 1679), whose praises as a devotional writer and controversialist were sung by an admirable chorus of royalist divines including Dr. Henry Hammond and the Bishops John Fell, George Morley, John Pearson, Humphrey Henchman, and Peter Gunning. It was widely accepted that she was the author of *The Whole Duty of Man* (1658), a work acknowledged to be well within her capacities even by those who disagreed over its authorship.[61] Her prayers and devotions enjoyed manuscript circulation for many years after her death; copies were made by "E. Eyre" of six of her prayers, now in the Bodleian, and others were in the hands of Elizabeth Elstob at the turn of the century. Elstob's reply to George Ballard's request to see them gives some indication of the mechanics of manuscript transmission, which was not particularly efficient in this instance.

> I have made the most diligent search I possible cou'd, for Lady Pakington's two Prayers, but have not found them, but will search once more and if I don't find them it is probable Mrs. Chapone will be able to get you a sight of them for the Lady who lent them to me is married in her neighborhood.[62]

Although Lady Pakington's prayers and devotions were not published, it is clear from the correspondence about the authorship of *The Whole Duty of Man* that it was not necessary to have her name appear in print in order to establish a reputation both as a learned lady and as an author.

Other women writers left even fainter traces, but they can be found in secondary correspondence. Elizabeth Fisher Bland (fl. 1681–1712) had a reputation as a Hebraicist as seen in references to her by Ralph Thoresby and a single surviving transcript of hers in the British Library. Another

elusive author appears in a gracious letter written by the learned clergy-
man Peter Du Moulin to Lucy Hastings, Countess of Huntingdon, to
express his appreciation of her translations of his Latin verses into English. He is touched, he declares, that

> my verse could moue a person of such high parts and dignity to
> honour them with a traduction. . . . Our young Ladys reape the
> benefit of your Lsps verses which they write & learne, & more per-
> sons that are not for Latin are obliged to your Lps golden veine, for
> helping them to the way of Christian felicity.[63]

The only surviving example of the countess's verses is a manuscript piece
on the death of her son, inscribed by her in her copy of the collected
elegies, *Lachrymae Musarum* (1650).[64] These two items by the countess,
who was the daughter of the poet Sir John Davies and the prophetess
Lady Eleanor Davies Douglas, prove that she did engage in literary pursuits, although none were published. For her, like Elizabeth Bland, the
exchange of such translations and verses in letters with a select circle
satisfied the author's desire for readership.

A more sustained record of women's participation in the intellectual
controversies of the day through epistolary means can be found in John
Locke's extensive correspondence. In addition to his close friend Lady
Masham, Locke was also in correspondence with several other women,
discussing his books, their essays, and topics of mutual interest, in addition to acting as a matrimonial go-between. Lady Elizabeth Guise in
Utrecht writes to him with thanks for his letter and present; a mutual
acquaintance apparently had suggested that Locke contact her because of
her interest in his writings. "Curiosity is you know Insident to my Sex,"
she explains, "neither am I exempt from it in some perticulers. That was it
which first perswaded me to looke into your booke" where she found
much of interest and an excellent style.[65] Locke then sent her another
treatise of his to comment on, and she answers later that month,

> You have hitt right when you request me to peruse your booke; since
> I doe it with all the pleasure Imaginable and shall ascrib it wholy to
> my own dulnes if it be not as well to my advantage; but you must
> choose some other person to describe the Errors you would have
> found ther, since in my opinion there are non. (4: 439)

Other women correspondents did not let him off so lightly. Locke and
Elizabeth Burnet (1661–1709) corresponded for more than six years. She
had written to him in 1696 after reading *The Reasonableness of Christianity*,
quite concerned that he would be misunderstood (as he was) about his
stand on the existence of a "positive obligation from Scripture or Primitive practice for the use of the Sacraments" (5: 664). Locke responded

sympathetically and in 1697 he sent her a copy of his letter to Bishop Edward Stillingfleet. Although she politely demurred that "the subject is much too nice for me" in one letter, in another she favored him with a page-by-page critique of the piece (6: 138, 197–204). Locke seems to have taken this quite well:

> I am extreamly sensible of the favour you have done me in perusing my Book and makeing those observations you have done, and you have answered the expectations I had from the Friendship you honoured me with in being at the pains to remark to me, what you judge faulty in my management of this controversie. (6: 216–17)

Locke urges her to make more comments so that "where I finde you continue to think me in an error I shall know what use to make of it another time." Burnet hastens to assure him that "there needs no care or thought to Justify your self to me" but she is concerned that he will be misunderstood, since "I conclude your aim is to make people better and wiser, and hope you will remember the world is mostly made up of Children in the worst sense . . . many deprived them selves of the benefit they might reap by your books by carelessly taking in prejudices and caractures without examination" (6: 225–26).

At the same time, Burnet was sending her own writings in manuscript for Locke's critique. Late in 1699, she mentions that while perusing the New Testament, she wrote down her thoughts on "the state of the soul after death" (6: 707–8). Some six months later, she is apologizing for the delay in sending, at his request, her essay. Finally, in March of 1701, there is a brief mention of this piece again—Burnet wanted to have it back from Locke (7: 265). Locke had been very ill during this period, which explains in part why it is not until July 1701 that Burnet writes to thank him for his comments; apparently he had also requested to see more, for she adds, "you may be sure you have a right to command any thing of this Nature" (7: 359–61).

Besides transmitting their own writings in these letters, Burnet and Locke were reviewing the efforts of others. Burnet mentions Benjamin Whichcote's *Select Sermons* (1698) with approval. She notes, "I hear Dr. Bentleys late Book is condemned by some as too reflecting etc: but 'tis perhaps because," she concludes shrewdly, "they don't take his advise and put them selves in the place of the injured" (7: 575–76). Stillingfleet's works, which had sparked the controversy with Locke, were well known to Burnet, and being acquainted with both men, she laments in one letter "finding two persons so capable of thinking truely and consequently of thinking alike, so seemingly opposite to each other" (6: 509–11). She also was familiar with John Norris's *An Essay Towards the Theory of the Ideal or Intelligible World* (1701) and was eager to hear Locke's views on it (7: 61).

The copious correspondence of Rachel, Lady Russell, also displays her lively and informed interest in the religious and philosophical issues of the day, even if she shows little inclination to join the fray directly. Her network of correspondents ranged from her former tutor and close friend Dr. Fitzwilliam and Bishop Tillotson to Bishop Burnet (who praised her epistolary style), Lord Cavendish, Sir James Forbes, Dr. Simon Patrick, Sir Robert Worsley, and Lord Halifax. Fitzwilliam, Tillotson, and the Earl of Galway maintained a frequent exchange of books, papers, and opinions with Lady Russell. In 1685 she writes to Fitzwilliam, "I have not the book you mention of Seraphical Meditations of the Bishop of B. and Wells, and should willingly see one here . . . I have sent you the last sheet of your papers, as the surest course; you can return it with the book."[66] With Fitzwilliam she discusses *The Anatomy of an Equivalent*, lent to her by another friend, and *The Letter to a Dissenter on the Declaration of Indulgence* by the Marquis of Halifax (*Letters*, pp. 414, 378–79). On another occasion, she sends him an unidentified text, "cry'd up to be very well writ, by which has offended the States in a high measure; so much, 'tis said, they have desired the licence to be called in" (*Letters*, p. 394). With Tillotson, she passes on Fitzwilliam's opinions about a certain Samuel Johnson's *Way to Peace Among All Protestants*, adding her own view that "if it hath not fully pleased both [sides], it hath the good fortune to have provoked neither" (*Letters*, pp. 409–10).

Lady Russell's letters to the Earl of Galway in the early part of the century are evidence that she also circulated her own devotional writings. On receiving some of his papers to read, she comments, "Neither you nor myself have the smile of fortune too lavishly bestowed upon us, or to abide by us, as to draw our hearts or minds as to choose, and be fond of what the world at present affords us." To his request that she send her writings, she replies,

> Pray, my Lord, be not in care about my writings. Indeed, they are not worth your reading, nor the postage: but I consider, if any body living will think them so, it is yourself and Lady Norton [her niece]; and I often feel myself willing to relieve my thoughts, so apart to reflect on times past, when to look forward to what is to come, should be my care, my comfort, or my dread. (*Some Account*, pp. 315–16)

It is easy to receive the impression that only titled ladies or bishops' wives participated in epistolary exchange, but the letter books and files of the nonconformist and Quaker ministers reveal similar contacts with women of lower social rank but equal thirst for knowledge. Richard Baxter maintained theological and philosophical correspondence with several women, some aristocrats, and some not. Mary Rogers, the wife of the governor of Hereford, opened her exchange with Baxter declaring "your book of mortification (of the crucifying this world) hath peirsed into the secrets of my soule and shewed mine iniquity."[67] Katherine Gell also used the opportunity of commenting on Baxter's publications to introduce the subject of her own theological doubts and concerns. She wrote to him in July 1655 expressing her fears over her state of grace, hoping

> yr Leasure will permit some lines back to me, I heartily wish we could see you one weeke in ye Country yt we might also heare you . . . had I not to great a family to leaue I should indeauor ye fullfilling my desires in coming to you; ye great care you haue shewed to poore soules made me willinge to write.[68]

Their correspondence lasted more than three years, and included spiritual comfort offered by Baxter and a mutual exchange of interesting treatises and sermons. Gell was in communication with other religious figures as well, for she writes to Baxter with some disapproval of one Mr. Billingsly, whom she heard preach on grace, "I haue herein sent yu [three treatises] one of ym yt I may see was to chide me & yerfore being on such a point I haue sent a copy of my answere wch he never answered agayne."[69]

Unlike Gell, Elizabeth Throckmorton had a personal acquaintance with her correspondent, the controversial Bishop Stillingfleet. She writes to him concerning the arrangements for a theological gathering and her letter makes her role in the proceedings quite clear.

> The gentlemen are willing to attend you wherever you please, I think it will bee less trouble to you & more privatt, att your house but that I leave to your appointment, & if I hear nothing from you to the contrary on thusday we will be at your house att 3 in the afternoon. Schism is the point we desire to haue discuss'd: not to be wors than my word I have sent you Mr. Thorndicks papers: which pray oblige me with your care of.[70]

The other surviving pieces of this correspondence indicate the same strong tendency in Mrs. Throckmorton for the disputation of heavy subjects. "I discoursed with some persons since I was with you about the Greek Churches admitting us in communion, which they say agrees with them in the doctrine of transubstantiation," she opens one letter enthusiastically. She deftly abstracts their arguments about the Catholic Church, noting that "they offered to dispute any point I pleased either in person or writings, but I was very desirous to haue them proue the Ch. of Rome the Catholick Ch: soe as to include all the <?> of her comunion: and the Pope the head of it," which she admits is not really a fair question. She concludes her discussion of the issues by asking Stillingfleet "if you haue any thing you think materiall for mee & reasonable to urge" to send it to her in writing and let her know his address "that I may give you their answers."[71]

Also misleading is the impression that literate women relied solely on men for their intellectual fuel in these epistolary exchanges. The correspondence between educated English women such as Bathsua Makin and Gertrude More with the celebrated European scholar Anna Maria van Schurman was originally part of this network of "private" exchange. Van Schurman's replies to their letters, in Greek and Latin, were later included in her published papers.[72] Elizabeth Thomas, in addition to her educational discussions with John Norris and "Pylades" (Richard Gwinnet)— "Since you desire my Thoughts at large concerning *Philosophy*" begins one letter—also sought out the company of learned ladies such as Lady Hester Pakington and Lady Mary Chudleigh, the author of *The Ladies Defence* (1701).[73] Chudleigh encourages "Corinna" to write on the role of women in marriage, "since you write so incomparably well both in Prose and Verse."[74] Chudleigh concludes her letter desiring that the "Correspondence you have so generously begun, I hope you will be so kind to continue." Elizabeth Burnet, after her initial hesitation over Catherine Cockburn's theatrical acquaintances, became her patron, introducing her to Locke and, through her husband, circulating Cockburn's writings on the Continent.[75] Mary Astell also attracted a large circle of female correspondents interested in intellectual issues pertaining to women, among whom were Lady Anne Coventry of Smithfield, Elizabeth Elstob, Lady Catherine Jones, and Lady Elizabeth Hastings, the latter of whom unfortunately burned all her correspondence.[76]

The overall impression left by a survey of these different methods of manuscript exchange is not of intellectual stagnation or isolation of intellectually inclined women, but of the existence of personal networks along which manuscripts and letters traveled in Britain and Europe. Patriarchal sentiments may have dissuaded some women from publishing their writings—along with reasons of geography, social status, and expense, which also deterred male writers—but it did not stop the act of writing itself. As Isaac Watts observed of Elizabeth Bury (1664–1720), another well-educated daughter of a supportive mother, there were many Stuart women "rich in Learning, yet averse to Show."[77] Elizabeth Burnet and her family are a case in point. Although she published a book of devotions, the majority of her intellectual activities were conducted through chains of correspondence. She read and criticized the works of Stillingfleet and Locke, in manuscript and print, and cultivated her acquaintance with Astell and Cockburn. While she was pursuing the state of the soul, her husband, Bishop Burnet, was corresponding with the poet Anne Wharton (d. 1685), who, in turn, was simultaneously composing a drama for her friends' entertainment and exchanging verses with Edmund Waller, Aphra Behn, and the Earl of Rochester.[78]

Through manuscript circulation and epistolary exchange, channels did exist for women to cultivate their intellectual and literary interests. This method also provided the opportunity for a readership outside their own families without losing control over their productions. It could lead to a reputation as a poet, scholar, or controversialist without a word having been published. Particularly striking is the degree to which women felt free to approach, and, with polite formalities, criticize the writings of leading male controversialists of their day. Equally important are the ways in which women preserved female writings through family commonplace books and, in a wider sphere, sought out other women interested in philosophical or literary pursuits to establish networks of women writers.

Patterns of Publication

When one turns from the manuscripts to the printed texts written by women, the recent efforts to construct bibliographies become extremely valuable. They reveal as incorrect the impression that women did not engage in public literary activity and controversy in any numbers; although women wrote only a small fraction of all titles published during the 1600s, Patricia Crawford names nearly 300 who have been identified as the authors of pamphlets, books, and broadsides.[79] This number, as we have seen, cannot be taken to represent the total number of women actively engaged in literary and intellectual pursuits; apart from its omission of manuscript works, there is no way of determining how many of the remaining anonymous entries in the catalogues are by women. Also, the cut-off date at 1700 excludes writers such as Elizabeth Burnet, whose minds and attitudes were the product of Stuart education, but whose writings appeared in print in 1701.

The other intriguing feature of Crawford's bibliography is that of these women, only sixty-two felt the need to conceal their identities with initials, pseudonyms, or anonymous publications. Furthermore, many of those who did so in one instance, such as Jane Lead and Dorothy White, used their names in other works. Finally, the fact that neither Catherine Cockburn nor Mary Astell put their names on their publications did not bar their recognition as authors and controversialists. Obviously, not all of Aphra Behn's contemporaries were cowed into silence or felt their modesty slipping.

Given this respectable number of women openly engaged in authorship, even if the output was only a small proportion of the whole, why does the impression continue that women were effectively barred from the press? One interesting phenomenon apparent in the new bibliographies is the degree to which earlier cataloguing efforts hide women writers. There has been a tendency to condense the number of women writing by attributing all "female books" on certain subjects with similar titles to one or two well-known women. Mary Astell has frequently been credited with titles more likely to have been written by Judith Drake, and Lady Chudleigh has been attributed the authorship of several "ladies' defenses" that are not hers.[80]

The most obvious reason for the invisibility of women writers is their subject matter. Twentieth-century critics concentrate on poets and playwrights, although during the seventeenth century the most popular topics for both sexes were matters of religious controversy, which have proved to have little lasting appeal. Many seventeenth-century authors who were "popular" in their period are unreadable today. As Edmund Gosse observes, a bit unfairly, of Catherine Cockburn's works, "her later writings, on philosophy, on morality, on the principles of the Christian religion are so dull that merely to think of them brings tears into one's eyes."[81] Today, no one analyzes the fine points of Margery Clipsham's *The Spirit that Works Abomination* (1685) which generated sufficient enthusiasm among her contemporaries to require a second edition. The question to be asked, therefore, is not how many seventeenth-century women writers produced works of interest to a modern audience, but the extent to which their writings were printed and attracted a readership among their contemporaries.

More influential than these two explanations, however, is the extent to which seventeenth-century women writers gave this impression themselves. "It is not ambitious design of gaining a Name in print (a thing as rare for a Woman to endeavour as obtain)," asserts Hannah Woolley in her comprehensive encyclopedia of domestic skills, *The Gentlewoman's Companion* (1675). The only reason she printed her autobiography (and portrait) in it was "to stop the mouths of such who may be so maliciously censorious as to believe I pretend what I cannot perform."[82] In introducing a book of a completely different character, Dorothy Leigh feels a similar need to explain her reasons for publishing *The Mother's Blessing* (1636), "lest you should marvell, my children, why I doe not according to the usuall custome of Women, exhort you by words and admonitions rather than by writing."[83] According to Mrs. Leigh, it was "motherly Affection" that overrode any objections, and her prudent fear that her eldest child would hoard a manuscript copy.

How much do such declarations reveal about the state of feminine authorship? When one examines the context of these two works, the women's protestations of the uncommonness of their activities is shown to be a bit misleading. Both women were writing on subjects and in forms which had been successfully undertaken by previous women writers in that century. Woolley herself was highly successful, with eight titles to her credit, all of which went through multiple editions. She also wrote in a tradition established by the Countess of Kent, whose *A Choice Manuall, or Rare and Select Secrets in Physick and Chirugery* (1653) went through nineteen editions by the end of the century. Leigh, likewise, had her predecessor in the genre of the mother's advice to children in Elizabeth Joceline's manuscript book *The Mother's Legacie to her Unborne Childe* (1625). The popularity of this subject was capitalized on a few years after Leigh's book by Elizabeth Richardson, Baroness Crommond's *A Ladies Legacie to her Daughters* (1645).

Were these disclaimers, or the use of pastoral psuedonyms, indications of feminine fears of social censure? Certainly, the most celebrated incident of a woman's distress over appearing in print is that of Katherine Philips, the "matchless Orinda," when her verses were published under her initals in a pirated edition in 1664. "I must never show my face [in London] or among any reasonable people again," she wrote in chagrin to Dorothy, Lady Temple; one of her biographers observes heatedly that "there are no records of any man suffering as Katherine Philips did over the publication of his literary work."[84] Disregarding the issue of men's publication fears for the moment (they, too, published anonymously), one is left wondering what Philips suffered on this occasion and why—did her fears and those of her fellow writers who printed anonymously arise out of concern for their reputations as chaste, sheltered females or as poets and thinkers?

The first feature of the case to consider is that Philips already had a reputation as a writer when the pirated edition appeared, having printed her translation of Corneille's *Pompey* to critical acclaim in the previous year. Lord Orrey was the instigating force behind her translation and presentation of this piece, which won her a literary reputation in court circles.[85] Not only did she solicit criticism of *Pompey* from him, but Sir Charles Cotterell ("Poliarchus") and Sir Edward Derring were also invited to comment critically on it and her other writings.[86] Nor was Philips unduly alarmed at the thought of strangers reading *Pompey*; her prime concern over the large number of manuscript copies floating about before its official appearance was that they would lessen the force of "that particular Respect intended" by her dedication of the piece to the Duchess of York.[87] In light of these prior literary activities, Philips's dismay over the theft and publication of her verses appears to have been more complex than a modest attempt to hide the fact that she was a poet.

Was it actually, then, a fear of critical response? As is known after the fact, her verses brought her enormous praise and reputation. Before this period, however, her correspondence with Cotterell reveals that she was neither unwilling to have her verses read outside her immediate circle of friends, nor was she afraid of masculine criticism. Although many of her poems were directed to special women friends such as Mary Aubrey ("Roseiana"), Philips also composed several at the desire of Poliarchus, too. It is his "repeated Commands," she writes him, which have "at length compell'd a very melancholy Muse to appear in a more Chearfull Dress than she usually wears" (p. 37).

Her letters to Cotterell and Lady Temple show that she views the pirated edition as a violation of privacy, but "impudence" is the word she selects most frequently to characterize the act. " ' Tis impossible for Malice it self to have printed those Rhymes, which you tell me are got abroad so impudently, with so much Wrong and Abuse to them, as the very Publication of them at all, tho' never so correct, had been to me, who never writ a Line in my Life with the Intention to have it printed" (p. 228). Since she had just supervised the publication of *Pompey* the year before, this remark deserves closer attention. She repeats her claims in a later letter that she had only written verse for "want of Company and better Employment, or [when] the Commands of others have seduc'd me to write" and she would have preferred "never to have those Trifles seen at all, than that they should be expos'd to all the World in this impudent manner" (p. 229).

The force of her indignation is directed at the printer of her poems, not at the publisher of her translation. Her principle objection is the "manner" in which her poems are being "exposed," made public. Her indignation reaches its height when she thinks of her verses,

> my Imaginations and idle Notions rifled and expos'd to play the Mountebanks and dance upon the Ropes to entertain the Rabble, to undergo all the Raillery of the Wits, and all the Severity of the Wise, to be the Sport of some that can and Derision of others that cannot read a Verse. (p. 230)

The pirated edition was published under her initials, not her name, and it is further proof of the wide readership enjoyed by her verse in manuscript that she knew they would not conceal her identity. Nowhere in their correspondence, however, do Katherine Philips and her friends suggest that her femininity or reputation as a chaste wife is at stake. In fact her male acquaintances advised her to print immediately yet another edition, an authorized one, as the best counteraction to the pirated version (p. 220). There is no question that Philips felt herself badly used by the booksellers, but her desire to suppress the pirated 1664 edition is more than mere female modesty or fear of recognition as a writer. It is also the distress of an author over inaccurate transcriptions, mixed equally with indignation that "the Rabble" and those that "cannot read a Verse" would now be free to make ill-informed judgments on her and her poetry.

A related matter which also distressed Philips was that these same ill-disposed readers would believe "that wretched Artifice of a secret Consent, of which I fear I am suspected" (p. 231). She vigorously denies such schemes in her letters to her friends, declaring that both she and her poems were exploited as a "pittiful design of a knave to get a groat."[88] There are no such complaints made about the publisher of *Pompey*. Her denunciations of the pirating publisher who hurried her verses into print are as much the reaction of an author outraged as of a female violated.

If Katherine Philips is placed in the wider context of all publishing writers in the seventeenth century, then we may ask, Could this insistence on the oddity or exceptional nature of the author and the insignificance of her literary output be a literary convention rather than an actual reflection of the individual author's experiences? Were the disclaimers included in the prefaces specifically a characteristic of women's writings, were they autobiographical revelations, or did they mirror larger literary tradition?

In the prefaces of books by women, certain patterns emerge. Those women who printed under their own names took great pains to assure their readers that it was not a desire for personal fame and fortune that prompted them to print. It was "meer pity [which] I have intertain'd for such Ladies, Gentlewomen, and others, as have not received the benefits of the tythe of the ensueing Accomplishments" that moved Mrs. Woolley to share her domestic secrets.[89] "Not in Affectation to be Popular (for that I do not desire)," astringently maintains Elizabeth Bathurst, who printed three treatises defending the Quakers, "but in Obedience to Christ Jesus . . . have I pen'd this matter, so that the Innocency of his Truth and People may more conspicuously appear." As for personal gratification as an author, she declares, "neither have I fondly desired to get my Name in Print, for 'tis not Inky Character can make a Saint."[90] Elinor James, in her support of the king and the Anglican Church, was ideologically opposed to Bathurst, but similarly announces on the title page of her *Vindication of the Church of England* (1687) that "it is not Interest that moves me to this, for I never made Gain of anything that ever I did, nor none do I desire; for it was nothing but the Fear of Gods Judgements that hath been the sole Cause of all my Actions for above these Twenty years."[91]

Even those women who had the protective shield of a pseudonym felt the need to announce their lack of worldly concerns. Whether anonymous or otherwise, poetry or theology, in the preface the work is presented as a public duty of the author, which, even so, appeared only because of the solicitation of *several* friends. Elizabeth Singer Rowe finally permitted her verses to be published at the end of the century only "at the desire of two of her friends," but the preface also implies coyly that a further volume might be produced should the urging be renewed.[92] Lady Mary Chudleigh declares of *The Ladies Defense* (1701) that "'twas written with no other Design, but that innocent one of diverting some of my Friends; who, when they read it, were pleas'd to tell me they lik'd it, and desir'd me to Print it, which I should never have had the Vanity to have done, but in a Compliment to them."[93] Such repetitious assertions of reluctance and the insistence on the inconsequential nature of the piece have been read as autobiographical statements or feminine defense mechanisms. Although he is careful to urge caution in interpreting such remarks, Keith Thomas nevertheless feels that such statements "must have served to perpetuate the legend of women's inferiority."[94]

In the context of the period, however, such modesty is not unusual. When one reads the prefaces of works comparable in subject and scope by men, not by professional writers but amateurs, one is struck by the similarity of the protestations. "This which was at first *conceived* for the use and direction of my own Congregation," quips John Flowres, "I have at the desire of some private Friends, suffered to be *brought forth* to a more publick view."[95] Edward Reyner is even shyer, claiming that he was "assayled by friends to publish some pieces, which cost me pains, but could never be overcome till now." "I am sensible," he concludes with adamant modesty, "of the curiousity and criticalness of the times, and of my own tenuity and insufficiency. I am able to bring nothing out of my poor Treasury which may seem new."[96] The anonymous T.M., who is also in print only because of the enthusiasm of his friends, has a higher opinion of his own rhetoric, but an equally low one of his readers:

> this Task was first undertaken by me not onely for the satisfaction of some private intimate Friends and honest-minded Protestants, who did much sollicite and intreat me hereunto, but also for the confutation of all such peevish and perverse opposers of the Truth and to stop the mouthes (if it were possible) of such Malignant Antilegions, Antagonists, and Gainsayers.[97]

Read in this company, women authors seem no more modest than their male contemporaries; rather than pleading pressing business or spiritual concerns which prevent the author from attempting true scholarship as many male writers do, however, they simply plead their sex.

Regardless of the subject matter, male and female writers shared a low opinion of the scholarly discrimination of their readers. Comments about the "nicety" of the age abound and references to narrow-minded critics were commonplace. Richard Ferrers in *The Worth of Women* (1622) speaks sadly of his past experiences; no sooner did he pick up a pen "But all the carping-criticks-squint-eyd rout / Like dogs to carion did about me runne, / And fortie faults in twentie words found out."[98] Even the clergy were not exempt; Thomas Brookes, the author of *The Unseasonable Riches of Christ* (1655), declares defiantly that he has no intention of trying to please "the captious Critick or the sullen Cinnic."[99]

Needless to say, women writers shared this defensive attitude toward readers. When the noted Old English scholar Elizabeth Elstob sent one of her books to the Yorkshire antiquarian Ralph Thoresby, her only remark was "as you find it deserves, I doubt not you will defend it against the Censure of the Criticks."[100] Dorothy Leigh announced her intention to publish, "not regarding what censure for this shall be laid upon me."[101] Lucy Hutchinson was more explicit about her feelings for the reading public at large in her dedication of her translation of Lucretius to the Duke of Anglesey. She calls Anglesey "the iustly celebrated Micenas of our dayes where Learning & Ingenuitie finds it most honorable, I had allmost sayd, its only refuge in this drolling degenerate age, that has hissed out all sober & serious studies."[102] Whether or not readers and critics were as contentious and narrow-minded as these authors claim is one matter, but it appears from the conventions followed by both male and female writers that anyone entering the arena of publication had better be wearing armor.

If it is recognized that self-deprecation and the repeated insistence on lack of financial motive were at least partially literary conventions, shared by seventeenth-century male and female writers, rather than a strictly personal revelation, then it is possible to reestablish the literary environment for women writers specifically. Such attitudes appear to be more closely tied to attitudes toward print than toward gender. As seen in the preceding chapter, the antifemale satirists rebuked women for getting "out of their place" with their writings during the seventeenth century. But, as also seen, there was no unanimous opinion of exactly what their place was during the century. The harshest and most frequent criticism, whether by men or women, is directed at the "gainsayer," the person who writes for personal profit and glory. Such a writer seems to violate the notion of print as a public medium, one intended to spread general moral improvement, not to exploit for private gain.

Providing they had sufficient public spirit and "friends" to encourage them to print, what subjects attracted women writers? Crawford's analysis shows that works by Quaker women were by far the most numerous publications, followed by books of prophecy, "literature," and political writings.[103] In short, women who did publish chose to do so most frequently on controversial subjects or in defense of a beleaguered faith. Appeals, defenses, and petitions round out this body of printed materials. Print was apparently an acceptable medium for women who felt themselves grievously wounded under the law and their purpose was to attract as wide as possible public attention to their authors—not a very "modest" proceeding.

Particularly visible and interesting are the female petitioners during the Commonwealth. During the 1640s and 1650s, large groups of women presented petitions to Parliament covering matters of national importance as well as private grievance, martial law, tithes, and the bankruptcy laws as well as for the release of husbands and fathers. The prefaces of these petitions begin courteously enough with modest disclaimers, but as Patricia Higgins notes in her study of them, once into the heart of the matter, deference is dropped.[104] When Mistress Anne Stagg, a brewer's wife, presented a petition in 1642 on the dangers of episcopacy, it is plain that she and the other signers expect from Parliament "the same gracious acceptance with you [found by men], for the easing of these grievances, which, in regard of our frail condition, do more nearly concern us and do deeply terrify our souls."[105] Other petitions are much less restrained in their language. One protesting the use of martial law in peacetime made its case in blunt terms.

> Are any of our lives, limbs, liberties or goods to be taken from us more then from men, but by due processe of Law and conviction of twelve men of the Neighborhood? And can you imagine us to be so sottish or stupid, as not to perceive, or not to be sencible when daily those strong defenses of our Peace and wellfare are broken down and trod underfoot by force of arbitrary power?[106]

Another interesting feature of these petitions is the large number of women signers who supported and presented them. On 23 April 1649, one was brought to Westminster by nearly 500 women, according to witnesses, which had nearly 10,000 women's signatures.[107] The petition condemning the death of the Leveller Robert Lockyer and the use of martial law during peacetime was worded to "plead the Rights and Libertyes of all Peticoat Petitioners, and then demand Justice against all that had a hand in the murther of Mr. Lockyer together with an inlargement of the rest of their Champions in the Tower and at Windsor" and carried at the end several thousand signatures.[108] The petition signed by Mary Forster in 1659 opened with a brief comment that "it may seem strange to some that women should appear in so publick a manner, in a matter of so great concernment as this of *Tithes*," but it is the women's duty to "bring in our testimony even as our brethren against that Anti-christian law and oppression . . . by which many of the Servants of the Lord have suffered in filthy holes and dungeons until death."[109] The first of the declared 7,000 signatures is that of Margaret Fell, followed by those of her daughters. The roll continues, divided by districts, some prefaced with a separate statement; London women urged "you which should do Justice, we who are of the female kind, whose names are underwritten, do bear our Testimony against Priests and Tithes, who have spoiled our Friends good, and prisonned many of them to death."[110] Mothers and daughters together signed this and other documents, two generations uniting in public political action. Those activities, therefore, cannot be dismissed as eccentric behavior by a few women, manipulated by men. In order to gain these impressive numbers, the women themselves would have had to have both good organization and strong commitment.

Although the large group petitions stopped after the Commonwealth, the older practice of an individual petitioning for justice or appealing to the public in a printed defense persisted. Whether the author is upholding her religious practices, her character, or her business, the tone in these petitions is open aggression. Anne Levington turned to print to declare the true *State of the Case in Brief* (1655) between her and the Countess of Sterling. Elizabeth Cellier, the London midwife accused of involvement in the Gunpowder Plot, showed the same fighting spirit in print with *Malice Defeated* (1680) as she had shown in the stocks. There, according to one spectator, she held a "kind of battledore" to protect her head from the crowd's rocks, and "all the stones that were thrown within her reach, she took up and put into her pocket."[111]

More common, perhaps, than Cellier's sensational treason trial, was the case of Mrs. Hester Shaw. She was, confusingly enough, another successful London midwife who also had an unfortunate experience with gunpowder. Her neighbor's secret supply blew up Shaw's house and killed several of her relatives. To add to her woes, Shaw's local minister, to whom she had entrusted some of the goods saved from the house, refused to give them up, thereby casting aspersions on her character. *A Plaine Relation of my Sufferings* (1653) and *Mrs. Shaws Innocency Restored and Mr. Glendons Calumny Retorted* (1653) threw the matter open to the public. Again, friends were involved in Mrs. Shaw's decision to publish her grievances.

> I am necessitated to publish this Narrative, in Answer to a Relation of my Sufferings by that sad Accident of Gunpowder which befell me and others the 4 of January 1650 and set forth by Mr. *Thomas Glendon* Minister in that Parish . . . finding myself crowded into print with calumny and reproach; I was rather prevailed upon by some of my best friends, not to be silent least mine innocency might thereby suffer.[112]

It is significant that Mrs. Shaw's opponent (who also published his defense) was none other than the local minister, a strong source, one would have thought, of patriarchal authority and moral superiority. In view of this fact, together with the supposed reluctance of seventeenth-century women to appear in print, it is notable that Mrs. Shaw's best friends, like Katherine Philips's, considered publication the most certain means to confirm her good name and to restore her goods.

While the Quaker women dominated the field of religious writings, other women writers' publications ranged from the eccentric, highly personal outpourings of the numerous prolific prophets of the century to the scholarly quibbles over Anglican communion practices. All of these topics, however, are characterized by their aggressive public stands and appeals to the wider audience to support the authors' views rather than those of the rival theologians'. On the far end of the spectrum were women such as Lady Eleanor Davies Douglas (1609–52); neither the wrath of husbands nor the orders of a king could suppress the fifty-three pamphlets she published between 1625 and 1652.[113] The daughter of Baron Audeley, a fellow of Magdalen College, Oxford, who gave her a "learned" education, Lady Eleanor was undaunted when her first husband burned some of her manuscripts in 1625 after she developed her "spirit of prophecy." She predicted, in addition to her husband's death, the assassination of Buckingham, and, by 1633, her other woeful predictions about the fate of the English nation landed her in prison. Instead of remaining silent, she transferred her publishing activities to Amsterdam and survived a crushing £3,000 fine for importing her books into England.[114] Her second husband, Sir Archibald Douglas, also disapproved of his wife's activities, but she continued her writing with unabated enthusiasm nevertheless.

A less flamboyant and antagonistic character than Lady Eleanor (though nearly as prolific) was Mrs. Jane Lead, who founded the English Philadelphian Society based on the teachings of the mystic Jakob Boehme. Through her books concerning Boehme's revelations and the testaments of her own experiences, this blind visionary held together an international network of devotees. In her early days, she had been a student of Dr. John Pordage, the author of *Theologia Mystica*, whose wife, according to Lead, was the actual originator of the movement.[115] Lead's own publications such as *The Heavenly Cloud* (1681) and *The Fountain of Gardens, Watered by the Rivers of Divine Pleasure* (1696) were "much sought after and praised" according to her son-in-law Francis Lee, and were responsible for drawing the two young Oxford scholars, Lee and Richard Roach, into her circle.

Lead maintained her standing with mystics on the Continent through her lifetime and it was "the Blessed Virago" to whom they sent their own manuscripts for an opinion, not to the scholarly Roach or Lee.[116] By her death in 1704, Lead's English reputation had declined, even though her son-in-law loyally declared to the European brethren that "the learned

Dodwell . . . a man celebrated throughout Europe, *thinks* [her writings] *not to be altogether despised.*"[117] Like many movements directed by a charismatic figure, after Lead's death the Philadelphians lost momentum and eventually faded away, although offshoots revived throughout the eighteenth century. In his biography of her, Roach comments that although Lead's writings are now "overlook'd by the wise of the world & almost Unknown in her own Country; [they are] high valued in others, & Testified to by Numbers of all Ranks and Quality as to their Blessed & Powerfull operation upon their Souls in such manner as no Product of these Latter Ages has been."[118]

Certainly as radical in their own time as the Philadelphians, the Quakers produced the single largest group of women who published their writings, both during the Commonwealth and afterward.[119] Almost no work has yet been done on the content of these women's writings as a body of feminine theology. Many of their titles are extremely rare, and in twentieth-century studies only the most prominent member of the society, Margaret Fell, usually identified only as the wife of George Fox (her second husband), has received much attention. Some Quaker women such as Dorothea Gotherson, *To All that are Unregenerated* (1661), and Elizabeth Redford, *The Love of God is to Gather the Seasons* (1690), made one contribution and disappeared. But others continued to write and publish over several decades. During the early years of the Restoration, Judith Boulbie made her debut with a fiery pamphlet, *A Testimony for Truth Against All Hireling Priests* (1665), and concluded just as vigorously nearly fifteen years later with *A Warning and Lamentation over England* (1679). Joan Vokins was less prolific but equally persistent, appearing first in 1670 with *A Loving Advertisement*, then in 1687 offering *A Tender Invitation*, and finishing in 1691 with a description of *God's Mighty Power Magnified*.

Several Quaker women's publications called for second and third editions. Although unfamiliar to most modern readers, *A Lamentation for the Lost Sheep* (1665) by Martha Simmonds and Anne Whitehead's *An Epistle for True Love* (1680) earned enough popular readership to make it worthwhile for printers to bring out new editions. Dorothy White, who had published nineteen titles under her name between 1660 and 1684, also had several reprinted. Very little is known about her and in spite of her literary output she has slipped through the historians' nets, leaving behind only her zeal for her faith.

The life and career of Margaret Fell, "the mother of Quakerism," spanned almost the whole century. Born in 1614, in Lancashire, she married Thomas Fell of Swarthmore Hall, with whom she had nine children. After her conversion to Quakerism, she wrote twenty-three inspirational works, including her most famous, *Womens Speaking Justified* (1666). The Swarthmore manuscripts preserve her extensive correspondence from other Quakers, which testifies to the importance of her writings and correspondence, as well as her public life, as a model to other Quaker women.[120]

These examples are not meant to imply that only women charged with treason or involved in eccentric or radical groups used the printed word to make public their views. Conservative religious and political views, which often went hand in hand, did not lack enthusiastic women authors to defend them. Mary Pope delivered her support of monarchy in *Treatise on Magistracy* (1647), a subject further explored during the Restoration by Elinor James, who produced thirteen titles defending royalty and the Church of England against enthusiasts and papists alike, giving in to "the earnest desires of some [friends] . . . to Publish them."[121] Lady Pakington's *The Whole Duty of Man* displays both its author's erudition and orthodoxy, gaining approval from conservative clergy. Elizabeth Burnet's *A Method of Devotion* is a model of conservative Anglicanism. These women, and others such as Lady Masham with her *Discourse Concerning the Love of God*, were all publicly recognized as seventeenth-century defenders of orthodoxy both in their lives and in their writings.

Another category of women writers who escape the label of radical, eccentric, or persecuted females are those who published on domestic subjects such as cookery, medicine, and domestic conduct. There is no indication that Hannah Woolley was considered to be a "loose woman" for her numerous publications, although many must have found her tone of smug superiority irritating. Mary Tillinghurst's *Rare and Excellent Recepts* (1678) enjoyed a second edition twelve years later with no apparent blemish on the author's character, and there is no record that Mrs. Mary Tyre, the author of *Medicatrix, or the Woman-Physician* (1675), faced ridicule for her publication. Ann Scarborow's *A Looking-Glass for Maids* (1655), a treatise on domestic piety which also required a second edition, appears to have raised no questions about the virtues of its author.

In this context, the career of Catherine Trotter Cockburn, whose publications spanned both the seventeenth and eighteenth centuries, and who succeeded in publishing in both philosophy and drama, offers several interesting features. Her career epitomizes that of the woman writer who chose public print as her medium. Elizabeth Burnet's hesitation over making her acquaintance is closely tied to Cockburn's early success in Restoration drama, in addition to the fact that Cockburn was at that time a Catholic. As one of Burnet's letters makes clear, she *knows* nothing against Cockburn's character personally, but she dislikes intensely the environment in which she has passed her time: Cockburn's poverty "forced as it were [her] to write plays, and consequently to contract Idle acquaintance, [which] has left great blemishes on her reputation . . . tho I am very willing to think her in great measure injured."[122] When one recalls the unsavory reputation of Cockburn's fellow male dramatists such as Buckingham and Wycherley, it is easy to understand why the bishop's wife might have been a bit leery. John Locke, however, had no such scruples. When Cockburn's defense of his *Essay Concerning Human Understanding* was published, he wrote to his young advocate, "As the rest of the world takes notice of the strength and clearness of your reasoning, so I cannot but be extremely sensible, that it was employed in my defense. You have herein not only vanquished my adversary, but reduced me also absolutely under your power."[123] The Burnets eventually followed Locke's lead, but there is no question that Cockburn's early theatrical ties made her much less desirable as a personal acquaintance then than in her later life when she was the wife of a clergyman writing theological treatises.

This shift in attitude is apparent in her final printed defense of Locke. A sermon by Dr. Winch Holdsworth against Locke's views on Christianity provoked her to compose "some animadversions, which she threw together in the form of a *Letter* to the doctor." According to her eighteenth-century biographer, Cockburn had every intention of suppressing the letter "if it should have the desired effect upon him," namely, that Holdsworth retract his statements about Locke. However, nine months passed, and Holdsworth's only response was "a large and particular answer [to her letter]," which he refused to let her see until she committed hers to print. Eventually, she convinced the cautious doctor to send her his piece, but "not meeting with conviction from it, which would have made her give up her cause, she was prevailed on to let the world judge between them."[124] She then published *A Letter to Dr. Holdsworth* (1728) without using her name, but identifying herself on the title page as the author of *A Defense of Mr. Locke's Essay of Human Understanding*, her most famous nondramatic work. For Cockburn, the decision to print was tantamount to announcing that the philosophical differences between her and Holdsworth were irreconcilable and that it was up to the public to decide the case. As for her reputation, there was no longer any trace of her theatrical associations to cast a shadow on her Christian disputations.

This conversion to the role of "the good author" separated Cockburn from the group of women writers whose careers have been used to demonstrate the typical obstacles faced by female writers during the 1600s—the satirists, dramatists, and versifiers who wrote to support themselves. Rather than being the norm, however, the open professionalism of these women was atypical of the majority of authors of either sex in the seventeenth century. Mary Fage lays claim to being, if not the first female professional writer, then the one most blatant in her search for patronage. In *Fames Roule* (1637) this industrious writer composed an anagram and acrostic on the names of every member of the royal family, all the peers of the realm, and various and sundry other important people. The whole volume is designed to attract attention to its author, who announces on the title page that she is the wife of "Robert Fage the younger, Gentleman," a hack writer who produced rather dreary histories. There are two dedications, one to the royal family and one to the Earl of Arundell, the Duke of Buckingham, and others. A clever opening poem acts as a preface where Fage makes the conventional gestures of shooing away hostile critics and explaining the rules behind her composition.

> *Momus*, I know, at this my worke will wonder,
> And blaming me, will belching envy thunder,
> By blusterous words, out of his mouth, which he
> Shall seconded by *Zoilus* likewise be.
> Tush say they, what! A Woman this worke frame?
> Her wit will not attaine an Anagramme;
> There many may be false within her Booke.
> Yet Monsier *Critick*, notwithstanding looke
> I pray thee on these following Roules, and than
> Anagrammes here according to them scan.[125]

As did male writers, Fage is warding off the evil critics by accusing them of jealousy and petty-mindedness. She has effectively defused the issue of her sex by bringing it up first, thus anticipating her opponents who might use this fact against her, by making them look like blustering windbags.

In addition to this technique, Fage also arms her efforts with commendatory verses by Thomas Heywood and "T.B." These verses stress the unusual nature of her enterprise and the ingenuity involved in assembling the enormous collection of anagrams and acrostics (both forms were very popular pastimes for amateur writers throughout the seventeenth century). They also address the fact that the author is a woman; "Shee's (as all women should be) modest, claimes / But what becomes her Sex," announces Heywood, "yet to our shames / and iust taxation, hath late undergone / A difficult attempt, which hereton none / Of us durst enterprise." T.B. adds his warning to the "snarling Critickes" not to "taxe these lines" since when the muse inspires "though her poetick lines / Not full so rich appeare, her glory shines / Equall to his." The whole construction of the volume is intended to attract patrons. The insistence on flaunting the gender of the author is part of this strategy of presenting a novelty in the poetry and also in its "modest" female author. Moreover, if each person whose name was used in the volume bought one copy, Mary Fage would have sold a tidy number of books.

There were women who also pursued public poetic careers in less voluminous forms by using other time-tested avenues to literary fame and patronage. They wrote commendatory verses and celebratory pieces on public occasions. Mary Oxlie of Morpeth (who is frequently referred to as

Mary Morpeth) aroused her "rustic Muse" to praise William Drummond; even as she admires his verse, she gives dark hints about her own, "From an untroubled mind should Verses flow; / My discontents makes mine too muddy show."[126] These women poets also swelled the ranks of male writers including Andrew Marvell and John Dryden as they commented, celebrated, and condemned important public events. Rachel Jevon was only one of many English poets inspired to welcome Charles II on his return from exile. She goes one better than most and offers her *Exultationis Carmen* (1660) in both English and Latin. Joan Philips has a less happy event to address in her broadside warning the rebellious Duke of Monmouth that he was being misled, urging him to "Prove Your high Birth by Deed *Noble* and *Good*; / But *strive not to Legitimate Your Bloud*."[127] Alicia D'Anvers takes a lighter tone as she attempts to reassure the nation when William of Orange visits Belgium in *A Poem on His Sacred Majesty* (1690). This takes the form of a comic poetic dialogue where "Britannia" is the jealous lover who fears she is losing her man to "Belgia." Although none of these pieces offer any competition to Dryden's or Marvell's compositions on similar events, they demonstrate women writers' participation in this very public literary form, feminine voices commenting on affairs of state instead of domestic matters.

Women also found employment in less spectacular literary forms. The popularity of almanacs with the reading public provided at least two women steady work. Sarah Ginnor was the more prolific, contributing six almanacs in the mid-century, while her rival Mary Holden also had several years of producing *The Woman's Almanack*. The majority of women actively seeking to cultivate a steady public readership, however, were providing audiences with fiction and dramas. The fictionalized memoirs and exposés of court life, in which readers were invited to guess the true identities of the characters, began to appear in increasing numbers toward the end of the century and women were prominent contributors to this new genre. Mary de la Rivière Manley's *The Royal Mischief* (1696) and *New Atlantis* attracted both male and female readership with their suggestive scenes supposedly revealing intrigues of an amorous nature in high society.[128] Aphra Behn's *Oroonoko* (1688) answered this same desire of the English reading public with its tale of the noble savage in the strange new world. These English women had competition from the French in this genre: translations of the fictions of Marie Catherine La Mothe Aulnoy, such as *The Novels of Elizabeth Queen of England* (1680) and *Memoirs of the Court of France* (1692), and Marie Madline de La Vergne, Countess de La Fayette's *Zayde, A Spanish History* (1678) provided the exotic setting and the historical background still in demand by today's readers of romance fiction.

Drama, however, was virtually the only form of literary production at which a man or a woman could earn even a precarious living in the seventeenth century. So, it is not surprising to find that most of the professional women writers were involved with the theater in some degree. Cockburn used it to support herself after being left fatherless and it was the principal source of income for Aphra Behn for several years. Although the numerous dramas of the Duchess of Newcastle and *The Tragedie of Mariam, The Faire Queen of Jewry* (1613), attributed to Elizabeth Cary were not intended for commercial production, women such as Behn, Mary Pix, and Susannah Centlivre depended on the popular success of their plays on the London stage to earn a living.[129]

Like Mary Fage, female playwrights such as Frances Boothby used gender as part of their strategy, deliberately confronting the audience with the fact that a woman wrote the play and turning it into a clever prologue and epilogue. In *Marcelia* (1670), Boothby had an actor hesitantly address the audience in the prologue, "I'm hither come, but what d'ye think to say? / A Womans Pen presents you with a Play: / Who smiling told me I'd be sure to see, / That once confirm'd, the House wou'd empty be."[130] He is supposed then to feign astonishment that the aisles have not filled with fleeing spectators ("Not one yet gone!") and scurry offstage to receive further instructions. He returns to inform the audience that the author wants her viewers to leave, "You'l croud her Wit to death in such a Throng / Of Wits." Having thus ironically defused this element of the audience, the actor then makes the conventional swipe at the critics and their possible negative reactions, "For if that *Solomon* now liv'd, and writ; / They'd cry, Pish, hang't, there's nothing in't of Wit." In the epilogue, he reappears to offer the traditional appeal for the audience's applause, but with a twist. His author, he announces, "scorns such undermining ways" as mock humility, "Nor will she do her spirit so much wrong, / To beg what does not to her brow belong." She is determined to discover her fate truly. After making this brave declaration, he adds her warning, that she does this with full knowledge that "They'l Cowards be esteem'd that give her blows."

> Which strangely takes her! knowing that ye must
> Be to your Honour, or your Wit unjust.
> Mark how maliciously her snares sh'as laid:
> *Praise* or *Condemn*, you're equally betrayed.[131]

Boothby was not, as some critics interpret her prologue, offering a modest apology for presuming to be a female playwright. She, like Mary Fage, is using her gender for maximum effect, and in this comedy, it is the author who has the last laugh.

Reputations of women dramatists, however, were poor, both artistically and personally. The inference has been drawn repeatedly that the latter was directly the result of their being women who dared to compete in a man's world. This was certainly the view presented by the anonymous author of *The Female Wits*, which lampoons several of these dramatists. The male dramatists had no desire for competition from either sex. The slurs cast on the characters of these women in particular are so much worse than any made about women writers in general, though, that one is left pondering the effects of guilt by association and the example of Catherine Cockburn, who, as seen, went from a dubious creature to a respectable and respected commentator on the principles of Christian morality by severing her connections with the stage and becoming a cleric's wife.

Women satirists may have been less interested than poets and dramatists in patronage or profit, but they were equally concerned to attract a large audience. As mentioned in the preceding chapter, male antifemale satires drew numerous rebuttals. Rachel Speght, supposedly a minister's daughter, started the counterattack against Joseph Swetnam with *A Mouzell for Melastomus, The Cynciall Bayter and foule mouthe Barker against Evahs Sex* (1617). As Nussbaum's study shows, Speght's efforts were supported by two other women, who were apparently aware of Speght's planned attack: Ester Sowernam contributed *Ester hath hang'd Haman* (1617) and Constantia Mundi concluded with *The Worming of a Mad Dogge* (1617).[132] As mentioned before, John Taylor was answered by authors assuming female pseudonyms during the middle of the century. This tradition of women defending women was continued by Sarah Egerton Fige, who responded with conventional reluctance to Robert Gould's *Love Given O're* in the 1690s. "Pride is the Deity they most adore," charges Gould, and in his poem every women is at heart a whore. Fige, however, retorts briskly, "I am sorry you do Females hate, / But rather deem ourselves more fortunate, / Because I find, when you'r right understood, / You are at enmity with all that's good."[133] Female satirists such as Speght and Fige are using print in much the same way that the female petitioners and writers of appeals did, to confirm their female "modesty" by seeking the widest possible public readership in order to redress the wrong done to their sex.

Considering the overall pattern of women's writings, therefore, it is evident that although few in number proportionally, female authors were not on the whole timid creatures, veiled in feminine modesty, inhibited by social censure from expressing their thoughts. Of the women publishing, the majority used their names and chose subjects of public controversy. Manuscript networks and epistolary exchanges expanded the range of options available to women interested in philosophical issues as well as literary ones. Such methods provided opportunities for intellectual and artistic development which a superficial view of a "lady's life" might not suggest.

By placing manuscript literature back in its proper context, women's participation in such practices is not so much a mark of "modesty" as conservativism, the preference for the older form of literary transmission which left control of the text in the author's hands rather than signing it over to the bookseller. These types of intellectual exchange, printed and manuscript, taken together suggest a much more active participation in the literary, philosophical, and political events of the times by women and a much larger sphere for women writers. They also bring into question the current theory that women writers lacked sufficient numbers to form "an alternative literary society."[134] Furthermore, the content of these women's writings suggests that the patriarch's wife had definite views on the roles of women in marriage and society and was quite aware of a female audience waiting to read them.

Women Writers

The Female Perspective

Books discussing women's roles by women writers are far fewer in the seventeenth century than those by men. This is not to say that women did not have any comments on the subject, but their views less frequently take the form of specific treatises on the issues than interjections in the midst of other subjects. There were, as seen, women satirists and petitioners who attacked the antifeminist writers and in doing so directly addressed the questions concerning women's equality and opportunities. In addition to these writers, who formed what one reader calls "a large and well-defined movement" during the Restoration, many more women writers were using less obvious routes to comment on their status and roles in society.[1] In ballads, almanacs, prefaces to translations and verses, religious meditations, and poems on female friendships, women throughout the century were considering the role of the patriarch's wife and, indirectly, suggesting feminist alternatives.

Just as the men had their image of the Good Wife, women had their comparable figure of the Good Husband. Ballads gave the same type of advice to young women considering matrimony as they did to young men. In the ballads women are evaluated in terms of their housekeeping and constancy; men are ranked as husbands for their ability to handle money and sex. The Bad Husband is portrayed as either a playboy spendthrift or an impotent miser.

One ballad helpfully categorizes all potential husbands by the color of their hair.

> Young-men that are freckled and fair,
>   are commonly given to lies;
> But black men and brown, I declare,
>   are known to be vertuous and wise;
> They hate for to wrangle and brawl,
>   they honor and nourish their Wives,
> And never will wrong them at all,
>   But love them as dear as their lives.

Flaxen-haired men, warns this ballad, "poor innocent Girls" betray, but worse yet, those with "the Yellow curl'd locks" "get the young Lasses with Child." "For pleasure abroad they will Roam, / and lay the young Females along, / Yet they'l do but little at home. / What Woman can bear with this wrong," it concludes plaintively. On the other hand, men with "whey beards" are so feeble that even if they wished they cannot fool around away from home. And, asserts the balladeer, no wife deserves that, either.[2]

In another song, "The Kind and Careful Mother" summarizes men's weaknesses. She warns her dutiful daughter that Bad Husbands "To gaming, and hawking and hunting they'l tide, / With drinking and feasting with harlots besides; / Full quickly will squander and waste their Estate, / And they may be sorry when it is too late."[3] To add insult to injury, Mother adds, the estate they lose is likely to be that of their bride.

The Good Wife earns praise for her industrious labors on behalf of her family, and the Good Husband must likewise "be the First man up; & ye Last in Bed."

> With the Sun rising he must walke his grounds;
> See this uiew that & all other bounds
> Shut euery Gate; mend euery hedge thats torne,
> Either with old, or plant them new Thorne;
> Tread or'e his gleab, but with such care, yt where
> He sets his foot, he leaues rich compost there.[4]

The images of the Good Wife and her Good Husband insist that there be a division of labors instead of one party working in order to maintain the idle ease of the other. The Good Husband does not cheat his family of either his money or himself.

> They, like the industrious Bee, will delight
> To labour, and bring home their profit at night;

> If such a kind Husband you happen to have,
> Your duty, dear Daughter, will then be to save;
> And likewise be loving, not given to scold,
> Good Husbands are Jewels far better than Gold.[5]

In these portraits, the ideal family is represented as a working unit, with the husband and wife combining their efforts to ensure the security of the whole.

In addition to his peculiar ability to spread compost where he walks, the Good Husband is also characterized by his nurturing of his wife. As Spufford's study of popular literature demonstrates, the concept of romantic love in marriage was very much present in literature from the most courtly pastorals to the crudest chapbooks. Mary Ridley, the seventeenth-century commentator, agrees with male writers on matrimony when she declares that "one end of marriage is mutuall societye and comfort."[6] Balladeers declare that the Good Husband cherishes his spouse: "When Wives by their Husbands are dearly ador'd, / No greater a Blessing the world can afford." The Bad Husband, in contrast, is oblivious to the distress he causes his wife; he ignores her tears, spends her money, and pursues his selfish pleasures. The Good Husband does not create trouble for his family and "In troubles or crosses, or what may befall, / Good Husbands will still bear a share in them all; / And in their kind arms their sweet Wives will infold."[7]

In her treatise, Dorothy Leigh advises her sons how to select wives and in the process also describes the duties of the Good Husband. Do not, she urges, as some men do, "taketh a woman, to make her a companion and fellow, and after he hath her, hee makes her both a servant and drudge." Such a husband mistakes both his spouse and the nature of marriage. If she is good enough to be your wife, Leigh admonishes, "shee is alwayes too good to bee thy servant, and worthy to be thy fellow." "If thou wilt have a good wife," she concludes, "thou must goe before her in all goodness."[8] A Bad Husband will never make a Good Wife or a happy marriage.

An anonymous young lady sets out her criteria in verse in "How to Choose a Husband." Her ideal man would shun all extremes in appearance and behavior. "His features should be comely, but not faire, / Not curious, or carelesse in his hayre / In euery part strong, yet in each part should bee / A Descent grace, an equall [with] symetrie." He must not be "a Niggard of his Purse / But content to use it as is wise," and "Care and discretion duly should attend / Each seuerall action to its generall end." In his personality, he must not be "Foolish or Humourous, or Phantasticall," neither caught up in superstition nor "intemperate wth wine." The only matter in which he should not be moderate is that his life must be "ye Emblem of a constant Hart," and he himself should be "as chast as he would haue his Wife." If she ever finds this paragon of prudence, temperance, and passion, and he is "Readie to entertaine my Loue," the author warns, the reader must not be surprised or "Thinke it no immodestie, yt when wee two / Shall meet together I begin to woo."[9]

Women's portraits of the Good Husband present him as a man of moderation, whose labor and love is directed toward the benefit of his family. Above all, he is characterized by his fidelity and affection for his Good Wife. Like the criticism leveled at bad wives for unfaithfulness and extravagance, in these representations men are rebuked for being drunkards, gamblers, and adulterers. To be a Good Husband, he must not undermine the family by squandering its estate nor create disharmony by forgetting to cherish his spouse, whom he should acknowledge as his companion and fellow. He must not be given to "wrangles" and brawls any more than his Good Wife would scold or nag. In short, the conventional representation of the Good Husband holds him accountable to the family in the same ways as the Good Wife is, only his sphere is commercial and hers domestic. This image depicts the ideal marriage as a fellowship, not a master/servant bond.

Matrimony of this nature is a source of inspiration for many seventeenth-century women writers. Their depictions of their husbands and their domestic lives stress strongly the mutual affection and esteem created by wedlock. Gertrude Aston Thimelby celebrates her marriage in several poems, including one written in 1651 to her husband on New Year's Day.

> How swiftly time doth passe away,
> Wher happines compleates the day!
> Weeks, months, and years, but moments prove
> To those that nobly are in love.
> This computation's only knowne
> To them that our pure flame can owne.
> Succeeding yeares example take
> By those are past; ther numbers wake
> Envy, whilst with a will resignd
> No wil is knowne til th'others mind.[10]

Under less happy circumstances, Mary Monck composed a poem of consolation for her husband on her deathbed. She calls him "Thou who dost all my worldly thoughts employ, / Thou pleasing source of all my earthly joy, / Thou tend'rest husband, and thou best of friends, / To thee, this first, this last adieu I send."[11] Anne Bradstreet uses similar terms to describe her husband: "My head, my heart, mine eyes, my life, nay more / My joy, my magazine of earthly store, / If two be one, as surely thou and I, / How stayest thou there, while I at Ipswich lie?"[12] The Countess of Winchilsea, not known for her high opinion of men and their treatment of women, nevertheless writes a verse letter to her husband "Daphnis" in 1685, calling him "the Crown and Blessing" of her life, declaring he "to the world by tenderest proof discovers / They err, who say that husbands can't be lovers."[13]

This type of poetry eulogizes husbands who are first and foremost "best of friends" with their wives. In these marriages, the desires and aspirations of husband and wife are so compatible that they cease to be distinguishable, merging into one "pure flame." The women in these poems stress that their husbands are the highest of their earthly joys, and the conventional imagery used to depict their union is that marriage is the experience closest to being in paradise on earth.

The loss of such Good Husbands produced numerous epitaphs by disconsolate widows praising their departed spouses. Lady Katherine Dyer (d. 1641) is credited with the inscription on her husband's monument, whose poignant intimacy is included in several modern anthologies: "My dearest dust, could not thy hasty day / Afford thy drowsy patience leave to stay / One hour longer, so that we might either / Sat up, or gone to bed together?"[14] An unknown seventeenth-century manuscript collector was moved by Diana Wharburton's less skillful tribute to her husband, Sir George, "Dearest of Husbands," to record it in his commonplace book.

> . . . what Rhetorick can express my loss
> Thou wearest the Crown; thy Di must bear the Cross
> Only thy presence can afford reliefe
> To this sad heart, oppressed thus with griefe.[15]

"I live in patience," she concludes, "but dye in desire." Elizabeth Singer Rowe wrote her verses on "The Anniversary of her Husband's Death" and had them circulated in manuscript rather than carving them on his tombstone.[16] Lucy Hutchinson and Lady Fanshawe chose prose to immortalize their departed spouses, Fanshawe explaining to her son in her preface that she wishes the book to serve as a vindication and a momument to her late husband's memory. "*Glory be to God* we never had but one mind through our lives," avows Lady Fanshawe, "our soules were wrapped up in each other, our aims and designs one, our love one, and our resentments one." "What ever was reall happiness," she writes her son, "God gave it me in him."[17]

The image of "the good man" in women's writings is as a husband; the ideal is a man who is both a friend and a lover. The ballads and chapbooks make it clear that the Good Husband provides for his wife's conjugal needs as well as housekeeping expenses. Poems and epitaphs written by women of the middle and upper classes, on the whole, while not denying married love, tend to stress the spiritual nature of the union. Marriage is represented as the combining of two natures, two wills, into one force.

As attractive as this image is, there were women who did not accept this picture of domestic bliss. In the same fashion as male wits complained about the hard-hearted, empty-headedness of women, female poets reviled men for being fickle seducers. For women, declare this group of female writers, love is a trap. From her, charges Aphra Behn in "Love Armed," Cupid took sighs and tears, while from her lover, "his pride and cruelty." It is "My poor heart alone" that is harmed in this affair, "Whilst thine the victor is, and freed." Behn's wish in another song echoed throughout the century: "*Pan*, grant that I may never prove / So great a *Slave* to fall in love, / And to an Unknown *Deity* / Resign my happy Liberty."[18] There is nothing in the content of this verse to distinguish it from the laments of disillusioned Sons of Ben or later libertines. Women as well as men found this vehicle suitable to express distrust and disatisfaction with the social games expected of courting couples.

Women, too, caution female poets, can fall into the trap of marrying for the wrong reasons. Elizabeth With warns "All you young women that live here in health / Marry not old men, hoping to get wealth." Mercenary marriages by women are depicted in no less admonishing manner than those by men. "For riches have wings and flie like the wind," With concludes glumly, "I married for riches, but none could I find."[19]

The ballad "The Maiden's Counsellor: Or, a Fair Warning Before Marriage" carries on this convention of cautioning women against hasty marriages or marriage for the wrong reasons. It warns young women, "You Damosels fair, take special care, / And not too hasty be, / A Marriage Life brings Care and Strife, / When single Maids live free."[20] Apart from the pain of a faithless lover, such songs proclaim, the whole institution of marriage is objectionable. Single life, these songs declare, means liberty for women. The manuscript verse "Advice to Virgins. By a Lady" bluntly states that "the Married Life affords but little ease, / The best of Husbands are so hard to please." There is little faith in love as the basis for marriage. A woman in love, the author charges, imagines her future spouse to be her ideal man and accepts his offers "with Ideas of a God like Man." Marriage, however, "lets us see the falsity of Love" and the men who appear "Gods 'till Marry'd, but prov'd Divels then."[21]

Jane Barker announces in "The Preference of a Single Life before Marriage" that she loves being a spinster and cannot see why her friends ever marry.

> *She* that intends ever in *rest*, to be,
> Both for the *present* and the *future*, free
> From *cares* and *troubles*, intermix'd with *strife*,
> Must flee the hazard of a *Nuptial Life*.[22]

Single life represents a happy and carefree state for women. Men and love are the complicating factors and, poets such as Barker inform their women readers, women can get along quite nicely on their own, without lovers or husbands. As the balladeers sing to young unmarried females, "Let not young Men your hearts insnare, / *A Single Life is free from Care*."²³

The imagery found in the women's antimarriage poems is very similar to that in the men's libertine lyrics. Marriage is a "snare" or "trap" where the true, unpleasant character of the spouse is revealed. Love acts as "fetters" which "enslave" those foolish enough to get caught. The particular danger from love, however, which is cited only in women's poems, is that once married, women fall under the legal authority of their spouses. "But when once subject to the *Jugal Bands*," Barker concludes, "Her *Will's* confin'd, she's under a Command."²⁴ In "To the Ladies," with heavy irony Lady Chudleigh depicts the fate of women after marriage.

> Wife and Servant are the same,
> But only differ in the Name:
> For when that fatal Knot is ty'd,
> Which nothing, nothing can divide:
> When she the word *obey* has said,
> And Man by Law supreme has made,
> Then all that's kind is laid aside,
> And nothing left but State and Pride;
> Fierce as an Eastern Prince he grows,
> And all his innate Rigor shows:
> Then but to look, to laugh, or speak,
> Will the Nuptial Contract break.
> Like Mutes she Signs alone must make,
> And never any Freedom take:
> But still be govern'd by a Nod,
> And fear her Husband as her God;
> Him still must serve, him still obey,
> And nothing act, and nothing say,
> But what her haughty Lord thinks fit,
> Who with the Pow'r, has all the Wit.
> Then shun, oh! shun that wretched State,
> And all the fawning Flatt'rers hate:
> Value your selves, and Men despise,
> You must be proud, if you'll be wise.²⁵

As the author of "Advice to Virgins" notes, there is nothing more galling than a woman being legally bound to obey a man who is manifestly her inferior: "Obedience do's a grating duty prove, / If Husband's cannot teach as well as Love. / A Womans humour hardly can submit / To be a Slave to One She do's Out Wit."[26] Some women, "Ephelia" (Joan Philips) maintains, are just too good to be wasted on men. "To one that Affronted the Excellent *Eugenia*," she begins pointedly, "Thing, call'd a Man! Ambition cheats thy Sense, / Or, thou'rt deceiv'd with too much Impudence; / To think that Divine Creature you pursue, / Can be deserv'd, or merited by you."[27] The popular image of the "conjugal knot" in these poems is depicted as the equivalent of a noose drawn tight around the woman's neck.

Such antilove, antimarriage sentiments have their equivalents in male writings, notably the Cavalier and libertine lyrics. Certainly, if women's antimarriage verses are viewed only as autobiographical revelations it would be a disservice to the authors and their works. The significance of them is less as a window into the private lives of the authors than as a female literary convention, where women are not portrayed as doting wives, lovesick girls, or desperate spinsters. The antimarriage poems offer an alternative female voice, characterized by wry sophistication and detachment, where the speaker is not so absorbed in snaring her man that she cannot see the pitfalls around her. The convention furthermore suggests that the way for women to improve their happiness in life is not by collaborating with men, but by banding together with women, a point of view brought to its fullest expression in female friendship verses discussed later in this chapter. Finally, although the antimarriage writings do not directly embrace feminist issues such as the equality of the sexes or the deficiencies of women's education, the presence of a female voice protesting against marriage and advocating the single life suggests a consciousness of the disadvantages of contemporary women's roles and status.

There were women writers throughout the century who did choose to address feminist issues directly, and who selected the roles played by their sex as their literary battleground. This group, a small but determined voice in seventeenth-century literature, proceeds from a variety of bases—theology, linguistics, poetics, and education. Their general arguments and conclusions concerning women in English society were consistent and also in agreement with the views expressed simultaneously by the male profemale writers.

In the same fashion that an examination of the narrative of Genesis and the scriptures led men into considering the true nature of women, female writers debating theological matters were drawn into discussions of women's abilities and their opportunities for spiritual and intellectual advancement. The most prominent women writing in this area were in separatist sects such as the Quakers, Brownists, and Baptists. These women were not arguing the social, worldly equality of the sexes as their primary point, but the equality of their souls and their calling to work in their religion.

In her book *The Justification of the Independent Churches of Christ* (1641), the seventeenth-century preacher Katherine Chidley remarks tartly, "I know of no true Divinity that teacheth men to be Lords over the Conscience." This attitude characterizes women's writings on female participation in the church from the Restoration Quakers to the earlier independent prophecies of Lady Eleanor Davies Douglas who stoutly declares that God's spirit is revealed "as soon to his handmaids as his men servants."[28] This line of argument, the equality of male and female spirits in the Lord, is also used by the women petitioners to protest against unjust and immoral laws such as tithes.

The best known of these women religious writers is Margaret Fell, who, in her treatise *Womens Speaking Justified* (1667), attempts to remove the central stumbling block for women's preaching—Paul. She tackles his injunctions in 1 Corinthians 14.34 and 1 Timothy 2.11 that women must be silent in church ("If they will learn any thing, let them ask their Husbands at home, for it is a shame for a Woman to speak in the Church"). She first points out that Christ "is the Husband, and his Wife is the Church, and God hath said, that his *Daughters* should Prophesie as well as his *Sons*."[29] Because it is Christ, not a mortal man, from whom women must learn, "in this True Church, Sons and Daughters do Prophesie, Women labour in the Gospel." The women to whom Paul refers are the "tatlers, busiebodies, and such as usurp authority over the Man[,] would not have Christ Reign," those who do not acknowledge Christ as their head.[30] "Christ in the Male and in the Female is one," explains Fell patiently, "where he hath poured forth his Spirit upon them, they must prophesie, though blind Priests say to the contrary and will not permit holy women to speak."[31]

Although Margaret Fell is the most widely read woman writer on this subject by modern readers, she was but one voice among many. "As Male and Female are made one in Christ Jesus," asserts Quaker Elizabeth Bathurst (1655–85), "so Women receive an Office in the Truth as Well as Men, and they have a Stewardship, and must give an Account of their Stewardship to their Lord, as well as the men."[32] Sarah Blackborow (fl. 1650s-60s) explains with her characteristic touch of impatience that the Apostles were obviously not referring to women in general when they commanded female silence, but only those who were not "of the Life." "This is no mistery to those that are Ministers in the spirit, whose eye is in their Head," she states firmly, "these saw both Male and Female, in the Gospell were true labourers with them . . . and these knew that Christ was one in the Male and in the *Fe*male."

Christ the power was one in the Male and in the *Fe*male one Spirit, one Light, one Life, one Power, which brings forth the same Witness and Ministers forth it self, in the Male as in the *Fe*male, And both comes to learn the Scriptures by one Teacher, even the Holy Ghost, and so both are of a good understanding.[33]

In such writings, women represent themselves as not only having equal abilities to preach and proselytize, but also the duty to do so. Women, like men, see themselves as "stewards" who "must prophesie" in obedience to their True Husband, Christ.

In an interesting parallel, the loyalist Mary Pope offers the same justification for women's participation in politics as did the radical Quaker women for their preaching. She, too, feels it her "duty" to publish her views on the current political situation. In the preface to *A Treatise of Magistracy* (1647), Pope announces that she published her opinions seeking to "put [out] my helping hand, having good warrant out of God's word so to doe." She cites as her justification for participating in the politics of her day the "examples from the women that brought the work of their hands to *Moses*, for the helping forward of the building of the Tabernacle."[34] Even though women do not have authority within the institution, Pope seems to be arguing, they have a duty to help construct the edifice.

The conservative Elinor James likewise pleads the call of duty as the reason for her written defenses of the Church of England and the monarchy. *"How do you think I can bear it*, when God hath fill'd my Heart full of Love and Loyalty, and I know you Abuse [Church and king]," she exclaims at one point.

I know you will say *I am a Woman, and why should I trouble my selfe?* Why was I not always so, when I pleaded with Parliament about the *Right of Succession*, and with *Shaftesbury*, and *Monmouth*, and at *Guild-Hall*, and elsewhere; and I made Applications to my late Sovereign Lord the King (whom my Soul Loved) That he would be pleas'd to let me Undertake for the City, and to make me a God Mother . . . and the King granted my desire. . . .[35]

According to James, she has the same duty to protect the institutions that she loves as she would human relations. She is stretching the concept of maternal responsibility to include her involvement with politics and in a reversal of the patriarchal argument, she declares that being a woman is no bar to political participation, but a natural extension of feminine nurturing activities.

Women writers engaging in politics, or belonging to groups such as the Quakers which were active in political areas, share a vocabulary in spite of their religious or philosophical differences. Radical or conservative, they first establish their grounds for participation by arguing scriptural precedents. They also place their activities in a domestic framework, pointing out the practical effect of politics on women whose husbands are imprisoned for debt or religious beliefs. Finally, they assert their duty as women—mothers and wives—to protest the corruption of "their" institutions, their church, their monarchy.

Religious radicals and women involved in politics were not the only advocates of women's roles outside the household. Other women writers, along with the male controversialists, were discussing the theoretical aspects underlying women's roles in society such as education and legal status after marriage. Sarah Ginnor, "Student of Physic" and the author of *The Womans Almanack* (1659), takes a completely secular approach to the question of the true nature of women's abilities. She states her intention in this book to "rowse up our spirits, and show forth our Vertues," by reminding readers of accomplishments by women in medicine and astrology (two sciences closely allied in her work).

The gift of learning being so little set by in these days amongst those of our Sex, is the chief invitation which hath caused me to publish this final Tract, thereby to strip up others, not to let their great worth with other learned Authors of our Sex ly in obscurity. I need not quote them, for I think few of our Sex so ignorant but they have either read or heard of them, and though some of them have been abused by the quacksalving Montibanks that would engrosse al knowledge into their own hands, yet have great and wonderful cures been done by our Sex, after these paper-sculd Mongrels left them.[36]

Ginnor is not arguing directly for the equality of the sexes. She is, instead, attempting to remove notions of inferiority by offering examples of previous successes by women. In this fashion, she hopes to encourage women readers to enrich their own circumstances and their self-esteem.

Ginnor raises the central issue for women who were arguing the status of women in secular terms—the opportunities for women's education. Bathsua Makin's *An Essay to Revive the Antient Education of Gentlewomen* (1673) and Mary Astell's *A Serious Proposal to the Ladies* (1694) are the best-known treatises written by women urging reform in education, but they were not written in a vacuum, nor were they without female precedents. As seen, male writers throughout the century criticized the quality of women's education, and other women writers were equally censorious.

Margaret Cavendish, the Duchess of Newcastle, certainly considered herself to be a learned lady, but in her writings, she lashed out against her own sex, as well as parents who fail to educate their daughters. In *Sociable Letters* (1664), in which she uses the convention of an exchange of epistolary essays between two female friends to comment on "the Humours of Mankind," Cavendish's characters are sharply critical of women's abilities and pastimes. "Womens Minds or Souls are like Shops of small-Wares, wherein some have pretty toyes, but nothing of any great value," observes one lady tartly. "I imagine you will chide me for this opinion, and I should deserve to be chidden, if all women were like you; but you are but one, and I speak of Women . . . I wish with all my heart our whole Sex were like you."[37] Cavendish did not permit her characters to challenge male superiority; instead, they attempt to emulate it. After a day spent reading history, one is filled with the desire to "Fight Valiantly, to Suffer Patiently, to Govern Justly, and to Speak Rationally, Movingly, Timely, and Properly," qualities she finds sadly lacking in her own sex (p. 52). Most women, she remarks in another letter, spend their time reading trashy romances, not fortifying and elevating their minds, so it is little wonder that they are sillier than men.

Women's faults, however, are in part the result of their upbringing. Concerning adultery, one of Cavendish's characters explains that it is "caused by unruly Appetites" which women in particular should learn to govern.

> But for the most part women are not Educated as they should be, I mean those of Quality, oft their Education is onely to Dance, Sing, and Fiddle, to write Complemental Letters, to read Romances, to speak some Languages that is not their Native . . . [which shows that] their Parents take more care of their Feet than their Head, more of their Words than their Reason. (p. 50)

Women are not fit to govern with only these skills at their disposal and Cavendish's characters are witheringly scornful of those who try. Such misguided women are only exposing the deficiencies in their education.

Cavendish was unrelenting in her criticism of women who make public displays of their ignorance (as she herself was frequently accused of doing). Although Cavendish acknowledges that the husband is the head of the family, she does not accept the notion of women in a subordinate role in society. Because women cannot vote or hold office, they are not true citizens and "if we be not citizens in the Commonwealth, I know no reason we should be Subjects." The only authority over women is that of their husbands, but, because of men's susceptibilities to female charms, although men "seem to govern the world, . . . we really govern the world, in that we govern men" (p. 27).

Cavendish was not content, however, with this indirect form of power based on flattery and sexual manipulation. The success of this form of power is dependent on the woman's physical charms, not rational standards. "If Nature had not befriended us with Beauty, and other good Graces, to help us to insinuate our selves into Men's Affections, we should have been more inslaved than any other of Natur's Creatures she hath made" (p. 27). Although Cavendish was outspokenly critical of her own sex, sounding at times just as strident as the antifemale satirists, it does not mean that she felt that women's roles in society were fair and reasonable. Without "Beauty" women are slaves; because their parents do not educate them, women grow up to be the fools misogynists claim them to be.

Margaret Cavendish did not offer any formal plan to correct this fault in women's upbringing other than suggesting that they could employ their reading hours better. Lettice, Lady Falkland (1612–47), the wife of the gallant Cavalier Sir Lucius Cary, on the other hand, devised a scheme to improve women's education on a wider scale. Lucius Cary's mother was the highly independent and learned lady Elizabeth Cary, to whom *Miriam* is attributed, and historians suggest that it was in part Lettice's well-educated mind that attracted Lucius Cary—certainly it was not her fortune, which was so small that Cary married her over the strenuous objections of his father.[38] After her husband's death, Lettice Cary devoted herself to charitable works and meditation. "She was *second* to none of her *Sex*, and *Age* (I believe) among us," declares her seventeenth-century biographer, "for perspicacity of *understanding*, & clearness of *judgement*."[39] One of her ambitions was to establish "*places* for the *education* of young *Gentlewomen*, & for retirement of *Widows*, (as *Colleges* and the *Inns of Court* and *Chancery* are for men)." It was her hope that "*learning* and *religion* might flourish more in *her own Sex*, then heretofore, having such opportunities to *serve* the *Lord, without distraction*." She envisioned setting up several of these female colleges around the country and her biographer believes that the project was "not beyond the *power* and *interest*, she had with great ones, to have affected it." Unfortunately for her, "these *evil times*" under Cromwell prevented her plan, the whole notion appearing much too close to Catholic practices to be acceptable to a Puritan government.[40]

There are no records of Lettice Cary's specific plans for her female colleges apart from those published in the seventeenth-century biography, but it is obvious that she perceived a need for greater intellectual opportunities for her sex. Her biographer's depiction of the project stresses that it was not merely to be a religious retreat, but one where "learning" flourished in the same mixture of religious, secular, and classical training that men received at Oxford or Cambridge. Disapproval for the scheme seems to have arisen primarily because of the Catholic connections; an interesting parallel can be found in the history of the Anglican community set up by Nicholas Ferrar (1592–1637) at Little Gidding, where women received the same education as men. It, too, drew criticism as being too "papist" and in 1646 was disbanded by Parliamentary troops.

During the 1640s, as we have seen, books such as *The Womens Sharpe Revenge* kept the issue of women's education in the forefront of the controversy. In 1659, a fresh attack was added with the translation of Anna Maria van Schurman's *The Learned Maid: Or, Whether a Maid May Be a Scholar*. Van Schurman, the "Star of Utrecht" and pupil of Descartes, was frequently cited by seventeenth-century male writers as the epitome of female scholarship. She also had strong ties with educated Englishwomen as her collection of letters, *Opuscula* (1648), demonstrates. *The Learned Maid* breaks new ground in the women's education controversy in both its methods and the points argued; instead of searching for biblical precedents or claiming moral duty, van Schurman approaches the issue as an exercise in logic.

> Objection II.
> Whose mind is not *inclined* to studies, they are not fit to study.
> But the minds of Women are not inclined to studies.
> They prove the *Major*, because nothing is to be done *invita Minerva*, as we say, *Against the hair*.
> The *Minor* they will prove from use and custome; because very seldom do Women apply their mind to study.
> We answer to the *Major*. It should be thus: *Whose mind*, after all means duly tried, *is not inclined to studies*: otherwise it is denied.
> To the *Minor* we say, no man can rightly judge of our Inclination to studies, before he hath encouraged us by the best reasons and means to set upon them.[41]

Van Schurman is using the intellectual apparatus of her male opponents; the effect is to safeguard her efforts from being dismissed as private grievance. This use of academic form signals the seriousness of the writer's intentions and of the subject itself; it could support rigorous scholarly examination. *The Learned Maid* provides women with an attack on seventeenth-century attitudes toward women's abilities based on secular logic to add to the arguments based on scripture and maternal privilege.

Although van Schurman is offering a critique of women's education and attitudes about women's true nature, she does not offer a practical alternative. It is not until Bathsua Makin's 1673 treatise *An Essay to Revive the Antient Education of Gentlewomen* that another practical plan for improving women's education is put forth. Makin (c. 1612–?), the tutor of Charles I's daughters, friend of van Schurman and Lucy Hastings, Countess of Huntingdon, was a professional educator. Makin's vision, like that of Lady Falkland, is to provide a "competent number of Schools [to be] erected to Educate Ladyes ingenuously."[42] In these schools, girls would be given a "liberal" education including classical and modern languages, mathematics, philosophy, history, and astronomy.

Makin turns to the traditional form practiced by male writers celebrating illustrious females, and uses examples of accomplished women in the past to argue that women can benefit from education. Although Makin acknowledges the controversy over the true nature of women and the equality of the sexes, she is at pains to make it clear this is not the issue of her book. Her intention is "not to equalize Women to Men, much less to make them superior. They are the weaker Sex, yet capable of impressions of great things, something like to the best of Men" (p. 29). She is quite aware that this tactic will not go over well with many of her women readers; in the preface she asks them not to be "offended, that I do not (as some have wittily done) plead for Female Preeminence." She makes it plain that she has a particular strategy for her treatise—"To ask too much is the way to be denied all" (p. 4). Makin has very concrete goals in mind; as the postscript to *An Essay* indicates, her methods of education, unlike those of Lady Falkland, are not the results of her charitable leisure time, but of her livelihood, an actual school at Tottenham (p. 42). She had to choose either to "offend" some women readers by refusing to deal with the abstract issue of the equality of the sexes, or to offend the fathers, whose money paid for the school. Therefore, to gain some ground to achieve better-quality education for more girls at schools such as the one at Tottenham Court, in her essay Makin does not urge the greater issue of the general nature of men and women.[43]

Her language, however, is not entirely conciliatory. She, too, uses the imagery of slavery and imprisonment to depict the effects of ignorance which the most fervent of the profemale writers adopt. She comments in unflattering terms on men who may dismiss her proposal: "it is an easie matter to quibble and droll upon a subject of this nature, to scoff at Women kept ignorant, on purpose to be made slaves. This savours not at all of a Manly Spirit" (p. 5). To those who plead custom, she is equally unrelenting. "Bad Customs (when it is evident they are so) ought to be broken, or else good Customs can never come into use. That this is a bad Custom, is evident, continued upon a bad ground. Let Women be Fools, and then you may easily make them Slaves" (p. 34). To the anticipated objection that "Women are of low Parts," Makin curtly replies, "So are many Men." To the fear that "If we bring up our Daughters to Learning, no Persons will adventure to Marry them," she answers coldly that the only reason would be the men's sense of inferiority: "Many men, silly enough, (God knows) think themselves wise, and will not dare to marry a wise Woman, lest they should be over-topt" (p. 30).

Thus, although *An Essay to Revive the Antient Education of Gentlewomen* has as its primary goal the gathering of pupils for a real school, it also has absorbed the imagery and tone of many of the polemical works on the equality of the sexes. Women denied education, Makin is implying, end up as "Fools" and this condition permits them to become no more than "slaves." Although she declares that she does not challenge the superiority of men, Makin nevertheless argues strongly against the notion of the natural inferiority of women.

The image of women enslaved by ignorance was brought to its extreme presentation in a work frequently attributed to Mary Astell, but more likely to be by Judith Drake, *An Essay in Defence of the Female Sex* (1696). James Drake wrote the commendatory verse that sets the tone for the ensuing argument.

> Our Sex have long thro' Usurpation reign'd
> And by their Tyranny their Rule maintain'd.
> Till wanton grown with Arbitrary Sway
> Depos'd by you They practice to obey.

Judith Drake accuses men of endeavoring "to train us up altogether to Ease and Ignorance," thus following the pattern of conquerors to demoralize the vanquished tribe and "disarm 'em, both of Courage and Wit."[44] She views the current submission of women to men as based on physical force, not mental superiority.

This dominion over women has its roots in ancient history, according to Drake.

> . . . nothing makes one Party slavishly depress another, but their fear that they may at one time or other become Strong or Couragious enough to make themselves equal to, if not superior to their Masters. This is [women's] Case; for Men being sensible as well of the Abilities of Mind in our Sex, as the strength of Body in their own, began to grow Jealous, that we, who in the Infancy of the World were their Equals and Partners in Dominion, might in the process of Time, by Subtlety and Strategem, become their Superiors; and therefore began in good time to make use of Force (the Origine of Power) to compell us to a Subjection, Nature never meant. (pp. 20–21)

In Drake's analysis of the contemporary status of women echoes of Hobbes and Locke on the origins of civil goverment are heard. Drake also continues this line of argument to compare the conditions of married women and slave labor. "By degrees, [men's domination of women] came to that height of Severity, I may say Cruelty, it is now at in all the Eastern parts of the World, where the Women, like our Negroes in our Western Plantations, are born slaves, and live Prisoners all their Lives" (p. 22). This equation of housewives and plantation slaves is a startling and provocative image, even for twentieth-century readers; Drake does not hesitate to apply it even to "civilized" countries such as France with its Salic Law and England, where "our Sex can hardly boast of so great Privileges, and so easie a Servitude any where" but "Fetters of Gold are still Fetters, and the softest Lining can never make 'em so easy, as Liberty" (p. 25).

With her brisk, ironic style, Drake does not let women escape uncriticized, either. Her solution to this unhappy situation is less institutional than Falkland's or Makin's: she encourages women to help themselves. In the section entitled "The Education of the Female Sex not so deficient as commonly thought," she examines the opportunities available to Englishwomen who wish to pursue meaningful studies. She points out that the education given to young children is the same for both sexes, "for after Children can Talk, they are promiscuously taught to Read and Write by the same Persons" (p. 36). The division comes when boys are sent to grammar schools and girls to boarding schools to learn "Needle Work, Dancing, Singing, Musick, Drawing, Painting, and other Accomplishments." The main problem is that girls are taught only English, or perhaps French, but no classical languages. Given their early deprivation, however, Drake is "very confident that 'tis possible for an ingenious Person to make a very considerable progress in most parts of Learning, by the help of English only" (p. 41).

As Drake sensibly points out, the prime function of learning classical languages is to master the contents of the works. "The obliging Humour" of translators, "has so far prevail'd, that scarce any thing either Ancient or Modern that might be of general use either for Pleasure, or Instruction is left untouch'd" (p. 42). What is required, therefore, is a determination to master a course of study, a self-motivated improvement. "Assist'd by these helps," Drake concludes, "'tis impossible for any Woman to be ignorant that is but desirous to be otherwise, though she know no part of Speech out of her Mother Tongue" (p. 44). If women remain foolish, Drake charges, they are in part to blame.

As had Makin, Drake refuses to be drawn into the controversy over the equality of accomplishments of the sexes.

> I shall not enter into any dispute, whether Men, or Women, be generally the more ingenious, or learned; that Point must be given up to the advantages Men have over us by their Education, Freedom of Converse, and variety of Business and Company. But when any Comparison is made between 'em, great allowances must be made for the disparity of those Circumstances. (p. 6)

The important issue for Drake is that women realize their own abilities and opportunities. Instead of endlessly debating equality, women can and should improve themselves by their own efforts.

Mary Astell's *Serious Proposal to the Ladies* utilizes both this concept of feminine self-determination rather than depending on masculine assistance and Lady Falkland's concept of a female academy. It opens with the premise that women's "Incapacity, if there be any, is acquired, not natural; and none of their Follies are so necessary, but they might avoid them if they pleas'd themselves."⁴⁵ The thesis, that ignorance results in vice, is the same propounded by Locke in *On Education* (1693). She uses his gardening images to depict the potential of women's moral and intellectual growth under proper management: "the Soil is rich, and would, if well cultivated, produce a noble Harvest; if then the Unskillful Managers, not only permit, but incourage noxious Weeds, tho' we shall suffer by their Neglect, yet they ought not in justice to blame any but themselves, if they reap the Fruit of this their foolish Conduct" (p. 21). Women, in short, are the products of the care and attention given them.

Her solution is to "erect a *Monastery*, or if you will (to avoid giving offence to the scrupulous and injudicious, by names which tho' innocent in themselves, have been abus'd by superstitious Practices,) we will call it a *Religious Retirement*" (p. 49). Here, those women who have discovered "the vanity of the world and its impertinencies" and those "desirous to know and fortify their weak side, first do good to themselves, that hereafter they may be capable of doing more good to others" may retreat from the temptations of worldly life. Their "Employment will be . . . to magnify G O D, to love one another, and to communicate that useful *knowledge*, by which the due improvement of your time in Study and Contemplation you will obtain" (p. 57).

Not only was Astell seeking to improve the educational opportunity of women, but she was also seeking to provide an alternative way of life. Astell imagines a utopian female society which "will be but one Body, whose Soul is love, animating and informing it, and perpetually breathing forth it self in flames of holy desires after G O D and acts of Benevolence to each other" (p. 79). The pure flame created in the ideal marriage would be replaced by one growing from a spiritual sisterhood. Unlike Lady Falkland's retreat, which was envisioned as a female college or Inns of Court, Astell's model was a religious institution, combining a mentality of withdrawal as well as a physical structure.

In Astell's remarks on men and marriage, one hears the same tone as in the antimarriage poems. The retreat would provide a place where women "may get out of that danger which a continual stay in view of the Enemy, and the familiarity and unwearied application of the Temptation may expose them to" (p. 50). Seventeenth-century women have few defenses, for "Custom, that merciless current that carries all before it," has taught women to resign control over themselves to others and to consider themselves inferior. Society in its present state, asserts Astell, is designed to ruin women. Women cursed with fortunes are at the mercy of "the rude attempts of designing Men . . . expos'd a prey to bold importunate and rapacious Vultures" (p. 120). Only by withdrawing from society, Astell maintains, will a young heiress avoid being "inveigled and impos'd on." She "will neither be bought nor sold, nor be forc'd to marry for her own quiet, when she has no inclination to it but what the being tir'd out with a restless importunity occasions" (p. 120).

As Joan Kinnaird notes, Astell's particular vision of a female society was not "born of liberal impulses but conservative values."[46] Astell was not attempting to create a new solution or a novel mentality; in spite of her disclaimer, her "monastery" was very close in spirit and rhetoric to the Catholic ideal. Her plan for correcting the existing evils in English society was not to abolish or change the institutions, but to withdraw from them, a theory espoused by many minority groups before and since. She does not attempt to reeducate men, but to separate women from them and from poisonous practices corrupting the divine institution of marriage.

To replace this damaged institution, Astell offers in her writings the notion of female friendship, "a Blessing the purchase of which were richly worth all the World besides!"[47] Ruth Perry points out that Astell's own strongest emotional ties were with other women, although she enjoyed the friendship and admiration of many of the leading male intellectuals of her day, and her deepest concern was that women are kept "groveling here below, . . . catching Flies, when [they] should be busied in obtaining Empires."[48] Perry writes, commenting on Astell's female connections, "In a sense, her advocacy of chastity was but a veil for the protective love and ambition she felt for other women."[49] In offering the benefits of female friendship over the possible snares of matrimony, Astell was drawing on a much older literary tradition of women turning to women for support and assistance.

It is demonstrated in the prefaces and dedications of seventeenth-century books and poems that women were writing for women. Patricia Crawford notes that slightly more of the books written by women are dedicated to other women than to men.[50] Lady Chudleigh makes her intended readership clear in the preface to her essays, announcing that they are designed primarily for women in order that they will be "persuaded to cultivate their Minds, to heighten and refine their Reason, and to render all their Passions subservient to its Dictates."[51] Sarah Ginnor, likewise, identified her audience as a female one, which she hoped to "rowse." Whether they chose to dedicate their writings to royalty such as Princess Elizabeth of Bohemia or an unknown female friend such as Elizabeth Middleton's Sara Edmondes, or even to a man, women writers acknowledged the fact that they were being read by women and that their works would be of particular interest to them.

As Crawford also points out, seventeenth-century women writers were aware of accomplished women in the past and called attention to their achievements. At the beginning of the century the obvious choice for Protestant female authors was Queen Elizabeth. Diana Primrose eulogizes Elizabeth's heroic virtues in *A Chaine of Pearle* (1630), citing her prudence in government, temperance, justice, fortitude, and abilities in "science." By the end of the century, Bathsua Makin was able to cite a roster of admirable women up to Anna Maria van Schurman.

Crawford also mentions the popularity of women who had achieved fame through their literary efforts, such as Katherine Philips, Anne Bradstreet, and Aphra Behn. "Orinda! Sappho! Sister! Friend!" begins one enthusiastic manuscript verse salute to Katherine Philips.[52] Aphra Behn drew similar worship from her female readers, and although some professed shock at the boldness of her language, other women applauded it. Joan Philips sees Behn's passionate descriptions as one of her strengths.

> Madam! permit a Muse, that has been long
> Silent with wonder, now to find a Tongue.
> Forgive that Zeal I can no longer hide,
> And pardon a necessitated Pride.
> When first your strenuous polite Lines I read,
> At once it Wonder and Amazement bred,
> To see such things flow from a Womans Pen,
> As might be Envy'd by the wittiest Men:
>
> .   .   .   .
>
> As in your Self, so in your Verses meet,
> A rare connexion of Strong and Sweet;
> This I admir'd at, and my Pride to show,
> Have took the Vanity to tell you so
> In humble Verse, that has the Luck to please
> Some Rustick Swains, or silly Shepherdess:
> But far unfit to reach your Sacred Ears,
> Or stand your Judgement: Oh! my conscious Fears
> Check my Presumption, yet I must go on,
> And finish the rash Task I have begun.
> Condemn it Madam, if you please, to th'Fire,
> It gladly will your Sacrifice expire,
> As sent by one, that rather chose to shew
> Her want of Skill, than want of Zeal you.[53]

Although skittish in its poetics, the verse is forthright and solid in the sincerity of its praise and admiration for Behn's successes. Joan Philips

saw Behn as a reigning female writer and in her request for approval, Joan
Philips was asking in effect to become one of the Daughters of Behn.

In addition to the dedications and commendatory verses to women by
women, the theme of female friendship also forms an important part of
women's writings. Henrietta Maria's court is credited with elevating the
concept of a platonic union to dizzying heights with its cult of friendship
in the 1630s and 1640s. Katherine Philips is the best-known female cele-
brant of this poetic convention, but other women engaged in similar
exchanges and female friendship was a frequent subject of verse epistles
throughout the century.

The verses written by Katherine Thimelby Aston and Lady Dorothy
Shirley in the 1650s illustrate the form and tone of this convention. While
their friend and sister-in-law Gertrude Aston Thimelby was rejoicing in
the "pure flame" of love between her husband and herself and declaring
that there is "No Love Like that of the Soul," Katherine Thimelby and
Lady Dorothy were finding a similar spiritual bond between themselves.
Their verses were often paired responses on conventional occasions, such
as "Upon the L D saying K T could be sad in her Company."

> . . . I am grieued that my exterior show
> Shuld contradick the joy I haue from you.
> For madam doe me wright I doe protest
> Ther is no Joy if not by me posset.
> When in your conuersation I can find
> Ther be al treasures to delight the mind
> And I unworthy I shuld this possesse
> Which might reward the worthyes and blesse
> Those that had uent'd most for your Deare sake.[54]

Lady Dorothy hastens to explain: "Deare Cosen pardon me if I mistawke /
I thought thy face had bin the truest booke / To reade the hart in."

> I fear'd you sad because that smileing grace
> which oft hath Joy'd me was not in your face
> Joy me it did because it made me see
> You pleas'd to tollerate this place and mee.

Following the conventions of friendship, the verse declares that knowing
Miss Thimelby has enriched Lady Dorothy's life; Katherine's presence
magnifies her own scanty virtues. Wishing to be worthy of her friend,
Lady Dorothy must first borrow some of Katherine's luster in order to be
a fit companion for her.

> Friendship occassions this, and you alasse
> Doe uiew me thre a multiplying glasse

> But what I can be unto you I will
> And wish increase in me for your sake still
> which by your company I hope that I
> shall gaine soe much I shall you satisfye
> But thinke not like a thefe I will conceale
> From whome I stole, the truth I will reueale
> And say tis you that haue inriched mee
> For whose sake I did wish to steal from thee.[55]

The poem concludes with the notion that just as in the perfect friendship of husband and wife celebrated by women writers in matrimonial poems, the strengths of these two women combine to overcome their individual weaknesses, forming one strong, pure mind.

A further glimpse into the nature of the friendship extolled by women is found in the letters of Constance Aston Fowler. Like her sister Gertrude, Constance enjoyed a deep, emotional bond with her future sister-in-law Katherine; initially, she began this friendship in order to help her brother Herbert's suit, but soon she, too, fell under Katherine's spell. Constance writes to her brother in her usual exuberant style, "never creture was more fortunate then I in gaining afection from her. For I beleeve I am blest with the most perfectest and constant lover as ever women was blest with."[56] After furthering her acquaintance, Constance was convinced that Katherine would be the perfect wife for her brother in addition to being the perfect friend: "she is soe rich in her selfe, that none can be poore that has the possession of so unvallewable a jewel . . . you two are deare partners in my hart, and it is soe holly devided betwixt you, that I have much a doe to gett leave of it to place any other friend of mine there."[57] Constance uses the same terms found in the matrimonial verses to depict the friendship between Katherine and herself. When she sends Herbert copies of Katherine's letters, she tells him, "you will say, I am certaine, when you peruse them, that ther was never any more passionat afectionat lovers then she and I, and that you never knew two cretures more truely and deadly in love with one another than we are."[58] Female friendship in the Tixall poems and letters has an intensity equal to that of a marriage relationship and provides the single woman with the same qualities of spirituality and refined sensibility extolled as the ideal in marriage.

Katherine Philips has left the largest body of female friendship poems, including "To Mrs. M.A. at Parting," "To My Dearest Friend," "Parting with Lucasia," "Orinda to Lucasia," and "Friendship." Love is the basis of friendship, married or otherwise, maintains Philips. In "Friendship" she declares, "Let the dull, brutish World that know not Love / Continue heretics, and disaprove / That noble flame; but the refined know / 'Tis all the Heaven we have here below." Love "chains the different elements in one / Great harmony, linked to the heavenly Throne."[59]

Love, however, is also subject to decay in this fallen world. "All Love is sacred," she begins, "and the marriage-tie / Hath much honour and divinity, / But Lust, Design, or some unworthy ends / May mingle there, which are despised by Friends." The purest form of love, Philips states, in "To Mrs. M.A. at Parting" is that of friendship, unmixed with sexual desires. Only then can two souls so mingle that "each is in the union lost."[60] Earthly marriages, on the other hand, have too many snares from lust and greed and are inferior spiritually to female friendship.

In her letters to Poliarchus, Katherine Philips believes men disrupt women's relationships with each other by demanding all their wives' attentions. She writes, "I find too there are few Friendships in the world Marriage-proof . . . we may generally conclude the Marriage of a Friend to be the Funeral of a Friendship."[61] Once married, not only is the woman legally tied down, but also no longer

> . . . our twin-souls in one shall grow,
> And teach the World new love,
> Redeem the age and sex, and show
> A flame Fate dares not move:
> And courting Death to be our friend,
> Our lives, together, too, shall end.[62]

The nature of worldly marriage precludes this form of female friendship and although her own marriage was a contented one, in these poems Philips does not appear to find conjugal bonds as congenial as those of friendship with other women. Female friendship for Philips and the Astons is nurturing, redemptive, edifying, and, with its pure, unwavering flame, a means of transcending mortal limitations.

This vision of friendship was not confined to the platonic gentry or those with Catholic ties. "Upon Parting with a Friend" by the Quaker Mary Mollineux dwells on the sadness that results when such a relationship is broken, even though their bonds are much deeper than mere physical presence. The intensity of feminine friendship is such that their separation causes great pain for both parties and Mollineux questions whether anything that produces so much anguish can possibly be good: "May we not Innocently then rejoyce / In the Society of Bosom Friends?" she queries.[63] Even with the pain, Mollineux feels that this female friendship is too valuable to be lost; just as in the Aston/Thimelby exchange and Katherine Philips's verses, Mollineux's poem recognizes the spiritual debt she owes to her friend, whose conversation has so enlarged Mollineux's sphere.

One finds the same qualities being praised, if not in the same rhetoric, in women's epitaphs for their female friends. Typically, the departed is a paragon of piety and wisdom and steadfast in her support of her grieving friend. Dorothy Bayly writes with more sincerity than style on the loss of her sister-in-law Pen Bayly, "the world a better friend did neuer Try." "Shal death thus Rob me of so braue a friend," she asks at the beginning, whom "grace, nature edication al expier / To make her that which all the world admier."

> So that great Soul she acted by
> Affliction euer her perpard did finde
> and had not will enough to crush her mind
> whilest others plesurs sought that falsly call
> She minded what was intilectual.[64]

For Dorothy Bayly, like the Astons and Katherine Philips, friendship with this woman of "quick solid judgement," modesty, and piety provided her with the example and the support she needed to improve her own life. Although the occasion is a far cry from the coterie poems on friendship, the sentiments and imagery found in such epitaphs celebrate in similar terms the power and importance of female bonds.

By the end of the century, no doubt in some measure the result of the models provided by Katherine Philips's verses, female friendship poems seem to be a feature of almost every woman poet's works. Anne Killigrew, for example, manipulates the convention to underline her own despondency and dissatisfaction with the worldly life in "The Discontent." Killigrew wonders about the possibility of achieving this pure friendship in a sordid secular world.

> But though True Friendship a Rich Cordial be,
>   Alas, by most 'tis so alay'd,
> Its Good so mixt will Ill we see,
>   That Dross for Gold is often paid.
> .   .   .   .
> Love in no Two was ever yet the same,
> No Happy Two ere felt an Equal Flame.[65]

In this poem, Killigrew is not challenging the theory of the perfect platonic flame, nor its value, but the validity of this ideal in a complex social world.

Lady Chudleigh, on the other hand, in "Friendship," has no doubts about its role in female life: "Friendship is a Bliss Divine / And does with radiant Lustre shine." It is perhaps a rare event to find the perfect match to form a pair "Whose Hearts are one, whose Souls combine, / And neither know of Mine, or Thine; / Who've but one Joy, one Grief, one

Love, / And by the self same Dictates move." Such relationships do exist, she declares, and women should strive to achieve them, not the mercenary marriages Chudleigh condemns in her other poems. This pair, while supportive and protective of each other's weaknesses, nevertheless seeks to "raise each other's Fame" by criticizing each other's faults. Their friendship is a relationship which, like Philips's, transcends circumstances, even death, for after their physical bodies die, they will "with a Passion more refin'd, / Become one pure celestial Mind."[66]

The female friendship poems are not overtly concerned with feminist issues. Education, dowries, and equality do not enter into the matters discussed. In one sense, however, they are allied in spirit with the separatist solution espoused by Lady Falkland and Mary Astell: only by withdrawing from a secular and sexual world can women improve themselves, expanding their spiritual and intellectual beings through true friendship. It is a state that excludes men entirely; although it is conceded by Philips that men may be capable of sustaining a platonic friendship with a woman, she implies in her verse that it is through female union, not marriage, that the true enlargement of a woman's sphere is achieved.

By the end of the century, women's writings in several disciplines showed a lively consciousness of the issues involved in the controversy over the true nature and roles of the sexes. Whether or not the work itself was a polemical one, the images and tone of the controversy permeate women's literary productions. In 1699, a vicar's daughter, Marie Burghope, opens the dedication of her landscape poem "The Vision" to Lady Mary Egerton by announcing, "It has been the comon Imputation of the Tyrants of the other Sex, that Women had neither Learning, Prudence nor conduct & therefore were fitt only to be the Drudges of Mankind." The poem itself is not in the slightest concerned with women's roles, but Burghope seizes the opportunity it presents to declare her beliefs in terms that would have been familiar to Mary Tattlewell and Ioan Hit-Him-Home:

> [men consider women to be] made up of Passion and Ignorance, & so to be govern'd as a higher sort of unreasonable Creatures. But these Men have seen themselues confuted by the numerous examples of our Sex in euery Age & Science, & in all Endowments of Body, & Mind. And now lest they shou'd be out done euery Way, they begin to declaime against our Acquisition of Knowledge as inconvenient, & pretend Policy to keep us in Ignorance.[67]

Sounding very much like Judith Drake and Lady Chudleigh, Burghope writes confidently of women's achievements and dismisses with scorn those males who would "use us as dumb Creatures, & make Slaues of us." Learning, she announces is the true source of all virtue, echoing Astell and

Makin. The lessons taught in the controversial works about women and in the women's writings themselves obviously had been absorbed by this young country poet.

By the end of the century, women readers such as Marie Burghope hardly could have avoided some acquaintance with such ideas, which had been flung back and forth between the satirists and the polemicists, celebrated in histories of admirable women, and even inserted in almanacs, medical treatises, and domestic conduct books, where Hannah Woolley's recipes mingle with her observations on female education. From those women who wrote and circulated their manuscript poems extolling the powers of female friendships to the marginally literate villager reading chapbooks and ballads, women formed a special audience, which received different female models than those depicted in domestic conduct books by men. Women writers, writing for women, were offering rebuttals to male criticism and suggesting alternatives to conventional women's roles in society. In addition to sincere celebration of the joys of marriage and satires on playboys, female authors also urged women to improve themselves through education and to "rowse up" their spirits. Even more radically, some women urged their readers to consider the pleasures of single life over marriage, to step out of the system entirely. Rather than wander into the only course of life represented in male writings, marriage, women writers encouraged their female readers to seek out the spiritual support and fulfillment that could only be found in the companionship of other women.

Case Studies

Sir Robert Filmer, Mary More, and Robert Whitehall

A final method for assessing the existing model of seventeenth-century domestic patriarchalism is to test it against writings from the period whose authors are either directly identified with or affected by its theory. The three manuscript essays included as appendices have very different origins and circumstances behind their composition. Sir Robert Filmer was a landowning country gentleman, educated at Cambridge and Lincoln's Inn, who enjoyed some reputation as a political writer before his death. His essay in praise of the virtuous wife was composed against the backdrop of his imprisonment and the raids on his home by Parliamentary troops during the Civil War. Mary More, on the other hand, was a twice-married London resident of unknown parentage and education. It is probable that she grew up during the Commonwealth and her essay explaining the true rights and duties of women was composed during the height of the Restoration from the perspective of both a wife and widow. Her adversary, Robert Whitehall, in contrast, had never been married and his life as an Oxford don seems to have left him with neither the inclination nor the opportunity to investigate the interesting condition of matrimony. An academic poetaster who owed his career to the patronage of Richard Cromwell, Whitehall nevertheless enjoyed the acquaintance and assistance of one of the most notorious libertines of the day, the Earl of Rochester. Closer in age to Filmer's generation, Whitehall stands as a bridge between the views of the earlier seventeenth-century writers and those of the Restoration.

How, then, can it be either useful or valid to read these three disparate spirits together? The obvious benefit is the plurality of perspective they provide and the opportunity to consider the relationship between their pieces and the conventions surveyed in previous chapters. The essays share several important underlying assumptions about both the nature of society and of women. All of the authors assume that marriage is the natural condition of adult life; to speak of women and women's roles, therefore, is to discuss marriage. As it is also assumed that all women desire to marry, these essayists are concerned with the question of a wife's duties and rights.

Second, all three authors reveal certain assumptions about the nature of women which are consistent with those expressed throughout the century. All three base their discussions of marriage on the unstated assumption that the wives about which they write are literate and capable of advanced studies in areas outside of strictly domestic spheres. They differ in their assumptions about the emotional nature of women—Filmer and More asserting independence and courage as feminine characteristics and Whitehall alleging fickleness—but all three implicitly acknowledge women's essential intellectual capabilities.

The essays also share a similar form of presentation. They were written for private circulation, as part of manuscript miscellanies. Filmer had followed this pattern with the majority of his other writings, even those published later, and the physical appearance of this essay on domestic virtues suggests a similar destiny. The More and Whitehall pieces were copied together and obviously meant to be read as a pair. Whitehall, who appears to have been the compiler of this miscellany, which includes several poems as well as the essays, was involved in an Oxford manuscript circle and also published some of his verse.

Finally, the authors of these pieces also share the less flattering characteristic of not being particularly outstanding writers or known controversialists during their own lifetimes. By and large, what contemporary reputations they did have were on a regional, not national level; Filmer's fame, for example, was not established until John Locke attacked his book *Patriarcha*, which was published nearly thirty years after Filmer's death. Not one of these authors was notorious for holding outrageous, outlandish, or controversial opinions—in short, not one of them appears to have drawn public attention for his or her life-style or challenge to contemporary values. In this sense, their writings fit into their generations' intellectual framework, neither standing outside them as radical or dangerous opinions, nor the result of personal circumstances, but the expressions of literate English thought at the time. These essays represent a traditional form of intellectual exchange and reveal the subject matters current and acceptable in such circles.

Sir Robert Filmer and the Patriarch's Wife

The life and writings of Sir Robert Filmer (c. 1588–1653) have served several generations of social and literary historians as prime examples of English patriarchal practices and philosophy in the seventeenth century. His most famous work, *Patriarcha*, is constructed on an analogy between political and domestic sovereignty; in recent years historians have interpreted it as his statement on family government as well. The duties of wives or mothers are noticeably absent in this piece. This omission of wives from governmental strategy (first pointed out with withering effect by John Locke in *Two Treatises of Government*) has led historians such as Lawrence Stone and literary critics such as Peter Malekin to regard Filmer as a "strong anti-feminist."[1] Filmer's "discreet" editing, to use Stone's phrase, of the Fifth Commandment to "honor thy father" is seen as typical of a rigid patriarchal attitude toward women supposedly held by men of Filmer's class and generation. This interpretation of Filmer's political writings has been supported by erroneous biographical information, such as the belief that Filmer took a child bride in a marriage arranged on purely financial grounds.[2]

Little attention, however, has been given to Filmer's writings specifically on domestic matters. In addition to his known published writings on legal and political subjects, three of Filmer's essays remain in manuscript, two completed and formally copied and one in rough draft, which address aspects of family government. In particular, his essays praising "the good wife" and "Touching Marriag and Adultery" have interest outside their unsung literary merit as patriarchal documents written by the leading theorist of political patriarchalism. Their content is of peculiar interest, therefore, in constructing an impression of the scope and nature of an English patriarch's domestic powers.

To understand the significance of these documents, they must be read in the context of the author's own domestic circumstances.[3] Filmer was the eldest of eighteen children, destined and educated to take control of the far-flung Filmer fortunes on the death of his father. He attended Trinity College, Cambridge, and then studied law in Lincoln's Inn from 1604 but, like many gentlemen of his day, took no degrees. In 1618, he married Anne

Heton, the daughter of Martin Heton, the bishop of Ely, and they lived in Westminster at The Porter's Lodge, where six of their children were born. Not until after the death of his father in 1639 did Filmer take up residence in the family home at East Sutton Park, Kent. During the Civil War Filmer was arrested for his royalist sympathies and from 1643 he was imprisoned for at least eighteen months in nearby Leeds Castle. Dame Anne took charge of the sizeable estate which was repeatedly raided by Parliamentary troops and is said to have sustained heavy losses. While in prison, Filmer's health began to deteriorate, but he did not die until 1653, and the estate was passed on to his eldest son Edward, then in exile with the court in Paris.

Such a career makes Filmer virtually indistinguishable from many of the country gentry with royalist ties. In the circumstances of his life and even in the events of the war years, Filmer's career was in no way unique. As his biographer Peter Laslett has noted, Filmer's publications, too, are not so important for their originality as for their representation of articulate, educated opinion of the day.[4] These publications, however, have preserved him from the fate of many of his contemporaries of disappearing into the black holes of biographical dictionaries.

Although the topics of Filmer's treatises are wide ranging—from political theory, to the practice of usury, to an analysis of English witchcraft trials—they seem to spring from the same cause: his intense desire to examine the conflicts between contemporary social and legal practices and those described in the Bible. Filmer's unpublished theological and domestic manuscripts display this same intellectually combative disposition. What is the true nature of "the good wife"? What is the difference between polygamy and adultery? In their analyses of these subjects, Filmer's essays implicitly question seventeenth-century definitions of marriage and suggest that a revision is needed in current interpretations of Filmer's patriarchalism which have been based on the political writings.

The history of these manuscripts has been documented by Gordon Schochet.[5] "In Praise of the Vertuous Wife" appears as Item 13 on the eighteenth-century list of Sir Robert's works. It is a fair copy, which comparison with Filmer's Civil War correspondence strongly suggests is a holograph; its abrupt ending and the blank sheet at the end of the volume suggest that although the argument set out in the opening of the piece is complete, the copy itself lacks some part of its conclusion. Two fair copies of "Theology or Divinity" are also listed among Filmer's papers; contrary to Schochet's assertion, neither copy appears to be in Filmer's hand.[6] The subject matter and its rhetorical treatment, however, along with the family evidence, point to Filmer as by far the most likely candidate as its author. The last of Filmer's domestic pieces is a very rough draft, written in an extremely shaky hand by Filmer, entitled "Touching Marriag and Adultery." It is not, as has been suggested by Schochet, a "lay sermon," but an investigation of the practice of polygamy in the Old Testament and its discussion by later commentators.[7]

In its subject, Filmer's essay "In Praise of the Vertuous Wife" belongs to the common convention celebrating the character the Good Wife discussed in chapter 2. In addition to the numerous literary precedents, in his own village church in East Sutton Filmer had the example of his uncle Edward Randolph's magnificent tribute to his wife Margaret, whose inscription begins, "Theis Stones cannot Express Love or Deserte: / My Love to thee, to God thy Reverence," and includes a lengthy account of her virtues as an ideal spouse. Like so many profemale writers before him, Filmer chose verses from Proverbs to frame his portrait.

The tone and treatment of the character in Filmer's essay are sophisticated blends of several types of discourse about women, all contained inside a scriptural framework, yet concerned with contemporary situation. This piece is undated, but speculation offers the possibility that it was one of the several theological pieces attributed by Laslett to the period during which Filmer was imprisoned in Leeds Castle, as internal evidence suggests that it was composed in the early 1640s.[8] For an essay in praise of domestic harmony, there are a remarkable number of references to warfare and besieged cities in this piece. Filmer chooses for his examples of virtuous women those heroic women in the Bible who repelled invading armies. That Filmer decided to use the admirable but extremely obscure wise women of Tekoa and Abel over better-known and more complete portraits of feminine virtue in the Bible suggests that the conditions under which he contemplated the qualities of the virtuous wife were equally unsettled.

The complexity of tone in this essay on a conventional topic is itself not surprising. As a member of a cultivated family, whose friends included Ben Jonson and George Herbert and who left an extensive collection of music manuscripts notable for including examples from all the major music types of the period, Filmer would have had the opportunity to become well acquainted with contemporary literature, continental and English, as well as the classics.[9] Filmer's younger brother Edward was also an author, publishing an important translation of French court songs; according to the family music manuscripts, the future author of *Patriarcha* appears to have passed his early days singing or being serenaded by his brothers and sisters with Richard Portman's "Phillis and her Myntor" and Thomas Home's "A Mournfull Shepherdess for the Loss of Laron."

Although his own life-style gives little indication of Cavalier excesses, certainly Filmer would also have been familiar with the courtly literary modes of flattering address to women. Elizabeth, his sister, was the subject of a rather awkward epitaph by their neighbor Sir Richard Lovelace: "Know that in that age when sin / Gave the world law, and govern'd queen, / A virgin liv'd, that still put on / White thoughts, though out of fashion." "In Praise of the Vertuous Wife" also suggests Filmer's acquaintance with less exalted Jacobean literature. Several of his "Objections" in this piece would go well in contemporary jest-books where the most blatant antifeminist slurs were to be found.

> *Obiection: A Crowne of gould is heavye so is a woman. . . . Answer:* It is better to have heavy persecution wthout then more heavie temptation wthin.[10]

Filmer's writings never trespass the bounds of scholarly humor, but this essay is unusual in its use of mild, witty paradoxes, showing a playful side of Filmer's style kept firmly in check in his published writings.

Dominating these varied literary voices is that source which Filmer knew best, the Bible. "In Praise of the Vertuous Wife" is essentially Filmer's interpretation of two passages from Proverbs as they relate to contemporary times: Proverbs 12:4, "a virtuous wife is the crown of her husband," and 31:10, "who can find a virtuous woman? for her price is above rubies." The essay meanders through the scriptures, frequently digressing into such issues as the benefits of early rising (for both sexes) and the biblical precedents for the sale of family land. Filmer constructs it in the form of a dialogue: observations are made, objections posed, and answers provided. One sees in this exercise a scrupulous intellect questioning the basis of its own beliefs rather than a complacent statement of received opinion. It is an exploration, using a scriptural framework of three themes: the nature of "virtue" in women, its manifestation in a wife, and finally, the value of a virtuous wife to her family.

Unquestionably, this essay, like his others, is based on the belief that a wife is second in command to her husband. Filmer states his position succinctly in "Theology or Divinity": the duty of a husband is to "teach his wife 1.Cor. 14:35 wch not to doe is sinne. Not to be able is miserie."[11] This sentiment, that the husband should naturally have the superior capacities in the pair, is implicit throughout "In Praise of the Vertuous Wife" and in this particular fulfills current definitions of a "patriarchal" document. The same sentiments are expressed in "Touching Marriag and Adultery" where, for example, Filmer finds no cause to deny the father's right to sell his daughter as a prostitute if he so wished. This stance and his flat declaration in this essay that based on God's presentation of Eve to Adam "the wife was given to the husband for a possession" cause these essays to appear as rigidly patriarchal in their attitudes toward women as the severest critic could wish.

Furthermore, like his contemporaries, Filmer believes that the dignity of a wife resides in her virtue, that bone of praise always tossed to the cheerfully subservient. Yet at this point Filmer swerves sharply from the expected path of patriarchal praise. Unlike the bulk of printed sources, Filmer does not define virtue as chastity, but as courage and strength. The good wife does not, of course, "shew [her husband] a cruel, bablinge, or lustful tricke," but her virtue is not limited to her chastity, nor indeed is it Filmer's prime concern. "The harte of her husbande trusteth in her," explains Filmer simply, "For her *Chastity* if she be free from adultery and the reasonable suspition thereof." Her husband's chastity is more problematic; not only can a husband trust his good wife for her own chastity, but also with the safekeeping of his own.

Courage is the key element in Filmer's praise of women. He cites 1 Peter 3:6, "whose Daughters ye are while ye do well, not being afraid of any terror." Filmer's exhaustive knowledge of the Bible furnishes him with numerous examples of courageous women: Deborah, Jael, Michal, and the wise women of Tekoa and of Abel (2 Samuel) are offered as instances of women acting valiantly, not simply for the good of their families, but also of their countries. "Theis examples should ca[use] men to emulate even the courage of weomen," observes Filmer. He then balances these heroines with a list of intrepid villainesses who tyrannized and betrayed their countries and spouses with as much success as any male, Delilah, Vashti, Athalia, and Cozbi. Men do not hesitate to credit wicked deeds to women, notes Filmer, and therefore, "if [women] be thus couragious in evill by nature why should we deny them good courage by grace?"

Filmer does not confine courage to heroic, warlike acts. It is also the self-discipline to live virtuously from day to day. "That courage is true vertue it appeare[th] bycause true vertue is the moderation of ye affections by faith and prudence[,] that one shewing what is lawful, the other what is possible and *convenient*. now this moderation is nothing but courage." It follows, therefore, that courage is best maintained by fortifying oneself against the tyranny of accidents and the despair of helplessness in the face of circumstances with both spiritual and secular skills to help maintain one's self-respect. Filmer's "meanes to attaine courage" are thus eminently practical: "First skill in Huswifrie and religion to prevent bodilie and ghostly terrors, secondly *Labour*. Thirdly *temperance*." "Leud companie," "*surfettinge* and al *vuluptiousnesse*" undermine the constitution of women as well as men and result in "*disuse of labour* wherby many [women] enfeeble their bodies and disable their mindes."

His insistence that women be good housewives in this context is neither patronizing nor bullying. It does not seem to spring out of a fear of usurping females, an attempt to keep them in the kitchen where they belong, but out of a more general and generous concern with human dignity in unsettled times. A woman's life, like a man's, needs both a purpose and the necessary skills that will enable her to "labour" rather than drift, a victim of situations.

Filmer regards with contempt the loss of either physical or mental capacities through destructive self-indulgence. More important to our picture of patriarchal attitudes, the stifling of a woman's powers by a man draws equal criticism from him. Unlike that other reputed "strong antifeminist," James I, Filmer has due respect for and knowledge of feminine attainments other than spinning.

> By the wheele and spindle are ment all labour not onely of body but of mind; if any woman excell in *Chirurgery, Phisick, government* of a commonwealth she shall be no more bound to the *wheele* then a prince is to ye *Plough.* Those husbands therefore are to *froward* that hinder theis eminent graces in their wives. . . .

Filmer does not assert that a wife is distinguished only in the role of her husband's consort; her own labors separate from those of her spouse determine her eminence. Underlining Filmer's insistence that lack of skills or the false restriction of them enfeebles women, he declares that a woman's accomplishments in whatever area her skills lie, are the source of nobility in women as "Armes and Learning [are for] men."

Filmer is not proposing the equality of the sexes. He does feel that there is "no vertue in men so differen[t] wch weomen may not hope in some sort to attaine, for e[ven] sayling and warre and government of kingdomes have been often times well handled by weomen, *Queene Dido* may be example for all, or rather *Q Elizabeth* in whose tim[e] theis things flourisht." Such observations do not reveal Filmer as a cryptofeminist. They do, however, display both his awareness of the potential capabilities of women and the existence of artificial limitations on them. They also indicate that Filmer, by his use of Elizabeth as an example, was not basing his analysis of women only on literary models from the Bible or the classics, but using earlier sources to illuminate contemporary situations.

Likewise, Filmer's interpretation of the creation of Eve as an important factor in his perception of the role of contemporary women is more apparent in his domestic writings than in his published political ones. On this issue, Filmer is firmly on the side of the female apologists such as William Heale.[12] Eve, he declares, was "a perfection to best, she was created in *Paradise,* lastily out of man['s] *Ribb* not out of the earth." This image of Eve as God's perfection of humanity leads Filmer to a spirited defense of her—

It is obiected. 1. *woman was the first sinner. Answer.* 1. Not the cause (for that was mans will) but the occasion. 2. she was the occasion not by hatefull knowledge (as Sathan) but by *ignorant love.* 3. As she was the first in sinninge so she was most griviously punished of al mankind. . . . The woman did decive out of error; the divel out of knowledge; the man did eate: so that she is to be pitied not hated.

In Filmer's opinion, God's punishment of Eve has left women in great "neede of patience against the day of *Sicknesse* and *Childbirth: widowhood* and *Martirdome.*" In "Theology or Divinity," Filmer seems to extend this to the trials endured by some wives, observing in the course of his exposition of the Fifth Commandment that "the mother is heere placed Second in authoritie: but in Levit: 19.3 at first, or earnestest in Love: too much neglected: and most to be pittied."[13] Like his contemporaries, Filmer sees the subjection of wives to husbands as the ordained result of Eve's transgressions; unlike some of them, he does not interpret women's subjection as the necessary result of inherent inferiority in female nature and he is sensitive to the difficulties of such a role.

Although the husband is his wife's governor, Filmer, in accord with most of seventeenth-century authors, does not see in this the license for tyranny. He again states his views succinctly in "Theology or Divinity" but the same principles underlie his discussion of the virtuous wife who never tests or usurps her husband's authority. Instead of presenting a formulaic statement of the wife's status and relationship to her husband's powers, however, Filmer finds the status of women after the Fall perplexing, for it is "not servile, yett intangled with froward accidents." He treads cautiously when traversing the subject of the nature of women. His hesitation is most marked at a critical point in his explanation of "Honour thy Father and Mother." The first, he begins, is either a father by nature, or by natural gifts "as wise, and good men." Furthermore, the father can be made by authority: "and yt either private (as maister, and tutors: and as some thinke husbands) or publique (as Pastors and Magistrates)" (chap. 12). "As some think" is a remarkably mild statement from a writer who supposedly modeled his domestic government on his political writings and a very shaky support for a theory of the absolute sovereignty of husbands.

In "Theology or Divinity," Filmer maintains that a husband does not have the authority to "exercise upon her any corporall restreynt or correction." Typically, he cautiously adds the qualification "unless he be a magistrate." Such careful distinction between the powers of a public official and those of a husband, between political and domestic authority, argues that Filmer would not have approved of subsequent critics' attempts to deduce his domestic government from his political theory. Otherwise, such state-

ments in his domestic manuscripts suggest that Filmer's political absolut-
ism is significantly qualified by the presence of a figure in the government,
a "wife," who is not far below the political "father" in authority.

Again, his perception of the women of his day stemmed from Filmer's
interpretation of key passages in the scriptures. His belief that Eve was the
perfection of mankind would not permit him to sanction the abuse of
wives. Filmer sees the diminution of women after the Fall as a corruption
of the best, "the best wine makes the strongest vinegar." Although he
advocates the husband's theoretical control over his wife's activities, Filmer is critical of the husband who in practice smothers his wife's talents.
In his essay on good wives, Filmer appears to be much more concerned
with encouraging wives to fulfill their roles in the family than warning
husbands to restrain their follies. "By trusting make her trustye," he urges.
Unlike Dod and Cleavor's edition of *A Godly Forme of Household Government* (1630) which condemns only the physical mistreatment of wives,
Filmer is aware of the damage that can be done without a hand being
raised: "againe, let not ye husband kill the spirit of the wife wth bitter
lookes, wordes, deedes; wch make of her a rib to become an excrement."

For Filmer, the trials of a woman's position as the most earnest and
loving member of the couple yet still second in authority are balanced by
the dignity of the theoretical and practical power she does wield. A virtuous wife is prized above rubies; she is "like pearles in vertue." Filmer
strongly implies that women are spiritually superior to men. He notes that
the first angel sent to comfort mankind was seen by a woman and that "the
incarnation and resurrection of Christ were first revealed to weomen, And
they loved Christ best alive and dead. . . . This ought to be their Comfort
in terror of Conscience and against the scoffes of the wicked." A virtuous
wife, concludes Filmer, is a living sign of God's favor to her husband, his
golden crown. God gives a virtuous wife to a man as a reward; Filmer
does not, however, speculate on the feelings of the virtuous wife about her
role as a prize.

Initially, Filmer seems to argue that "if any take a vicious wife it argues
his owne folly," but the implication that a wife's wickedness reflects her
husband's lack of grace plainly disturbs him. A virtuous wife is a mark of
God's blessing—but is a wicked one, like a wicked king, a sign of His
wrath? Or, is it merely a sign of the mismanagement of family government? Such questions bother Filmer and he returns to them repeatedly. A
careful sifting of the scriptures leads him to conclude that a good man
may indeed find himself wedded to a harridan, either as a *"Chastisement*
for some sinne past, or a preventinge of some to come, or else for a
Domestical martirdome." The evil or irresponsible wife, it appears, has
enough power in her secondary role to disrupt totally the peace of the
family, inflicting "domestical martirdome" on its head.

Filmer's depiction of such a "contintious wife" is as revealing as his image of the ideal one. Ignorance, idleness, luxurious self-indulgence, lust, and vanity are her characteristics. Of these, idleness and self-indulgence are the worst. For Filmer, idleness is more serious than the simple nonperformance of a task; it is indicative of a lack of commitment, a lack of love. Carelessness and "sloathfullness," "when in labour there is neither *earilynesse, vehemency, continuance*, nor *method*: sufficient *helpe*, or *allacritye*," betray the trust bestowed by the husband. Such traits rob the woman herself, lessening her self-respect and self-sufficiency and leaving her dependent on circumstances for her well-being.

There is no escape from marriage with such a wife. Unlike a rebellious son, who, significantly "is not equal to his father," a wife cannot be "restrained, disinherited, dismissed" ("Theology or Divinity," chap. 12). Her faults are magnified by her central role in domestic government; in the complicated scheme of domestic power, her deviance is capable of destroying the delicate balance of the family. Although in a subordinate role, the contentious wife is like "a *continual droppinge* wch eateth through the hardest stone, and being let in[,] rotteth the strongest houses." In a truly rigid patriachal system, one where all of the theoretical powers assigned to the husband were practiced, such "sloathfullness" would not have such a disruptive force.

Poor education and marriage contracted for the wrong reasons, not woman's essential nature, are blamed by Filmer for these faults. On the first, Filmer is quite insistent that girls should be trained before marriage to be self-sufficient housekeepers, capable of managing a household. He speaks of such preparation in terms of apprenticeship. It is significant that in this essay, Filmer's most-authoritarian statements are directed not at wives but children. Housewifery can only be learned, he insists brusquely, if girls "be broken of the[ir] will when they are younge" and "if they be kept in service farre from home." After marriage, such skills can only be maintained if full command is left in their hands, their husbands being "neither *spendthrifts* nor medlers wthin Doores," and if they have "no *concurrent mothers* or any other to command." This last comment highlights Filmer's concept of the position of the wife in family government. A wife has no shared powers: although she is second in command to her husband, within her sphere her authority is absolute.

The other cause of a good man finding himself with a bad wife lies in the circumstances under which their marriage was made. It is difficult to find a virtuous woman, warns Filmer, and even harder to win her as she may be "*promised* before, or *not affected to thee, or unfit for thy callinge*." Filmer advises his presumably male readers to choose a wife on the consideration of her mind, body, and estate. She must not be "grievously tainted" with pride, lust, covetousness, or an "eminent contagious disease." In the midst of these practical considerations in choosing a sound spouse, Filmer insists on the woman being equally attracted to her future husband, for "in particular she must affect thy Callinge and Person."

Filmer expands this theory of marital compatibility with his infamous political analogy. A virtuous wife is like a crown; crowns must come "*lawfully*, as by *iust warre, Election, Donation of god or man, Entrance in vacuity, Succession not by usurpation.*" Likewise, a good wife will be "given by God if she is vertuous and marrie willingly. not for *lust, Beauty, honor, wealth.* else she is a hellish screetchowle not a heavenly nightingale." In concert with his fellow commentators, Filmer sees no future in marriages made on the wrong basis, for either carnal or financial reasons, or to please a third party. The usurpation of power over an unwilling wife, or the abuse of authority by a tyrannical husband, will never lead to a good marriage, but will effectively bar both from entering the state Filmer calls "this heaven upon earth."

Filmer ends his essay in praise of the virtuous wife in celebration, comparing her virtues to precious stones and describing the happiness of the well-matched couple. He discusses her role as the benefactor of her neighbors as well as her family; it is the wife who practices the "arte of *Chirurgerie* and *Almes*," stretching forth her hand to relieve the poor. He concludes by emphasizing the respect and obedience owed to her by her children and by stating her rights as a widow to "*ye fruite of her handes.*"

This essay is a graceful tribute to practical, prosaic happiness and security in a patriarchal household as Filmer understood the concept. In "Touching Marriag and Adultery," Filmer changes his perspective to analyze the scriptural theory behind marriage and the wife's role in it. To distinguish polygamy from adultery, the main point of the essay, Filmer must first define the different roles and powers of women in the family— wives, concubines, and whores. The basis of the essay is the conflict between contemporary definitions of what constitutes adultery and the practices described in the Old Testament. Undaunted by the possibility of having to declare the majority of Old Testament prophets adulterers or Sarah a procuress, Filmer scrupulously dissects the opinions of Bellarmine and others on the possibility of lawfully having both "primary" and "divided wives."[14]

Filmer begins with the observation that in the original Hebrew, there are no equivalents for the English terms "husband" and "wife," only "man" and "woman." How, then, can one distinguish between the numerous wives and concubines who occupied Solomon's tents or explain why Sarah sent her maid Hagar to Abraham to conceive his child? Is not the first polygamy, the second adultery, and are not both unlawful and sinful?

The solution to this paradox lies in the definitions of a wife, a concubine, and a whore as opposed to other relationships that can exist between men and women. The differences between wives and concubines in the Old Testament are difficult to establish. Whereas the harlot in the Old Testament sells her body to many men, writes Filmer, a concubine occupies *"a kind of midle condition"* (515v). The concubine is bound to one man only, as is a wife, and thus, Filmer notes, annotators sometimes refer to her as a "divided wife," "halfe a wife and halfe a servant," whose offspring are acknowledged by the true wife as legitimate (515r).

Nevertheless, important distinctions remain between concubines and wives in the Old Testament. A wife is "publiquely and formaly married," while a concubine is "privately taken" (516v). The arrangement in the second instance is strictly between the man and the woman, a private agreement. In such a domestic arrangement, the woman retains a servant's status; Hagar remained subject to Sarah even after she bore Abraham's heir. An unmarried woman has the right to enter this relationship with a married man if she is not bound by any "matrimonial contract" to fulfill the command to increase and multiply, and the patriarchs in the Old Testament had the right to sell their daughters into such a situation if they chose (520r, 514v).

Marriage, on the other hand, is *"a diuine institution ioyning man & woman in a law fitly disposed to our helps and comforts of domestic life"* (521r). A wife occupies a very different position than a concubine in several respects: she is part of a formal institution, established by public contract, and is not a servant in the family but a partner in its government. The source of the public contract is the "original right of parents to give their children in marriage." Filmer does indeed advocate an extreme degree of control over adult children's lives, but it is not *patriarchal* power he is invoking but *parental*. "It is the right of Parents to dispose of their children in marriag. for they are in Gods sted and haue as iust a title to them as to any goods they haue" (514r). It is this power of the parents over their children that confirms marriage as an institution rather than a private agreement, for it is "the consent of the parents . . . wch makes the Contract or betrothing" (514v).

Parental rather than strictly patriarchal authority confirms such contracts because the mother who is a wife, not a concubine, is "solemly married," becoming a "partner in the gouerment of the family" (515v). In the Old Testament, according to Filmer's interpretation, a woman could be married without her consent, but she entered into a public, legal contract after which she assumed a position described by Filmer as a partnership with her husband in domestic government. As in his essay praising the virtues of the good wife, Filmer does seem to advocate very far-reaching authority over the lives of one's offspring, but the power is not defined as exclusively masculine, but as a plural, parental authority.

Filmer's primary concern is with the figures in the Old Testament, but his observations reveal information about the contemporary state of marriage with which he compares the powers of the patriarchs. As in his careful distinctions between public and private authority in "Theology or Divinity," Filmer is not making blanket statements about the power of the heads of families. According to Filmer's interpretation, the Old Testament patriarchs' authority and rights over their families no longer existed in Filmer's time, including the right of lawfully taking several wives. Although Filmer determines that concubinage was not sinful in earlier times, there is no indication that he himself was a closet polygamist or that he equated the scope of Abraham's power over his family with that practically available to a seventeenth-century English gentleman. The most obvious remnant of the parents' right to sell their daughters, in Filmer's opinion, exists in "the custom even to day of asking who gives this woman to be married to this man [which] is an acknowledgement of the original right of parents to give their children in marriage" (514r).

This is not to deny that Filmer himself was not the "head" of his own family in that he was its public spokesman, but instead to suggest that Filmer the author was quite aware of the difference between the authority available in theoretical and applied patriarchalism. Filmer's interest in the origins and extent of human authority in the scriptures has been confused in modern readings with what was actually practiced in his family. As a theory of human conduct, patriarchalism is derived from scriptural example in Filmer's opinion; even in the Old Testament version of it, however, Filmer establishes that, theoretically, a woman, once married, was "a partner" in the family government. Further undercutting the interpretation of him as a strict patriarchalist, Filmer concludes that the original formal, legal powers commanded by the patriarchs have in Filmer's analysis been reduced to mere social ceremonies that acknowledge the existence of former rights, such as the phrase in the marriage vows "who gives this woman."

These manuscripts on domestic issues establish Filmer's views on the theory of patriarchal authority as being both shared power and, by Filmer's day, greatly reduced from its scriptural origins. One means of confirming or invalidating their content is to compare Filmer's literature with his life. Externally, he bears all the trappings associated with the authoritarian patriarch defined by Stone. Filmer became the head of a large and not particularly sensible family when he was forty-one and maintained control of it for fourteen years. That the Filmer family viewed Sir Robert as its head, there can be no question. How far Filmer actively, effectively extended control over his wife and daughters, however, is another matter.

Little is known about the early years of the woman with whom Filmer chose to found his government, Anne Heton. From her father's will, one can deduce that she was born around the turn of the century; she married

Filmer in Saint Leonard's Church, 8 August 1618, not 1610 as has been written.[15] The speedy arrival of their first child who was baptized in February 1620, would seem to rule out the theory that Filmer wed a child bride.[16] The marriage was certainly suitable for both parties but to leap from that fact to the implication that it was a purely financial transaction arranged between parties probably unacquainted with each other seems a bit daring, especially as both Filmer and the Hetons resided in the same parish before the marriage.[17] Anne Heton was provided with a handsome settlement, but as her father died when she was still a child, it was parental not patriarchal authority that managed the match; Anne's mother signed the terms and gave her daughter away, as Dame Anne would later for her own daughter.[18] One could hardly jump to the opposite extreme and declare Filmer a romantic on such grounds, but his essay does condemn marriage not based on mutual "affecting" and this new biographical information, though not conclusive, lends credence to Filmer's later literary protestations.

What sort of woman, then, was the patriarch's wife, whom he seems to have had in mind when composing his praise of virtuous women? Her portrait shows Dame Anne as a strong-featured woman, not particularly handsome, but with fine eyes. Unlike the companion portrait of her husband, hers gives an indication of a durable sense of humor in her charming Mona Lisa smile. Dame Anne's production of a child on the average of every fourteen months for the first five years of her marriage suggests, according to current demographic theories on fertility during the period, that she married young, at the peak of her childbearing years. She was a wife for thirty-five years, a widow for eighteen; she survived most of her children. As mentioned in Filmer's will, she had discretion over his money and arranged the marriage of her daughter, as her mother had dealt with hers. She seems to have been a much-loved member of the Filmer family. Her mother-in-law Elizabeth Filmer left Dame Anne her "best Jewell" of diamond and pearl as the first personal bequest in her will.[19] She was well provided for in Sir Robert's will; in addition to life interest in his estates, he left his "beloved wife" the house in Westminster and all of his gold and jewels.[20] The sons she buried also remembered their "beloved Mother" in their wills with handsome bequests.[21]

More revealing than these references, which could be cynically interpreted as formulaic, is the confirmation contained in a letter from her feckless brother-in-law Henry in Virginia to her son:

Sr I should committ a grosse Solecisme in nature should I forget to present the humblest of my service to the Elect Lady my deare sister, your mother, whose ineffable favours are so deeply engraven upon the table of my hart.[22]

Unfortunately, her diary was lost after World War II, but from the excerpts published concerning the actions of the Parliamentary soldiers, she gives the impression of a resolute woman, not easily intimidated by marauding troops.[23]

Her correspondence in the 1660s with her second son Robert, or Robin as she calls him, gives a picture of a capable woman, a loving mother, and a doting grandparent. The purpose of these letters was to warn her son of her imminent arrival or departure—the virtuous wife in literature may have stayed planted indoors, but Dame Anne traveled back and forth between her houses in London and Kent and undertook an "eastern voiadge." The news in her letters is of a family nature, but of a rather unexpected sort. Part of it deals with the well-being of Robin's children, several of them who lived under Dame Anne's care, if not under her roof. The main topic, however, was East Sutton Park. In addition to overseeing her grandchildren, Dame Anne also ran the estate for her sons, first Edward in exile in Paris, then Robin in London, as she had done when her husband was imprisoned.[24] This included collecting rents and dealing with irate or obdurate tenants. "I have not yet received the honor of a visitt from goody spillett but I desired she should have one from Sam [Dame Anne's son] to whom she sputtered so much and so fast that he neither knew what she said nor what she ment[,] only perceived she thought she paid to much for the lease and was not so much considered for her paines," she wrote her son; "perhaps when she comes to me she will explaine herselfe more lardgly." [25] Incoherent Goody Spillett, however, was not nearly the trouble as "my old friend Piper," whose corn Dame Anne "thought it best to constraine and . . . [also to] lock up the barne." [26] This provoking gentleman, however, "took no notis" of Dame Anne's measures, causing her to request further suggestions from her barrister son.

Further difficulties arose over money matters on the estate. The failure of the cash crop, hops, combined with Robin's payments of his uncle's English debts, appear to have strained the family finances considerably. "The price of hopps is much fallen," she writes in concern, "they say yett all crop are as much shrunke as mine[,] therefore me thinks they should rise again; I have but five bags wch used to be 1200 and halfe[—]I am ashamed to come so to London in every bodies debt." [27] In spite of these pressing financial worries, which led Dame Anne to propose that they pawn some of her jewelry, and constant physical ailments, the sense of humor suggested in her portrait sustained Dame Anne.[28] "Heartely glad I am that you are so well mett," she greets Robin, "and wish we may all be so too as soone as any considering tennant will enable me." [29] Besides her dealings with the defaulting Mr. Swan, the oblivious Mr. Piper, and the sputtering Goody Spillett, Dame Anne also managed the harvesting and marketing of the hops. She watched the fluctuations of prices with the calculating eye of a modern options trader, with no mention of an intermediate steward dealing for her, observing the effects of foreign as well as domestic policies on prices. She was not, these letters suggest, completely independent in her activity. She requested and presumably followed her barrister son's legal advice about one of the tenants, and the money from East Sutton Park was channeled back to London for disposal. [30]

There is nothing in her background, marriage, or circumstances after Filmer's death to suggest that Dame Anne was distinguished for her "housewifery" or had extraordinary education or talents that led her husband and her adult sons to trust such important financial matters to her direction. If anything, one might receive the opposite impression from her scanty biographical information: her father's close friend and lifetime associate, William Gager, provoked Heale's published defense of women's rights in 1609 by maintaining in an Oxford debate that it was lawful for a husband to beat his wife. [31] The zest and thoroughness with which Dame Anne chronicles her activities suggest a capable woman with long experience. Nor does she appear to have been unique. During the Civil War there were numerous accounts of women running large estates single-handedly and conducting business affairs, the most famous of whom, because of their own written accounts, were Lady Fanshawe, Lady Halkett, the young Duchess of Newcastle, Lady Harley, the Countess of Pembroke, Lady Russell, and Lady Joan Barrington. The successful management of an estate, especially one the size of Filmer's, is not a skill quickly mastered, especially during times of crisis. The evidence of Dame Anne's letters and the fact that she continued to manage the estate when there were grown sons suggest that the competence displayed by women in general during the war years, which so surprises Thompson, was not so much a rising to meet new opportunities caused by social upheavals as a revelation of the scope of the domestic sphere of wives in this social class. [32]

Like the term "patriarchalism," twentieth-century definitions of "housewifery" have tended to restrict our perception of the scope of the activities followed by women in this period much more sharply than actually demonstrated in autobiographical accounts. The significant practical power in the family government as envisaged by Filmer and displayed in his own family was not "patriarchal" in the sense of belonging strictly to the males of the family, but parental in that it was shared with the wife, who, surviving her husband, wielded those powers of arranging marriages and estate management typically ascribed to the male head of a family. Based on his domestic writings and circumstances, one must either drop Sir Robert from the ranks of model patriarchs for this period, or form a new definition of "patriarchal" family government which takes into account the extent of the practical powers possessed by the English patriarch's wife.

Mary More and Robert Whitehall: The Equality of the Sexes

Sir Robert Filmer is an established figure in the canon of seventeenth-century studies; much less is known about the private circumstances and public career of the author of "The Womans Right," Mary More. Unlike Filmer, both Mary More and her antagonist, Robert Whitehall, seem to have slipped through the biographer's nets of parish records, personal correspondence, and family genealogies. Both received some public recognition—Whitehall during his life and More in the eighteenth century—but by and large, they were not among the century's celebrated.

What little was known about Mary More previously was recorded in Horace Walpole's account of her as an artist. She was

> a lady, who I believe painted for her amusement, [and] was the grandmother of Mr. Pitfield; in the family are her and her husband's portraits by herself. In the Bodleian Library in Oxford is a picture by her that she gave to it, which by a strange mistake is called Sir Thomas More, though it is evidently a copy of Cromwell, Earl of Essex. Nay, Robert Whitehall, a poetaster, wrote verses to her in 1674 on her sending this supposed picture of Sir Thomas More. [33]

For two centuries this has been the only source of information about her; as the art historian Ellen Clayton has observed, referring to the scarcity of information about women artists in general from this period, "Mary More flits by in the same noiseless, tantalizing way." [34]

Further information about the private individual can be gleaned from the essay she wrote defending the original equality of the sexes. "The Womans Right" is addressed to "my little daughter Elizabeth Waller." This same daughter Elizabeth married Alexander Pitfield, esquire, on 17 April 1680 in Saint Leonard's, Shoreditch, giving her age as seventeen. [35] From this, one can calculate that Mary More, listed as her mother, was married to a "Mr. Waller" for a period before 1663, when her daughter was born (the date of her son Richard's birth has not yet been found, although it has been erroneously stated as 1654 by his biographer). [36] She must have then been widowed and remarried a "Mr. More" by 1674, when Whitehall addressed his verses to her by that title.

Her daughter's marriage license also reveals that Mary More resided in the parish of Saint Andrew's Undershaft, Bishopsgate. Unfortunately, this hopeful lead turns out to be a dead end: Mary More and her husbands make no appearances in Saint Andrew's Undershaft's registers. The only possible trace of her there comes in the Parochial Visitation Book of 1693 when a "Mrs. Moor" gave "04.10" to charity. As a result of this biographical silence, the rest of her life must be derived indirectly, through the correspondence and circumstances of her children, in particular her son and son-in-law.

From Richard Waller's correspondence, one can reconstruct a skeleton of Mary More's later family life. For the last years of the seventeenth century and the first of the eighteenth, the Mores, the Pitfields, and Richard Waller and his family all lived within ten minutes' walk of each other, Mary More in Crosby Square, the Pitfields in Bishopsgate Street, and the Wallers in Broad Street next to Saint Peter-le-Poor.[37] From the steps leading into Crosby Square where Mary More lived, one could have seen the ruins of Crosby Hall, in which Sir Thomas More and Sir Philip Sidney's sister, the Countess of Pembroke, had resided. Its Great Hall, in which according to tradition Shakespeare had set Richard III's acceptance of the crown from the citizens of London, still was standing, but by Mary More's time, it had become a Presbyterian meeting house. She herself probably lived in one of the new houses built on the remains of the Old Hall. Today, looking straight forward from the square's steps, one can still see the steeple of Saint Andrew's Undershaft, in whose province two famous men whose accomplishments indirectly provided inspiration for Mary More's own had lived and died: Hans Holbein and the historian John Stow, who is buried there. Looking to the left, a hundred paces away, one sees Saint Helen's Bishopsgate, where Mary More's grandchildren were baptized.

Even in Mary More's day, this area was noted for its well-to-do merchants and bankers. John Aubrey's list of potential backers for his proposed school confirms this impression; he lists "Mr. Waller and his brother-in-law, both very ingenious and rich" as likely sponsors.[38] From his correspondence, we know that Waller owned land in Hertfordshire and Gloucestershire; in his will he leaves this property to his wife Anna "after the death of my mother Mrs. Mary Moore."[39] Obviously, the three families were comfortably well-off. She herself gives no direct information about her social position, but her warmth on the subject of mercenary marriages in her essay and her awareness of a wife's financial position under the law suggest that she had some experience with matters of this nature, or at least moved in circles where she could observe it. Given the events of her own life, she would be familiar with the legal position of widows and women's property rights during this time.

One social and intellectual circle to which she was linked by her offspring is that of the Royal Society, located at that time nearby in Gresham

College. Her son Richard was its secretary from 1687 to 1709 and from 1710 to 1714 and her son-in-law Alexander Pitfield was its treasurer from 1700 to 1728. The eminent scientist and inventor Robert Hooke had taken Richard Waller under his wing and Hooke's diary records paying visits with him to a Mrs. More who lived nearby and discussing her dreams with her.[40] In Waller's widespread correspondence, one finds other traces of his mother in her later years. Waller's letters to his fellow secretary, Sir Hans Sloane, reveal the close-knit nature of the three families: Waller writes from his country home in Hertfordshire that he was delayed in sending the editions of the *Philosophical Transactions* because "several of my Relations coming and staying with me a considerable time."[41] He protests that he does not have the keys to Edmond Halley's cabinets, having given them "to my Br. Pitfield"; his excuse for delaying a translation is that the manuscript had been misdirected and left "at my Mother's house in Crosby Square" and her servants did not immediately forward it.[42]

The last notice we have of Mary More comes in a letter from another of Hooke's friends, his editor William Derham. Derham also appears to have been on visiting terms with More. In 1713, Derham wrote to Waller and included an anxious inquiry about his mother's health.[43] No date has been found for Mary More's death, but one assumes it was after Waller drew up his will, but before his death in 1715, as his wife, not his mother, proved the will.

To discover more about Mary More's personality, one again must turn to the children she produced. John Evelyn described her son as an

> extraordinary young Gent: & of greate accomplishments: skild in Mathematics, Anatomie, Musick, Painting both in Oyle and Miniature to a greate perfection, and excellent Botanist, Ingraves rarely in Brasse, writes in Latine, & is a poet, & with all this exceedingly modest: His house is an Academy of itselfe.[44]

As we know nothing about his father except that he must have died when Waller was still a boy, it is a matter for speculation as to what degree he owed his impressive education and accomplishments to his mother. Certainly, his taste for sketching and painting may have come from her. As her essay shows, Mary More could read Greek and Latin, but unlike her son, her preference was for ecclesiastical rather than natural history. One imagines from her friendship with Hooke and Derham that she must have had at least a passing acquaintance with the principles involved in the new experimental sciences, but unlike her contemporary the Duchess of Newcastle, there is no record that Mary More ever attended a session of the Royal Society.

Mary More gives no clue about the source of her own education. At this point, one can only speculate that, like Lucy Hutchinson, Dudlyea North, and Mary Mollineux, she was the daughter of fond parents who encouraged their daughters to pursue the same studies as their sons. Possibly she was sent to one of the ladies' academies such as the one Katherine Philips attended, or, more likely, she may have been educated at home by a scholarly father or brother as was Damaris, Lady Masham. Whether or not she ever used her education and abilities with languages to support herself in the manner of Bathsua Makin or Elizabeth Elstob is unknown; perhaps, like Elizabeth Bland (another woman with private connections to the Royal Society), she contented herself with teaching her own children.

Mary More's original claim to public attention, however, was not as a "learned lady," but as an artist. Unfortunately, almost all of her paintings have vanished. Of the nine copies she made of the Holbein portrait which she mentions in her verse reply to Whitehall, two are known to have survived into the twentieth century. One of these she gave to the Bodleian in 1674 under the title of a portrait of Sir Thomas More and the other disappeared after being sold by Christie's in 1929. As Walpole pointed out, the painting is actually a copy of Holbein's portrait of Sir Thomas Cromwell; this ironic confusion of Cromwell and More suggests that Mary More was herself copying a copy, not the Holbein original, and most likely it was a copy out of its familial context. Given the numerous derivations of the Cromwell portrait that seem to have been floating around during this period (at least three are known to have existed at this time) and given the popularity of Sir Thomas More as a subject, confusion of the two seems less peculiar—Sir Thomas More's name was ascribed to several portraits by other artists in the seventeenth century which are now known to be of other sitters.

An interesting parallel to More's copying of the Holbein is found in the diary of one of her son's friends, Ralph Thoresby, the Yorkshire antiquarian, which may shed some light on a possible source for More's portrait. In 1677, as a young man living in London, but not yet formally acquainted with Waller, Thoresby records his pastime one day "at the Hall, an at home making Luther and Zuinglius pictures."[45] The Great Hall in Crosby Square apparently had Holbein portraits or copies of them hanging on its walls; Thoresby mentions elsewhere his habit of accompanying his relatives to the Presbyterian chapel in Crosby Square. It is tempting to speculate that Thoresby might have been copying pictures or panels left in Crosby Hall, which would have been a Holbein source for Mary More on her doorstep.

The surviving portrait itself in the Bodleian Library has been so heavily retouched that only the face is More's original work. One cannot help but feel that Germaine Greer's dismissal of it as an "undistinguished copy" is unfair: certainly the painting would be vastly improved if the enthusiastic restorer had not painted over the left-hand edge of Cromwell's face, destroying his profile.[46] In addition to this work, circumstantially, there are two other portraits still surviving that might be by Mary More. One is an unsigned pencil sketch of her son Richard which is the frontispiece of his manuscript translation of the appendix of *The Aeneid*. Waller himself did the other illustrations for the text, but each of them has his distinctive signature, which the portrait does not.[47] The other possible More portrait is one of the historian John Stow in Saint Andrew's Undershaft, her parish church, where Stow is buried. Its origin in the church is unknown, but the work itself is in a similar mode as the other verified portrait by More and it is from the proper time period.

The portrait in the Bodleian is also Mary More's first public tie to Robert Whitehall, the author of the rebuttal to her essay. As to the origins of their acquaintance, it is tempting to believe that Mary More was born or wed in Buckinghamshire, where there were several branches of the Waller family. Robert Whitehall was born there in 1625 and he also spent two years at his father's house in Addington after being ejected from Oxford by the Parliamentary visitors in 1648. Some acquaintance through either her husband's family or her own might thus account for a friendship which is puzzling not only in its exact nature, but also in its very existence. The possible common ground between a learned female theologian and an Oxford don whose only lasting claim to literary fame is that he appears to have started the young Earl of Rochester on his career as a debauchee, taxes the imagination.[48]

The More/Whitehall miscellany which contains their essays was compiled after More presented the Cromwell portrait to the Bodleian in 1674, for it contains Whitehall's verses to her on the subject. Because of the tone of this poem and More's response to it, one hesitates to use the word "friendship" to describe their relationship. Whitehall dedicates his poem to the "No Less Virtuous Than Ingenious Mris Mary More; upon her Sending Sr Thomas More's Picture (of her own drawing) to the Long Gallery at the Publick Schools in Oxon." The poem goes rapidly down hill from here.

> Madam:
> Your Benefaction has been such,
> That few can think it is a Womans touch:
> So to ye Life was Issa drawn (ye Bitch)
> That ye beholder doubted which was which:
> Seldom so Rare an Artist hath theere bin,
> Yet every Lady Knows to draw Man In.
> Since your Pencil far exceeds your Pen,

Let it be said I was ye first of Men
Could stop in Scribling—know we study thrift
And fancy this a Richer new yeares-Gift.
When one in Shadows, & other deals in Rime,
Painters & Poets should knock off in Time.
Janus will knit both Brows too, if I trouble You
Longer, or interrupt his.
Yours
R:W:[49]

Obviously, Whitehall intends to compliment the artist for drawing so well that one cannot tell the original from the painting, but the reference to Martial's disreputable bitch is not a particularly graceful one. Likewise, while praising her skill as an artist Whitehall also manages adroitly to cram in a cynical slap at the ability of all women to trap, "to draw in," men. Finally, surely no painter would appreciate being told to "knock off in Time," although one can rejoice in this poem that the poet did.

Mary More was certainly not overwhelmed by such scholarly praise. In her reply to "the most Ingenious Mr. Robert Whitehall, Fellow of Merton College in Oxon," she retorts with spirit, if not good poetry.

Sr.
Jear your Benefactress thats but Just
And I can bear't, but why no Woman must
An Artist bee in Painting, cause you see
I'm none, make ye whole Sex Suffer for me.
It made me Dogged Martials Bitch to read,
Besides I find his baudy Steps you tread.
Fellow and Batchelour, it must be soe
Hide yours sixt line, sure't it speaks more yn
you know.
The Holbin Coppyer yeilds, lets Pencils fall,
Scarce knows her poet from's Originall.
Three for our selves and six for friends beside
Nine ways at once, what ye Muse squint eyde.
Ile close them then, for ye vein I fear
May prove catching, I wish yould do so there:
Just what I thought, Oxford I knew before
How ere take Jear for Jear from
Mary More.[50]

In addition to accusing Whitehall of ingratitude for the gift, More objects heatedly to his implied criticism of her sex. Just because you find my painting unacceptable, or the source of jest, she charges, do not extend the criticism to the character of my whole sex. Although she says she has no desire to follow in Whitehall's "baudy steps," she nevertheless gets in a good crack at Whitehall's dubious sexual preferences as the source of his cynicism toward women. Nor does she seem much more charitable toward the patriarchal institution Whitehall represents: Oxford certainly does not seem to have been Mary More's touchstone of intellectual achievement any more than it had been for the satirist Alicia D'Anvers.

Significantly, More was not alone in her interpretation of Whitehall's verse to her. An anonymous writer responded to Whitehall's poem, which had been printed in Oxford in 1674. "Stranger to every Muse!" it opens, and the anonymous defender goes on to assert that there could be no complaint about Whitehall's execrable verses when they were devoted to such subjects as "Mother Loose," but "when thou'rt so fool hardy as to chuse / A theme, which if thou praise, thou must abuse, / Then know we'l knit our brows too, and you'le feele / Our pens as sharp as other peoples steele."

> Deare Friend!
>   Thy Poetry is such,
> That all will swear it is thy touch;
> So to the life thou'st drawn thy self,
> That none can doubt who is the Elfe.
> When once wee see thee at a pinch,
> Labouring for a Pun or clinch.
> Could'st thou not out of all thy breeding
> But to a Bitch thou must compare,
> The work of Artist thou call'st rare:
> And shew by drawn in quille thy braine
> Out weighs thy manners not half a graine.
> Since then her Pencil far transcends
> Thy pen, in vaine thy inke thou spends
> Endeavouring only to relate
> The Symmetry that did create;
> Nor could thy witt rival her hand,
> Tho't were inspir'd by her comand.
> Thou couldst not say enough by quibling
> Tho thou shouldst never stop in scribling
> Pre thee hence forward study thrift,
> Let's have no more such New-years gift:
> Bee not so prodigal of thy Time
> Knock of and deale no more in Rime
>   If this advice thou will oppose,
>   Lett thy next subject be thy Nose.[51]

Like More, this critic sees Whitehall's verses as essentially insulting. On the other hand, the Bodleian's acquisition records show that it was Whitehall himself who delivered the painting to the library. Further light on this matter and on Whitehall's personality comes after reading more of Whitehall's verse, especially his attempts at complimenting his former charge, the Earl of Rochester.[52] One comes to the conclusion that the anonymous poet may not have been so far wrong in his assessment of Whitehall's poetic abilities: Whitehall (who was thoroughly disliked by his associate at Merton, Anthony à Wood) had little sense of subtlety and a leadenly jocular sense of humor. Whitehall may have, with the best of intentions and with sincere admiration for Mrs. More's abilities, given offense to More and her defender purely by accident.

Whichever might have been the case, the unhappy and no doubt misunderstood Mr. Whitehall was born the second of nine children to Richard Whitehall, former vicar of Saint Mary Magdalen, Oxford, and from 1616, the rector of Addington, Buckinghamshire. The young Robert was educated under Richard Busby at Westminster, from whence he went to Christ Church, Oxford, in 1643. Ejected in 1648 for refusing to recognize the Parliamentary visitors, he next appears as a fellow of Merton College in 1650, having gained the favor of that party in the intervening years. "By virtue of the letters of Rich. Cromwell chancellor of this univ.," wrote Wood coldly, "[Whitehall] was actually created bach. of physic."[53] Apart from a year spent teaching in Dublin at the request of Henry Cromwell, Whitehall appears to have never practiced physic of any sort, but lived as a poetaster in Oxford. He kept his friendship with Rochester and his circle, sending him a rather obsequious, joking verse at New Year's and including the libertine "Satyr Against Marriage," attributed to Rochester by *Poems on Affairs of State*, in the same manuscript miscellany that contains More's essay and his reply.[54] Whitehall died in 1685 and was buried in Merton chapel. Today, not even a brass plate has survived to mark his grave.

The manuscript miscellany containing the two essays appears to have been compiled at his instigation and under his direction. The Whitehall text, "The Womans Right Proved False," shows signs of authorial amendments in its deletions and substitutions. This fact also points to its compilation between 1674 and 1685 when he died. The issue at stake in "The Womans Right," which Whitehall attempts to refute, is the usurpation of authority, framed in a challenge to that authority being wielded in the family. Underlying this specific argument is that of the original equality of the sexes and the effects of the Fall on the natures of women and men.

Men, says More, have based their authority over their wives on mistranslations and strained interpretations of key phrases in the New Testament. This original usurpation—whether intentional or not More never states, although the growing warmth of her argument over the course of the essay suggests the first—has been reinforced by custom, and the legal machinery, which, being made by men, enforces the injustice.

The framework of "The Womans Right" is quite conventional. More, too, depicts the ideal of the happy marriage as one based on love, in which the husband's and wife's interests are the same. She, like other women writers of the century, stresses mutual respect, duties, and love between husband and wife in contrast to a master/servant relationship. After the Fall, God assigned the two sexes different tasks and it is their duty to support each other.

> Neither [sex] have cause to brag, nor I am sure to oppress each other, by adding that to either which I am sure God never intended, but to help & ease each others burdens: Therefore are they called Yoke-fellows from a Yoke of Oxen drawing equally through ye cloddy troubles of this life.

The husband must provide maintenance for his family, "leaving no Lawfull way untried," and "with all tender affections comfort & cherish his wife." The wife, on her part, must show "all love and affection to her husband" and patiently bear the pains of childbirth; furthermore, she must "frugally use ye estate her husband so carefully gets, they both endeavouring ye promotion of Gods Glory & their own Salvation, forsaking all other Persons & Interests."

Like Filmer, More's examination of the distribution of power within marriage leads her to consider its historical forms. More continues to emphasize marriage as a partnership in her refutation of polygamy. "Marriage is ye indivisible conjunction of one man & woman onely," she declares firmly. She points out that Christ told his disciples that a man must cleave to his wife and they shall be one flesh, "not they 3 or they 4." Marriage, in More's presentation, is an exclusive partnership, where duties and affections cannot be distributed outside the pair.

In her depiction of the rights and duties of children, More also asserts the notion of marital partnership. The obedience owed by children to their parents, mother and father, is much greater than that owed by a wife to her husband. Christ, she states, obeyed his earthly parents; they had this power over him. The husband, however, does not stand in the place of the parents to his wife and she is not obliged to obey him as she would her parents. Parental power, even over a grown child, is depicted by More as much stronger than the husband's over his spouse.

In order to arrive at these conclusions, More, like her predecessors, has to deal with the issues surrounding Eve's creation. The punishment given to Eve that her husband shall rule over her "do shew something of a subjection to her husband after ye fall, tho not much," More maintains stoutly. Instead of a servile state, it is comparable to "the superiority of Eldership, which God seems to tell Cain was his due, if he did well." By making this parallel, More is suggesting the minimal nature of the formal obedience, that of a younger brother to an elder, and also suggesting it is conditional—"if he do well."

More does not pursue this last point, whether a wife need obey a husband who fails to "do well." She advises her daughter not to fight against a bad husband, if she should be so unlucky to marry one; because they are "yokefellows" she will only be hurting herself. "God will take thy part sooner or later," she consoles, "when we bear afflictions patiently (and leave him to revenge) [God will] doe it for us."

To avoid this unhappy situation, "The Womans Right," like Filmer's essay, offers counsel on choosing a partner. Both authors are remarkably consistent in their advice, only the sex whose traits are coolly scrutinized as potential helpmeets is reversed. Man or woman, one must choose by earnest prayer a God-fearing spouse, who is not foolish or harsh, and one "whom thou dost love and affect and that loves thee." Unlike Filmer and the majority of the profemale writers, More is highly conscious of the pitfalls for women under English law. A woman's need for care in this matter is vital, maintains More, "for the Laws of Our Country [give] a Man after marriage a greater Power of their Estate than ye Wife, unless ye Wife take care before hand to prevent it (which I advise thee to doe)." Throughout the essay, More demonstrates an awareness of such practical legal matters affecting a wife's position, an awareness that is absent from both Filmer's and Whitehall's considerations.

The current of concern underlying her advice, however, is the same that perturbs Filmer—the possibility of discord in a marriage from which there is no retreat. More does not offer Filmer's explanation which attributes a bad husband to God's will, but sees the problem in more immediate terms, the man's attempt to wield authority not rightly his. The poor education of men has led them to believe in the legitimacy of this usurped power; the neglected education of women has conspired against women's interests in support of men's claims.

Like Mary Tattlewell, Ioan Hit-Him-Home, and Mary Astell in her own century and Mary Wollstonecraft a century later, Mary More unhesitatingly identifies the source of this abuse of women's rights in parental neglect of the education of their daughters and the economic dependence of a wife on her husband. Also in common with Wollstonecraft, More considers that not only does the lack of general education for women put them in a false position but also what is received is different in nature from men's: "yt is ye want of learning, & ye same education in women, yt men have, wch makes them loose their right," she declares flatly. Unfortunately, rather than continue this argument and debate the responsiveness of society to the reforming powers of education, More chooses to close her line of thought here with a rhetorical flourish, declaring that if parents went about their duties better in the matter of educating their daughters, "then I doubt not but they would as much excel men in that as they do now in Virtue."

In her essay, More seems to be defining education as practical knowledge of law and finances relating to a woman's social circumstances and also as the classical university training available to men. Her whole argument is based on evidence derived from a combination of these two types of knowledge. The usurpation of women's rights has been accomplished and maintained because a lack of knowledge of practical legal matters has kept women at an unfair disadvantage and their lack of classical training in languages, philosophy, rhetoric, and theology has prevented women from discovering the true nature of their rights and the source of their current conditions.

Though More criticizes the "Errour in Parents . . . in their not bringing up their Daughter[s] learned," she offers no immediate practical solutions to change women's conditions outside of educating the family unit. More, like Judith Drake, seems to be advocating reform based on individual, personal accomplishment—parents, mothers in particular, must take the responsibility to see that their daughters are given the same opportunities as their sons. More does offer examples of exemplary females who have been successful in the realm of "masculine" academics. Like many other profemale writers, More chooses Anna Maria van Schurman as her example of a woman benefiting from education in the sense of formal university training; it would be interesting to know whether Mary More was part of the correspondence network including Gertrude More, Elizabeth Mackenzie, and Bathsua Makin in contact with van Schurman in her later years. [55] As there is no mention of Bathsua Makin in More's essay and vice versa, one can assume that the two London women were unacquainted. This omission is in itself interesting: Mary More, who read and wrote in several languages, sent her paintings to be displayed in the Bodleian, and circulated essays in Oxford circles, does not seem to have been singled out as an extraordinary female. The fact that her scholarly pursuits and critical views on the laws relating to marriage attracted no public praise or censure suggests again the scope of an upper-class woman's private and public spheres.

Although More is perhaps idealistic in her belief in the transforming powers of academic education, she is firmly practical about the financial position of wives, which is an effective block to a woman's activities, scholarly or otherwise. The right to control property is the second of a woman's usurped rights after education. Property is a recurring theme, accompanied by the observation that the laws concerning property are made by men, for men, as women are excluded from Parliament. More's advice to her daughter to tie up her property before marrying is, in this light, not so much a gesture of touchy independence as a refusal to admit property into the considerations of making a harmonious match. If property is settled beforehand, there is no question of the marriage being an easy way for a man to get a fortune for his own use. A woman's property can be administered in such a way to guarantee her control of it after marriage, More implies, but most women are ignorant of the methods of doing so. On the general level, her criticisms concerning women's property rights are directed at the formal laws relating to property, which, like the "laws" determining the equality of the sexes, are based on fallacies. On the practical, personal level, More is equally critical of parents who have failed in their parental responsibilities to ensure that their daughters' individual possessions are disposed of to their best advantage. More seems to imply that before the law of Parliament can be corrected, the ignorance of unmarried women about their own concerns and the irresponsibility of parents must be removed from social custom.

Also in this spirit, her anger is most visible on the subject of the legal marriage age in England. "It being lawfull in England for a girle of 12 years of age to marry," she observes, "thereby giving her husband all her estates . . . none can beleive any one marrys that child but for her Estate." Property and male control over it, she asserts, is the only logic behind the legality of child marriages. "Nor can any Reason be given for that Law, but to empower ye Man & enslave the Woman." Her use of the metaphor of slavery, common in other profemale writers, is unusual in this essay— obviously, this was a subject More found to epitomize the injustice of women's legal positions at the time and the dereliction of parental responsibility.

Throughout her essay, More is simultaneously critical of current laws that restrict a woman's ability to act on her own behalf and of the equally powerful social conventions that define women's "rights." She is, however, conscious of the fact that they have not restrained her as an individual. "It may seem strange to thee," she tells her daughter,

> that I thy Mother of all Women should concern my self in a Subject of this Nature, having never had any Reason as to my self to complain of the least Ill Cariage of my Husbands to me, nor hath any occasion or action in my whole life ever suffered anything, wherein the Power and Will of my husband hath been disputed on mee.

Her own situation, she feels, has put her in the position of an unbiased observer: she has seen "ye sad consequences & events that have fallen on men and their Wives" and has drawn her conclusion about the abuse of patriarchal authority accordingly. The individual woman, More seems to be stating, can overcome the inequalities inherent in the contemporary legal situation of women, but for women in general to achieve their true rights, there must be a general reeducation of society, beginning in the family with parents' responsibilities to their children.

More's adherence to her academic syllogistic structure throughout this intensely personal argument, though not as formal as van Schurman's, strikes the reader as strained and, given the vivacity in her prose during her flashes of wit and anger, not completely natural. Like van Schurman, she is using the intellectual paraphernalia of her ostensible opponents, perhaps to preserve her efforts from being dismissed as either mental needlepoint or private grievance. This use of masculine academic form, much like copious footnotes in modern studies, signals the seriousness of both the writer's intention and the subject itself. The necessity of declaring one's intellectual integrity in discussing the role of women, then as today, was made clear by the nature of the criticism her essay drew.

In his rebuttal to More's essay, Robert Whitehall, too, followed the conventions. Like earlier antifemale writers from Tudor times and throughout the century, he initially declares himself to be in sympathy with women's plight in marriage; it is More's methods, he asserts, with which he quarrels. He attempts to deflect anticipated criticism of his views by suggesting, as others had, that this essay was only a joke, an exercise in wit. He acknowledges that most readers will disagree with him and will assume that he is a jilted lover or has some other cause for revenge against women.

Although he opens with wit and urbanity, Whitehall soon falls into exasperation with More's linguistic legerdemain and is propelled into patronizing sarcasm about women's powers of reason. At this point in the essay, the conventional attacks on women's weaknesses begin to appear; "I should wonder you murmur (did not I know you are a Woman)," he remarks tactfully at one point. "What! could you Imagine men would be baffled with such Sophistry! no, tho they cannot find out all the Cunning of Women, yet some they can and subvert it to." Soon, like Swetnam, he falls back onto crude invective and ridicule.

Whitehall's principal grounds for contesting More's theories are, as he states, rhetorical and linguistic. He accuses More of straining words such as "yoke fellow" to indicate equality and using such faulty logic as the basis of her arguments. He challenges her interpretations of the scripture even more strongly: "What wresting of scripture! what perverting of texts, what subverting of Reason & Faith." He deflates her syllogism as sophistical and describes her examples of historical precedents as special pleading from isolated incidents. As for her formal argumentative technique, Whitehall handles More's points effectively, although in regrettable form—"your division of the 2d & 3rd cap. at first blush demonstrates it was done by one that is accustomed to divide onely with a pair of scissors." In short, he is denying the claim implicit in More's presentation that she has the intellectual apparatus to debate this issue in scholarly circles.

On the practical level, as an "Amorous Batchelour" Whitehall also feels his circumstances make him an unbiased observer. However, his evidence drawn from observation and contemporary practice is the weakest side of his argument and More's strongest. His references to this "peevish generation" imply that he viewed some of More's objections as symptomatic of a general contentiousness of a "younger generation" rather than any growing discontent among women. His treatment of More's contemporary evidence and her observations on Stuart husbands and wives is ambiguous when not positively evasive. For example, he sidesteps More's query as to why anyone should want to marry a child of twelve except to gain control of her property by attempting to shift the blame on women—

> I dare be confident there is not one Woman in a thousand but highly applaud and approve of that decree of the higher Powers, and would miserably repine at ye repeal of so gratefull an Act. Yea I beleeve should a Parliament of Women be assembled they would be so far from nullifiing it, that in ye first place they would call for the Statute Book, and for *twelve* write down *Seven* or *eight*.

—a witty reply, but hardly the point being debated. Whitehall here appears to be unable to come up with any logical reason why this law should indeed stand. He suggests, like Overbury's character of the Fine Dame, that it is not very fair for the man to have to labor to support his family and for the wife to bring in nothing. Instead of seeing property arrangements as a mercenary exploitation of marriage, he implies that it is in women's best interests to marry as early as possible and ducks the issue of the control of property entirely. Property itself is not an issue in Whitehall's view, but the nature of women is.

Likewise, Whitehall's response to More's comment about the law as an institution for the protection of men's rights avoids a serious engagement with the charge by adopting an apocalyptic tone. "And then what can we expect but to see those things which our Fathers dreaded to see, but saw not: and to hear those things which they dreaded to hear but heard not." These comparisons hark back to the Civil War, as do his remarks against women's preaching—"must we have now a new Generation (I had almost said of Vipors) of *Gifted Brethren*"—a revealing gesture that implicitly links More's criticism with those forces that drove England "posting to Confusion" in Whitehall's eyes. Whitehall, whose life and career had been batted back and forth between royal and Parliamentary favor, speaks from experience when he asserts that "it is dangerous to remove ANCIENT LANDMARKS: and that when EVIL SPIRITS have once got Posses-

sion its not every EXORCIST can cast them out." No matter what inequalities may be inherent in the legal "landmarks" that set out the boundaries of women's rights, to remove them would invite anarchy on a general
level, a far worse fate, Whitehall feels, than any localized inconvenience
experienced by only one sex.

Whitehall's refutation falters because of this refusal to deal directly with
More's contemporary arguments as well as her scholarly ones. In his ea-
gerness to score off More's (and Filmer's) observation that *Corrupta optima, pessima,* he overshoots the fact that More is not commenting on the
moral condition of women in general, but on, as she says, "bad Women,
of whom I know but few." Whitehall's rebuttal repeatedly refuses to engage More on the points she raises concerning legality; instead he turns to
assumptions about the nature of women as the basis for contemporary
conditions. For example, his attempt to dismiss More's precedent for
women's activities in spreading the Gospel by declaring that "Anna the
prophetess" in the Old Testament was only so styled because she was
"probably ye Surviving Wife of some deceased Prophet" avoids the issue
of whether women are fit to participate actively in the church. Again, this
is a particular issue associated with the inflammatory radical sects during
the Civil War and Whitehall's only response is to warn of possible abuse of
it and to appeal to conventional roles filled by women in contemporary
society.

This forms the ultimate weapon in Whitehall's armory, one that has
endured during centuries of debate on the subject: apart from any consideration of the legitimacy or equity, because of the "nature" of the sex, the
majority of women are content with the conditions More attacks. Whitehall's tone becomes shrill when he writes about those other women who
desire to "snatch at ye Reins of Government," who are "intoxicated with
proud desire," and "presently begin to aspire at Absolute monarchy, then
to challenge an equal Autority in State, to make Laws, bear Offices, vote
as Members in Parliament, and afterwards presume to sit in Moses his
Chair pretending they have power to TEACH as well as RULE." The
majority of women, he is confident, are not like this, but instead are
following their true inclinations, "what many of them passionately desire
to do viz marry." Like More, he sees marriage as the natural state of
women in society; unlike her, he sees it as an end in itself for women
which negates the need for independent education and control over
property.

To support this line of argument, Whitehall makes a veiled threat. Interpretations such as More's, he warns, are liable to backfire, and if taken
seriously "will prove so heavy that Woe indeed will be to the female Sex,
and Matrimony will be intollerable to them as it is pleasant." A close
examination of the issue of women's equality, suggests Whitehall, will

only result in wives' losing what freedom they now enjoy. If Stuart husbands exercised their full, legitimate powers, "Women many of them would have their Proper Right as some have in other Climates as Spain." For this reason, he suggests, wives had "much better rely on their Husbands Good nature, and be content with their allotment, than to lean on so short and broken a staff for Equality." By pressing for an acknowledgment of theoretical equality, wives may thus reduce the scope of the practical authority they now possess. In spite of his protestations that he himself does not believe the argument that he is presenting and that individual women are far superior to some men, implicit in this type of argument is that all women are married and so have a husband to guide, protect, and control them and that all husbands therefore are naturally more capable to perform these functions than their wives.

As with the other antifemale satirists in the century, much of the interest of Whitehall's refutation lies in this declared tension between what he declares are his true beliefs and the nature of his writing about them. As with his complimentary verses, Whitehall often seems to offend where most he desires to praise; one wonders how seriously he believes in the "rights" of women which he attacks with so much energy and enthusiasm. His insistence that he is playing devil's advocate seems more a protective device than a statement of principles. Throughout the essay he maintains that he is speaking against popular opinion, that part of the pleasure he takes in the refutation of More's argument is its perversity. The sentiments of the "Amorous Batchelour" who professes to be in sympathy with More's arguments, however, are much more restrictive and reductive than those of the patriarch Filmer.

In spite of this deliberate reduction of women's capabilities, Whitehall does not dismiss a woman's authority over her family apart from her husband. He does make the political analogy that Filmer does not, that the wife is subject to her husband in the same way that a magistrate is to his prince. One is reminded that women often do "rule" their husbands, even though theoretically, not legitimately, and also that not all husbands are naturally superior to their wives, even though they should be.

The debate between More and Whitehall comments on more than its stated subject, the original equality of the sexes before the Fall. The arguments put forth by More endeavor to refute the contemporary social structures that are manifestations of inequality between the sexes, property and marriage laws, by searching the scholarly realm for their theoretical source. She locates the source of the problem in a distortion of the model of family structure found in the Bible, which she implies is a deliberate distortion intended to keep women from sharing in their natural rights with men. What remains unclear in More's analysis is whether contemporary social structures would indeed respond to any correction in the theoretical base. The implication is that society, unlike scholarly theories, is not easily transformed or corrected. Individuals educated to see their true position and rights, however, could effectively change their private lives within the system, as she had done, and eventually through such personal gains could raise the general level of women's status as equal partners in marriage.

Whitehall's method of refuting this argument also reveals some of his assumptions about his society in general. As did the other antifemale satirists, Whitehall claims that the views expressed by the "Amorous Batchelour" are not widely supported. He furthermore implies that they belong to an earlier generation. Part of this generation's disapproval of such theories of equality is based on the obvious links between arguments for greater personal freedom and those of the radical sects during the Civil War. Both are seen as anarchic forces. Because of their potentially disruptive effect, the legitimacy of the content of More's arguments is not disputed directly; instead, he attacks her presentation and evidence. Yet by asserting as he does that all women desire to marry as soon as possible, Whitehall is in fact confirming More's observations of contemporary women's dependence on men for control of property. Finally, Whitehall offers the opinion that More's argument actually works against the welfare of women, that the good nature of husbands is a safer bet than the perils of independence which most women, he charges, do not wish to explore.

That such a lively and learned debate was carefully preserved in a formal manuscript miscellany designed for circulation suggests that such ideas as More's were current intellectual fodder at the time, an acceptable topic of controversy. There is a definite air of academic one-upmanship in both pieces; although More's essay is dedicated to her little daughter, it is not a closet devotion but a polished exercise designed for intellectual circles which could appreciate the finer points of Greek translation as well as the force of its arguments. Whatever his personal shortcomings as a poet and essayist, the "Amorous Batchelour" obviously considered it a topic worth his wit and his opponent worth his energies.

Conclusion

Theoretical and Practical Patriarchalism

The institutional structures of seventeenth-century England were patriarchal by tradition and law. Women had little or no formal part in government, education, or the hierarchy of the established religion. Although
the theory that formed the laws excluded female participation, the spirit
that governed the domestic practice was different. Domestic patriarchalism was a personal authority on the family level. In theory, the husband
was the head of the house. In practice, when death often removed him
before his spouse, or in a marriage where the wife possessed the stronger
will of the two, the woman often fulfilled "patriarchal" duties. The authority that is so frequently invoked in seventeenth-century writings is as
parental in nature as it is patriarchal. Inside this parental government,
women played a major part in determining the lives of their children.

The gap between theory and practice is suggested in the ongoing debates in the seventeenth century over women's roles and rights. Women's
roles were neither well-defined nor were they unquestioned by men and
women in the literature of this time. The issue of women's status was
viewed in the larger context of governance, a political issue as well as a
theological one. The usurpation and misuse of power is a central issue in
seventeenth-century writings; in the domestic sphere, it is held by both

sides to lead to discord and unhappy marriages. Tyranny by "the Cruel Shrew" or by the foolish husband is equally disruptive in the family and is equally condemned. In theory and by law, women were "subject to" men; in practice, controversy raged over exactly what "to be subject to" encompassed. In theory, education was supposed to be wasted on women because their minds were inferior; in practice, historians of female accomplishments pointed out, many women had excelled in studies and there was also a wider range of opportunities for girls to be educated. In theory, women's characters were supposed to be incapable of friendship, being fickle and jealous; in practice, women writers celebrated the excellence and harmony of female friendships which surpassed the state of marriage.

The twentieth-century interpretation of domestic life in seventeenth-century England restricts the activities of the patriarch's wife more than the actual practice did. By following an anachronistic view of "publish or perish," literary and social historians have dropped from consideration many women writers and thinkers noted in their own times. The distinctions are often blurred in modern interpretations between patriarchal theory, as codified in laws, doctrine, and literary conventions, and patriarchal practices, as seen in women's participation in marriage arrangements and in the intellectual and literary life of their day. The conventional, or stereotyped, representation of women in literature is often assumed to reflect actual practice, overlooking the possibility that even though a wife may have acknowledged the theory of "the Good Wife," if she was not wed to "the Good Husband" she may well have run the family. Although women writers may have shied away from debating the theory of the equality of the sexes, they nevertheless vigorously attacked manifestations of it, such as the property laws concerning women.

In analyzing women's participation in the intellectual life of the time, when one surveys the whole range of literary evidence available it becomes clear that although women writers may have made up a small percentage of publishing authors in the seventeenth century, their output was not negligible. They were not coerced into "private" forms of writing nor did they stop writing altogether. Many did choose to retain control over their writings by manuscript circulation rather than publication, but this convention itself did not preclude gaining a reputation outside their immediate circles as writers or controversialists. Writings by women during the century also show a well-established set of literary conventions, such as the antimarriage poems and the praise of female friendship in addition to those works celebrating "the Good Husband." Women writers in the seventeenth century wrote with the expectation that they would be read by other women, but they did not restrict their audience to females.

Even though men were writing vicious antifemale satires throughout the century, as they had done in previous ones, there was also a "female mythology" of learned and heroic women celebrated in books by men. Such female histories offered both male and female readers examples of women who were renowned as authors and scholars, supporting the notion of a tradition of female literary accomplishment largely lost to us today.

Finally, one must consider the extent of manuscript writings in prose and verse by women writers that existed in the seventeenth century. These pieces, including epistolary exchanges as well as circulated pages and miscellanies, are not currently part of our assessment of women's literary history. The mass of uncited, unexamined literature available from this period invites a reconsideration of women's literary activities during the seventeenth century and calls into question our current notion of the "canon" of women's literature.

The separation of literary evidence from other sources, such as demographic reconstruction, however, places a false emphasis on the theoretical and the conventional. This problem is increased when particular genres, such as drama or the conduct book, are isolated. To use literary evidence effectively, it must be considered within the context of the literary conventions of its time in addition to the patterns of life in the historical context. Otherwise, an overly simplistic model of a complex power relationship is constructed.

Domestic patriarchal authority was challenged, argued, and undermined by both men and women throughout the seventeenth century. Why then, in a period characterized by radical political change, did it remain in place? The very looseness of its structure may be the answer. Numerous seventeenth-century women such as Mary Astell and Mary More slipped through the meshes to criticize the theory, while simultaneously admitting that they themselves had not been confined by its dictates of their limitations. So many gaps existed between the rigid theory and the actual enforcement that its degrading and restrictive nature was not immediately felt. Conditions were not intolerable to the point of open rebellion for the majority of women in their everyday lives. The patriarch's wife, both in the family and in society, wielded considerable power, whether acknowledged in theory or not, but that power was to a large extent displayed on a private level, not through the public institutions.

Appendices

APPENDIX I

Sir Robert Filmer,
"In Praise of the Vertuous Wife"

APPENDIX II

Mary More,
"The Womans Right"

Robert Whitehall,
"The Womans Right Proved False"

Note on the Texts

Appendix I is a holograph in the hand of Sir Robert Filmer (c. 1588–1653), 19 centimeters by 15 centimeters, paper with twenty-two leaves of which seventeen are written upon recto and verso. The text is evidently incomplete. It is bound in parchment in fair condition, but the binding is discolored and mouse-nibbled; the edges of the paper leaves are in fragile condition with pieces coming away which affect the text. The title is a biblical text from Proverbs 12.4, "a virtuous wife is the crown of her husband." The manuscript was found by Peter Laslett at the Filmer seat, East Sutton Park, Kent, in 1939 and acquired by him in about 1946 from a purchaser of manuscripts at the Filmer sale. Its location in 1986 is in the rooms of Peter Laslett at Trinity College, Cambridge. For references, see G. J. Schochet, "Sir Robert Filmer: Some New Bibliographical Discoveries," *The Library* (June 1971): 136–60. (This bibliographic information was provided by Peter Laslett.)

This item as well as two copies of "Theology or Divinity" appear as items on an eighteenth-century list of Sir Robert's manuscript works. These last two do not, in this writer's opinion, seem to be in Filmer's hand; the subject matter of "Theology or Divinity," and more specifically its rhetorical treatment, however, combine with the family evidence to point to Filmer as by far the most likely author. The existence of multiple copies of Filmer's writings in manuscript again underlines the importance of manuscript circulation in seventeenth-century intellectual life.

The More and Whitehall essays are contained in the British Library's Harleian Manuscript 3198 in a leather-bound (octavo) fair copy manuscript miscellany. A previous owner's name has been scratched out on the front cover; no record exists of its origin or initial purchase. The book itself was apparently kept in the family for some years, as several of its originally blank sheets have been filled in with verse and recipes in an eighteenth-century feminine hand. The manuscript is listed in *The Index of Manuscripts in the British Library* (1984) only as "More's (Mary) Poems" (7: 206). In the Harleian index, it is described as "The Womans Right."

These texts have been transcribed preserving their original spelling and punctuation with the following exceptions: "ff" has been converted to "F" and "m̄" has been rendered "mm." All three authors have erratic notions of spelling and punctuation; not one uses an apostrophe to show possession. Filmer alone uses italics both to indicate direct quotation and for emphasis.

The following symbols have been inserted in the texts: [ ] = editor's addition, < > = author's deletion, and // = end of manuscript page.

Proverbs 12. 4. A vertuous woman is the
Crowne of her husband; But she that maketh
him ashamed is as corruption to his bones.

In ye fifte Comandement three Duties are enioyned
1. Towards Superiors and inferiors. 2. Towards
Aqualls. 3. Towards Our selues. Of ye first
kind some are Priuat or Publique. Priuat as ye
duty of ye wife, of Parents and Children, of Seruants
and Maisters. To these appertaineth ye Doctrine
of Chastisement, and ye respect to Age. Public
as ye office of a Kinge. To equalls appertaineth
ye Doctrine of Manners ye Contrary wherof is
Pride. To our selues appertaineth ye regard of
our owne good fame.

First of ye wife as being ye first estate. She is
described 1. by Salomon. 2. by Bath-sheba.
By Salomon she is set out by ye Effect and ye
Cause. The effect is threefold. 1. Honor in ye
verse. 2. Profit cap: 14. 1. 3. Pleasure or
is exprest by ye Contrary, cap: 19.13. The Dau
is gods fauor. cap: 18.22. and 19.14.

The honor is Demonstrated by ye Cause then amplifi
The Cause in these wordes A vertuous woman or
according to ye Ebrew A woman of strenght or

Sir Robert Filmer
"In Praise of the Vertuous Wife"

*Proverbes 12.4. A vertuous woman is the
Crowne of her husband; But she yt maket[h]
him ashamed is as corruption to his bones.*

In the fifthe commandement three duties are enioyne[d]
1. Betweene Superiors and inferiors. 2. Towar[des] æqualls.
3. Towardes Our selves. of the first kind some are Privat or Publique.
Privat as [the] duty of the wife, of Parents and Children, or Serv[ants] and
Maisters. To theis appertaineth the doctrin[e] of Chastisement, and the   5
respect to Age. Publi[que] as the office of a Kinge. To equals apper-
ten[eth] the doctrine of Manners the contrary where of is Pride. To ourselves apperteines the regard of our owne good fame.
    First of the wife as being the first estate. She [is] described 1. by
Salomon. 2. by Bath = sheba. By Salomon she is set out by the Effect and   10
the Cause. The effect is threefold. 1. Honor in the verse. 2. Profit Chap:
14.1. 3. Pleasure wc[h] is exprest by the contrary Chap: 19.13. The cau[se] is
gods favor. chap: 18.22 and 19.14.
    The honor is demonstrated by the Cause then amplifie[d.] The cause in
theis wordes *A vertuous woman* or according to the hebrew *A woman of*   15
strength or// *courage* as it <to> is taken chap: 31.10. Ruth 3.11. Hence we
learne that courage ought to be in weomen wch is proved by *Scripture,*
Reason, example. For scripture 1. Peter. 3.6. whose Daughters yee are whiles
ye do wel, not being afraid of any terror. For reason it thus is framed
Courage is true vertue, and true vertue may be and ought to be in weomen.   20
that Courage is true vertue it appeare[th] bycause true vertue is the mod-

12. Proverbs 14.1—"Every wise woman buildeth her house: but the foolish plucketh it
down with her hands." (References in notes are all taken from the King James Version.)
    12. Proverbs 19.13—"A foolish son is the calamitie of his father; and the contentions of a
wife are a continual dropping."
    13. Proverbs 18.22—"Whoso findeth a wife, findeth a good thing and obtaineth favour of
the Lord"; Proverbs 19.14—"House and riches are the inheritance of fathers; and a prudent
wife is from the Lord."
    16. Proverbs 31.10—"Who can find a virtuous woman? for her price is far above rubies";
Ruth 3.11—"And now my daughter, fear not, I will do to thee all that thou requireth: for all
the city of my people know that thou are a virtuous woman."

eration of ye affections by faith and prudence the one shewing what is lawful, the other what is *possible* and *Convenient*. now this moderation is nothing but courage. <Now> Besides that true vertue may be and ought to be in weomen is proved First by scriptures Gen: 1.27. Ephes: 4.24. out

5 of theis places it appeeres that women being made gods image ought to have Knowledge, holinesse, and righteousnesse, now to have theis is to have vertue. Againe gen: 3.7. where (by eyes) are ment *consciences*, now if *conscience* do accuse, it was made to excuse, for god makes nothing evil. Besides in foure commandements of the lawe *women* are named or implied

10 viz: the *fourth, fifth, seaventh,* and *tenth.* the law therefore was given to weomen. Lastly theis places are plaine *not withstanding through bearing children she shal be saved if they continue in faith and love and holynesse// wth modestie* or rather as our new translation hath it (she shal be saved in childbearing) 1. Tim. 2. [15]. Likewise ye husbands dwel wth them accord-

15 ing [to] knowledge givinge honor unto the wife as unto [the] weaker vessel, and as being heires together of th[e] grace of life that your praiers be not hindred. 1. Pet: 3.7. Secondly that vertue may be [and] ought to be in weomen it appeereth by the fouret[h,] priviledges of weomen, whereby they are not to b[e] puffed up, but to be made thankfull and hopefull in

20 regard of virtue. Theis priviledges are eithe[r] in the *narration* or in <thinge> the thinge. The narration of womans Creation is thrice re-peate[d] gen: 1.27. gen: 2.22 and 5.2. wch is of no creation else save man. In the thinge are three priviledges, first before the creation a double appr[o]bation of the woman 1. by god, gen.2.18. 2ly by man the exper-

25 mental feeling of his wante *but for Adam there was not found a helpe meete for him* gen: 2.20. Secondly in the Creation for she was ma[de] last in order and so was added as a perfection to the best, she was created in *Paradise,* lastly out of man['s] *Ribb* not out of the earth. Thirdly after the creati[on] the privilidges are in the law, or gospell. In the *Lawe* first

30 *Angelical,* for the first angel was seene by *Hagar* I meane by the way of Comfort. Secondly Judicial: Deut. 20.14 *thou shalt smite every male// thereof wth the edge of the sword, but the women and the little ones.* etc. In the gospell two waies[.] First as it was promised both by prophecie where in the

4. Genesis 1.27—"So God created man in his own image, in the image of God created he him: male and female created he them"; Ephesians 4.24—"And that ye put on the new man, which after God is created in righteousness and true holiness."

7. Genesis 3.7—"And the eyes of them both were opened, and they knew they were naked."

13. "our new Translation"—the Authorized Version (1611) was in preparation during Fil-mer's residence in Westminster. "Through the bearing of children" is from the Geneva Bible (1560).

24. Genesis 2.18—"And the Lord God said, It is not good that the man should be alone: I will make him an help meet for him."

30. "Hagar and the angel"—Genesis 16.7–14.

woman is first named gen: 3.15. and also by Ceremonie levit: 12.6. For a double purification for a double sinne of eatinge and deceiveinge as it implied a double repentance, so a double pardon and honour. Secondly as it was performed, For the incarnation and resurrection of Christ were first revealed to weomen, And they loved Christ best alive and dead. Theis privilidges had not beene granted if weomen could not be vertuous. This ought to be their Comfort in terror of Conscience and against the scoffes of the wicked.

It is obiected. 1. *woman was the first sinner.*
Answer. 1. Not the cause (for that was mans will) but the occasion. 2. She was the occasion not by hatefull knowledge (as Sathan) but by *ignorant love.* 3. As she was the first in sinninge so she was most griviously punished of al mankind, for Sathan had three punishments; the woman two; the man but one. The woman did decive out of error; the divel out of knowledge; the man did eate: so that she is to be pitied not hated. 4. She was the occasion though not the cause of our salvation in Christ.

Obiection: 2. *Weomen have beene most wicked.*
Answer. If some weomen have beene worst, then some weomen have beene better then men, As divels are// therefore worse because good angels are better then m[en.] The corruption of the best is worst, the best wine makes the strongest vineger. The examples that prove that courage may be or [ought] to be in weomen, are either *Direct* and commendable; or e[lse] *Indirect* and evill. The direct examples are twelve. Two in Exodus the 1.19. Fouer in the Judges, Debo[rah,] Jaell, she that stoned Abmelech, and Manoahs wife w[ho] had stronger faith at the sight of an angell than Jac[ob,] Daniell, John. Two in the first of Samuell Mich[al] in dismissing David, and Abigayl. Two in the second o[f] Samuell, the woman of Te-

5

10

15

20

25

1. Genesis 3.15—"And I will put enmity between thee and the woman, and between thy seed and his seed: it shall bruise thy head, and thou shalt bruise his heel"; Leviticus 12.6— verses 12.3–8 concern the ceremonies on the birth of a child and the ritual purification of the mother after childbirth.

24. Exodus 1.19—two Hebrew midwives, Shiphrah and Puah, disobeyed the King of Egypt's command to kill all the male newborn Hebrews. V. 15–19.

24. "Deborah"—a prophetess, who helped the Israelites defeat Sisear in battle, also cited by More and Whitehall. Judges 4.4–16. "Jaell"—killed Sisear, thus preventing the army of Canaan from overrunning the Israelites. Judges 4.17–23. "she that stoned Abmelech"—"And a certaine woman cast a piece of a millstone upon Abimelech's head, and all to break his skull. Then he called hastily unto the young armour-bearer, and said unto him, Draw thy sword, and slay me that men say not of me, A woman slew him." Judges 9.53–54. "Manoahs wife"—an angel appeared to her to tell her she would conceive Sampson. Judges 13.2–24.

26. "Michal"—Saul's daughter who was married to David and who helped him to escape from her father. 1 Samuel 19.12–13. "Abigayl"—she appeased David for her husband's lack of

koah, and of Abell. The eleventh in Esther. The last is in Hebrewes. 11.35.
taken out of the 2. Mac: 7. Theis examples should ca[use] men to emulate
even the courage of weomen. The indirect examples are twelve in eight
cases all e[vil.] First a woman had the Courage to abuse or deceive her
5 lou[er] as Dalila did Sampson. Secondly her father as Rach[al] did Laban.
Thirdly her King as Rachab. Fourthly h[er] husband as Eve, Jobs wife,
Rebecca, Zippora: Fiftly her husband and King as Michol, Vashti. Sixthly
he[r] children as Athalia. Seaventhly her subiects as did Jezabell. Eightly
neighbors or straungers as Cozbi. If they be thus couragious in evill by
10 nature why should we deny them good courage by grace.

Use. 1. Weomen had neede of patience against the day of *Sicknesse* and
Childbirth: *widowhood* and *Martirdome*, For Julietta said that the rib was as
wel bone as flesh. Use. 2. The meanes to attaine courage are three, First

---

hospitality, preventing David's retaliation. "And blessed be thy advice, and blessed be thou,
which hast kept me from avenging my self with mine own hand." 1 Samuel 25.14–42.

1. "woman of Tekoah"—she was used by Joab to effect the recall of the banished Absalom
by pleading with the king. 2 Samuel 14.1–20. "woman of Abell"—she prevented the attack of
Joab's army on the city. "Then the woman went unto all the people in her wisdom, and they
cut off the head of Sheba the son of Bichi, and cast it out to Joab: and he blew a trumpet,
and they retired from the city, every man to his tent."

1. Hebrews 11.35—"Women received their dead raised to life again: and others were tor-
tured, not accepting deliverance, that they might obtain a better resurrection"; 2 Maccabees
7—verse 20 states that "But the mother was marvellous above all, and worthy of honourable
memory: for when she saw her seven sons slain within the space of one day, she bare it with
good courage, because of the hope that she had in the Lord."

5. "Rachal and Laban"—"Now Rachal had taken the images, and put them in the camel's
furniture, and sat upon them: and Laban searched all the tent, but found them not." Genesis
31.34.

6. "Jobs wife"—she urged her husband to curse God and despair. Job 2.9. "Rebecca"—
Isaac's wife encouraged her son Jacob to deceive his father to obtain his blessing, intended
for Esau. Genesis 27.1–29. "Zippora"—Moses' wife, who rebuked her husband by circumcis-
ing their son. Exodus 4.25.

7. "Michol"—Michal, David's wife, rebuked him for his unseemly behavior and was made
barren as a consequence. 1 Chronicles 15.29 and 2 Samuel 6.20–23. "Vashti"—the wife of King
Ahasuerus, who refused to come at his command. "Likewise shall the Ladies of Persia and
Media say this day, unto all the king's princes, which have heard of the deed of the queen.
Thus shall there arise too much contempt and wrath." Esther 1.1–20.

8. "Athalia"—the daughter of Jezebel, who was the only queen to occupy the throne of
Judah; she seized power by assassinating the men of the house of David. 2 Kings 11.

8. "Jezabell"—the wife of Ahab, who among other crimes arranged Naboth's death in
order to obtain his vineyard by forging her husband's signature. 1 Kings 5.27.

9. "Cozbi"—a Midametess, she seduced the Israelites in Shittim and was slain by Phineas.
Numbers 25.1–18.

12. "Julietta"—presumably this refers to Julietta of Tarsus, who was martyred with her son
Saint Cyricus, c. A.D. 304. Although her acts were later declared apocryphal, she was widely
worshipped as a saint in Cornwall. An account of her martyrdom is contained in Baronius's

skill in Huswifrie and religion to prevent bodilie and// ghostly terrors, secondly *Labour*. Thirdly *temperance*.

Obiection. A woman is the weaker vessel. 1. Pet. 3.7.
Answer. I. That is in perseuerance, but not in a suddaine *act.* 2. her weaknesse is a fit middle terme to combine the father to his tender chil-   5
dren; againe if both were equally stronge neither should yeild and so no concord. 3. Gods power is seene in our infirmity 2. Cor: 12.9.

Hitherto of the demonstration by the cause, now followes the amplifica-tion by a *similitude* and *Contrary*. For the Similitude *she is the crowne of her husband or lord.* A crowne is a lawful purchased golden ornament of a   10
Kings head. Heere the working cause is that it must come *lawfully*, As by *iust warre, Election, Donation of god or man, Entrance into vacuity, Succesion not by usurpation.* So is a woman given by god if she be vertuous and marrie willingly. not for *lust, Beauty, honor, wealth.* else she is a hellish screetchowle not a heavenly nightingale. Secondly the matter of wch a   15
crowne is made of gold a great enemie to the *consumption* and *plague*, so a good woman preserves a man from the consumption of melancholie and plague of *Adulterie* which takes away the harte Osia 4.11.

Obiection: A Crowne of gould is heavye so is a woman. 1 *Corinth:* 7.26.
Answer: It is better to have heavy persecution wthout then more heauie   20
temptation wthin[.] In time of publique troubles god many times gives the gift of continence, but if he deny it it is better even then to marrie then to burne with distracting lust.// Againe the matter about which a crowne is employed is [the] head of a Kinge, for jewells and earerings are worne by other persons, but crownes onely by Kinges. that is absolute governors   25
as the word is taken Gen: 36.31. Now a King[e] may in sundry sortes dispose of his crowne yet may he [not] give or sell it away as king *John of England* did. S[o] may not a man put away his wife neither for sicknesse

---

Annales ecclesiastici of which there were numerous reprints during the first half of the seven-teenth century.

7. 2 Corinthians 12.9—"For my strength is made perfect in weakness. Most gladly there-fore will I rather glory in my infirmities, that the power of Christ may rest upon me."

16. "gold as an antidote to plague"—Robert Burton (*The Anatomy of Melancholy*, 1621) mentions this as a common, though disputed, remedy and it is found in Paracelsus and Leonardo Fioravanti's *Compendium*, translated in 1582 by John Hester. "Osia 4.11"—"Whore-dom and wine, and new wine take away the heart." Hosea 4.11.

19. 1 Corinthians 7.26—Paul says of the married state, "I suppose therefore that this is good for the present distress, I say that it is good for a man to be so [a virgin]."

26. Genesis 36.31—"And these are the kings that reigned in the land of Edom before these other reigned any king over the children of Israel."

28. "King John"—a reference to John's resigning his crown to Pope Innocent III in 1213

[of] bodie; as *leprosie, Epilepsie,* unlesse it were fraudelent[ly] concealed before mariage: For after wedlocke though separation be necessary in regard of *cohabitation,* yet [the] guift of contenencie may be hoped for in respect of the necessitye. Neither yet for the sinne of the minde, n[or] for
5 false religion unlesse she willingly depart and will n[ot] returne. Not for murther nor like *cryinge crimes* un[less] he be a magistrate, or complaine to him. Not for *Adulterye,* for if she repent the good Levite will receive her Judges 19.3. as Christ did his church, if she repent not, yet it is to be expected. And because of the outward *inconvenience* (though simply it be
10 lawfull) yet by our lawes it is held unfit: and to live wth out her is daungerous because we have no necessitie of callinge hereunto. All wch doubts would easily be dissolued if Adultery were death according to gods law wch bound ev[en] the verie *Pagans.* Ge[n]: 20.6. Jereme. 29. 22. 23. Thirdly the forme and end of a *Crowne* is in this word[e] *ornament,* For it
15 is a signe of honor to a prince for his victories and authoritie<s>, and is honored it self for the *Princes sake:* So a good *woman* is given to a man as a reward and signe of his authoritie and victorie over lust, and she is the more honored for his sake, as being not the cause but the signe and image of his honour. 1. Corinth. 11.7.//
20 Thus much of the similitude, now followes the *Contrarie* wherein we may consider the *workinge* and the *worke:* the workeing in theis wordes *she that shameth her husband.* This is done through want of *Obedience* in three thinges. 1. *good;* 2. *Bad:* 3. *Indifferent.* In good thinges three waies, First if She do not that wch is necessarily good unlesse her husband command it:
25 For besides her obedience to her spirituall husband Christ (who is the husband of the *Church*) her owne husband is also brought into Suspition by choosing an unfit wife. Secondly when that she refuseth to do good things though he comand it; herein she sinneth both against *god* and *man.* Thirdly when she doth not intreat, or persuade, but comand her husband
30 to do *good thinges.* In evill thinges their is a double error first on the left hand, namely when she forsakes not evill though he forbid it: or temptes

---

after his excommunication for refusing to acknowledge the papal legate, Stephen Langton. Matthew Paris in *Moanchi Santi Albani* (1571) phrased it in terms similar to Filmer's.

8. Judges 19.3—verse 2, "and his concubine played the whore against him, and went away from him unto her father's house . . . and her husband arose and went after her, to speak friendly unto her, and to bring her again."

13. Genesis 20.6—verse 3, "But God came to Abimelech in a dream by night, and said to him, Behold, thou art but a dead man, for the woman which thou hast taken: for she is a man's wife"; Jeremiah 29.22–23—"The Lord make thee like Zedekiah, and like Ahab: whom the king of Babylon wasted in the fire. Because thou have committed villainy in Israel, and have committed adultery with their neighbours' wives."

19. 1 Corinthians 11.7—"For a man indeed ought not to cover his head, for as much as he is the image and glory of God: but the woman is the glory of the man."

him to the comiting of *evill*. Secondly on the right hand, when she will
not indure his evill deedes, but reproveth him before others, or privatly
wthout leave: or speaketh of them to them to whome their knowledge
pertanes not.

Abygayl is obiected. 1. *Sam*: 25.25. *Answer* I. She was a prophetesse, for she   5
foretells the death of *Saul* and *Nabal*, the kingdome of *David*, and her
owne marriage to him. 2. She doth it not to accuse her husband but to
save his life. 3. She discloseth no secret but acknowledgeth a knowne sinne
to the Lords annointed being now armed and in furie. In things indifferent this is done three waies. First when she comandeth him to do thinges//   10
indifferent. Secondly when she refuseth to do thinges indifferent at his
charge. Thirdly when she doth th[em] upon her owne head. 1. *Tim*: 2.12.
*But I suffer not [a] woman to teach, nor to usurpe authoritie over ye ma[n] but
to be in silence. A bygail is againe objected. Answer.* her giftes are excused by
the extremity of the necessity.   15

Hitherto of the working, their remaineth the worke in the wordes she is
as rottinesse or consumption in his bones. heere is an allusion to the
disease too well knowne or some like, wch make a man sadd in his mind,
namely full of feare, dispaire, suspition for that wch is to come; gr[ief,]
disdane, anger for that wch is past. Also loathsome, for that he hath not   20
found or made her good. we read not in scripture that a *good* man had a
wicked wife.

Objection. I. *Adam was seduced by his wife.*
Answer. I. That Eve was a good woman appeareth because the promise
was made to her Gen: 3.15. and received the same Gen: 4.25. wch thinge   25
also is avouched wisedome 10.1. 2. She was deceived but was first deceivd
her self 1. Tim: 2.14./ 2 Corinth: 11.3. let none therefore wth Adam lay the
blame upon her, but rather blame him that should have beene the wiser of
the two.

Obiect: 2. *Jobes wife is obiected.* Job. 2.9. and 19.17.   30
Answ: In the first place she onely biddeth him blesse god and acknowledge his secret sinne, wch was also the error of his three freinds, three as
wise men as were then// of the world, and one of them a prophet Job. 4.12.
The other fact was but an error of humaine infirmity. *Obiect*: 3. *Zippora is*

---

5. 1 Samuel 25.25—Abigail pacified David by criticizing her husband Nabal.

27. 1 Timothy 2.14—"And Adam was not deceived, but the woman being deceived, was in
the transgression"; 2 Corinthians 11.3—"But I fear lest by any means, as the serpent beguiled
Eve through his subtlety."

30. Job 2.9—"Then said his wife unto him, Doest thou still retain thine integrity? Curse
God, and die"; Job 19.17—"My breath is strange to my wife, though I intreated for the
children's sake of mine own body."

33. Job 4.12—"Now a thing was secretly brought to me, and mine ear received a little
thereof."

pretended Exod. 4.25. *Answ*: She was not yet fully instructed then as Ra-[c]hel about images *Gen*: 31.19. Againe she returned with her father to *Moses*: and her brother was good to the *Israilit[es]* in all their journeis, lastly god punished *Miriam* wth leprosie that spake against her *Numb*: 12.2.

5

    Obiect: 4. *Michol is brought forth.* 2. *Sam*: 6.23.

    Answ: She thought *David* tooke upon him ye levites office, or that his ioy was too immoderat, or lesse beseeming princely gravity; For wch error though she were iustly punished wth barrenesse yet may we not count her

10 a scoffer that saved the life of David against her fathers will.

    Question: *may not then a good man have a wicked wife?*
    Answer: *He may, as shalbe shewed heereafter.*

    Thus farre of the honor wch a good woman bringeth, now followes the *Profit Chap*. 14.v: 1. Set out, First by the cause, Secondly by the worke.

15 Thirdly by the Contrary. The Cause in theis wordes wise weomen. The wisdome of a woman is twofold. 1. In spirituall things as she is a Christian. 2. In things of this life, and this is threefold. First for Pleasure as Musique. Secondly for Commodity as Huswifrie. Thirdly for Credit wch is twofold.<as>// 1. *Private As curious Artes.* 2. *Publique, As Phisicke and*

20 *Chirurgery.* Theis bring nobility to wom[en] as *Armes* and *Learninge* do to men. In this place is onely ment huswifrie wch must be attained, and kept Attained by three meanes. 1. If they be broken of the[ir] will when they are younge. 2. If they be kept in service farre from home. 3. If they be not marri[ed] untill they be skilfull in huswifrie. It is kept also by three

25 meanes. 1. If they marry husbands y[t] be neither *Spendthrifts* nor medlers wthin doores. 2. If they have no *concurrent mothers* or any other to comand. 3. If they change not servants yearly wanting courage to correct, and so be put every yeare to instruct a *new servant* in a new manner. Thus much of the cause, the worke followes, *shal build her house*, wch is done

30 three waies. First by saveinge. Secondly by encreasinge. Thirdly by *absolute raisinge of a mans estate.* This last is most noble to the woman but most daungerous to ye man[.] The *Contrary* in theis wordes *A foolish woman wth her owne handes destroieth her house.* A similitude taken from them who pull downe their owne houses, in time of fire or when the enemie ap-

35 proacheth.

    1. Exodus 4.25—"Then Ziporah took a sharp stone, and cut off the foreskin of her son, and cast it at his feet, and said, Surely a bloody husband art thou to me."
    2. "Rahel"—Rachal, Genesis 31.34.
    4. "Miriam"—spoke against Moses after his marriage to an Ethiopian and "Behold, Miriam became leprous, white as snow." Numbers 12.10.

That much of the honor and *Profit* of a virtuous woman. now remaines the Pleasure wch is described by ye *contrary*[,] namely the trouble of a *Contintious wife. Chap:* 19.v.13.// The word *Contentious* cometh of an hebrew word that signifieth to iudge. For strife ariseth when we iudge others wthout *Knowledge, Vocations,* and *Charity.* Theis are amplified by a   5
double comparision, First of ye *unequal,* wch is thus framed, *the foolish sonne is a heavynesse to the father,* much more *a contintious wife.* The sonne is not *equal* to his father, he is but a parte of him he may be *restrained, disinherited, dismissed, Other sonnes* may be had; all theise fail in a wife. The second comparison is of the like, namely a *continual droppinge* wch eateth   10
through the hardest stone, and being let in rotteth the strongest houses.
     Use.I. Man must learne to prevent Contention in wives by two meanes. *Chusinge* and *Usinge.* In choosing they must marke the *mind, body, estate.* In the mind her *understandinge,* and *Affection.* For her understanding she must knowe thy *language* and *Religion.* For her affections, first in general   15
she must not be greivously tainted wth *Pride, Lust, covetousnesse.* the last is most tolerable; And in particulare she must affect thy *Callinge* and *Person.* For her body, avoid an eminent *contagious* disease least it breed *separation* though not *perpetual divorce.* For her state either let thine answer hers, or attempt some heroicall and publique actions[.] So was the case of *Joseph*   20
and *Mahomet.* In the using her after marriage. First abrode give her no *Rule* but moderat *liberty.* At home both *Rule*// and *Liberty,* so that she be not tainted with ydlenesse[,] covetuousness, pride, or ignorance in extreme degree[.] Secondly communicat no secrets unto her above her capacity. Thirdly honor her in the presence of *Children, Servants, Strangers*:   25
unlesse her vices be *open* and *outragious*: If theis things be neglec[ted] thou shalt but blow the bellowes of *Contention.* Use.2. We must pray for *Constancie* for ye *drop[pings] of temptation* may eate into us though not by force yet by often fallinge.
     Use.3. If a contentious wife be such a purgatorie what a paradise is a   30
woman of meeke spirit. 1.P[et:] 3.5. Hitherto of the efforts of a good woman now foloweth the Cause of a good woman. Namely gods favor, set out partly by the *Institution.* cap: 18.12. *He that findeth a wife* that is such a one as *Issa* was before her fall (who afterwards was termed Eve) or he yt findeth a wife yt is a *good wife* (as Esay.1.[27].18 *wooll* is put for *white wooll*)   35
this man findeth good and receives her as an argument of gods favor. And partly by Comparison cap: 19.14. The doctrine is plaine that a good wife is <the> a symbole of gods favor.

31. 1 Peter 3.5—"For after this manner in the old time, the holy women also who trusted in God, adorned themselves, being in subjection to their own husbands."
33. Proverbs 18.12—verse 22, "Whoso findeth a wife findeth a good thing."
34. "Issa"—the Hebrew for Eve; "Esay. 1.27.18"—Ezekiel 27.18, "Damascus was thy merchant . . . in the wine of Helbon and white wool."

Obiect: *Nabal a sonne of Belial had Abigayl to wife*. 1.Samuell. 25.3 and 25.//
Answ: he had her for his further condemnation to make his impenitency
inexcusable, and for the trial of her patience, for indeed she was reserved
for *David*. *May not then a good man have a wicked wife?* Though we read
5   no<t> such example in scripture, yet this may fall out, either as a *Chastisement* for some sinne past, or a preventinge of some to come, or else for
a *Domestical martirdome*. Men theirfore that do intend to marrye 1. must
repent them for ye sinnes of their *youth* least they find their *mirrour* in
their wives iniquities. 2. They must pray yt they may enioye this heaven
10   upon earth if it be conuenient trusting more to gods providence then to
the experience of freinds or their own fancies. Thus farre go the words of
Salomon.
     Now we come to the song of *Beth = sheba* cap: 31.10 and so to the end.
This song is set downe according to the order of the Hebrew *letters*, As we
15   find seauen Psalmes so written the 25. 34. 37. 111. 112. 119. 145. and the foure
first chapters of the *Lamentations*. Now for as much as this was done to ye
ayding of *memory* we must endeavour to strenghten the same by al lawfull
meanes; And although we doubt of *artificial memory* by *places*, *images* and
actions whether it be rather a// *confusion* then a help: And though al men
20   cannot attaine to *Logique* wch is the true *art of memory* yet their is none so
rude, who by ladinge the same like a *Camill* may not make it stronger,
provided alwaies that he loades man bi Judgement; for it is not an orderly
but a barbarous memory wch reteneth things not understoode.
     This song hath two partes. *A proposition*. ver: 10. *An exposition* to the
25   end. The proposition is set out by a *question* and *compariso[n.]* The question in theis wordes *who shal find* etc. This is threefold. First *what kinde of
man shal[l] finde such a woman?* The answer is given by Salom[on:] He
that is in gods favor. Secondly *How hardly shal a man finde?* Answer; very
hardly: for where as there be but foure waies to knowe her. First, the
30   *Place, Nouit qua multo pisce natatur aqua<ti.>* So large being the visible
church, it is also most uncertaine because many lambes are wthout and
wolves wthin the *foulde*, that the knowledge is dificult. Secondly
Companie. This is also uncertaine, because a maide may have such company as she disliketh, though it be imposed by her freinds. Thirdly *Reporte*,
35   this may be *ignorant, Crafty, Partiall*. Fourthly *trial of her vertues*. This [is]
daungerous, and uncertaine for as Locustes lye hidde in a country till a
yeare of dearth: so sundry sinnes wch were smotherd in time of youth,
breake forth in *mariage* and *gouerment*.// Againe it is hard to obteine her,
As either beinge *promised* before, or *not affected to thee* or *unfit for thy*
40   *callinge*. We must pray theirefore that god will send his angell before us in
this businesse. Thirdly *How happie is he that findes her? Answer*: He is

     1. "Nabal"—Abigail's husband.

happy in his familie, and neighboures[.] in his families, first in himselfe
verse 23. *Her husband is knowne in the gates, when he sitteth wth the Elders of
the land.* Secondly in his Children, verse 28. *her children rise up and call her
blessed.* Thirdly in his servantes. verse 21. *She is not afraide of the snowe for
her householde, for her householde are cloathed wth skarlet.* In his neighboures.　5
I. the Poore. vers: 20. *she stretcheth out her hande to the poore, yea she
reacheth forth her hande to the needye.* 2. the Ritch. *both the Judges of the
lande whom she honoreth.* verse 23. *and the merchant whom she pleaseth* verse
24. From the question we come to the comparison, *Her price is above
pearles.* Pearles are esteemed not onely for their rarenesse but for their　10
vertues.

Use.1. Vertue is to be regarded in marriage.

Obiect.1. God *comandes the brother to raise up seede wthout regard to the
vertue of the woman* Deut: 25.5.

Answ: Some thinke that he was onely to adventure the penalty as　15
spitinge in his face, pluckinge// of his shoe and the like, But it is rather to
be thought that he was absolutely bound to doe it, for seeinge he married
her in faith and obedience to gods lawe, he had probability of hope concerning her amendement. *Obiect.2. Hosia was comanded to marry two harlots.* Os[ea] 1.2. and 3.1. *Answ*: we agree not to them yt make this a vision　20
or a parable but takeing it to be a real stor[ie] do thinke out of the 3.
Chap: verse 2. that the prophe[cy] of harlots was to make them *chast*:
neither was this entering into temptation, seeing god comanded it for a
typ[sic ? trial.]

Obiect: 3. *Isack, Jacob, Joseph and Moyses married Idolatrous women*; Gen:　25
31.19 and 41.45. Exod: 4.25.

Answ: It appeeres that *Rebecca* had true religion (thoug[h] somwhat
confused) by the author of Laban, gen: 24.31. and 59. As for Josephes wife

14. Deuteronomy 25.5—"If brethren dwell together, and one of them die, and have no
children, the wife of the dead shall not marry without, unto a stranger: her husband's
brother shall go in unto her, and take her to him to wife, and perform the duty of an
husband's brother unto her."

15. "the penalty"—"If the brother refuses her then shall his brother's wife come unto him
in the presence of the Elders, and loose his Shoe from off his foot, and spit in his face, and
shall answer, and say, So shall it be done unto that man that will not build up his brother's
house." Deuteronomy 25.9.

20. "Osea 1.2 and 3.1"—Hosea 1.2, "And the Lord said to Hosea, Go, take unto thee a wife
of whoredomes, and children of whoredomes: for the land hath committed great whoredome, departing from the Lord." 3.1, "Then said the Lord unto me, Go yet, love a woman
beloved of her friend, yet an adultress according to the love of the Lord toward the children
of Israel"; Hosea 3.2—"So I bought her to me for fifteen pieces of silver, and for an homer of
barley, and an half homer of barley."

26. Genesis 31.19—Rachal; Genesis 41.45—Joseph's wife was Asenoth, the daughter of the
priest of On; Exodus 4.25—Ziporah.

she was given him by *Pharoah* and so might not be refused, besides how knowe wee yt she was not a vertuous prosilyte. for Zippora we did answer beefore. Heere then; they first are condemned that will not marry where *vertue* is separated from *wealth*; the contrary we see in Jacob. gen: 29.17.

5 *Booz Ruth*: 3.10[,] *Hosia*. 3.3. who bought his wife at gods comandment. Secondly those that not regarding vertue marrye in respect of honor as Salomon did. 1.Kinges. 11.1 or of Beautye as Gen: 4.22 and 6.2.

Use.2. weomen must be like pearles in vertue. The pretious pearles and sweat before their owner be poysoned. A vertuous wife endevoureth to

10 foreshow her husband of the daunger to come. The *Berel* hath in yt the image of the sunne: the good wife the ymage of the sonne of god. The *Pyropus* shineth in the darke: so a good wife is most cheerfull in the time of trouble. The *Amathist* keepes a man from drunkinesse, and the *Bezoar* from ye plague. The first is literally in a good wife, by the latter is meant

15 keeping him from whoredome.

Thus much of the *proposition* now followes the *Exposition* weomen are two things. 1. the *workes* of a good woman. verse 11. to the 28. 2. The *Testimonie* given concerning her verse 28. to the end. In the workes two vertues are seene *faithfullnesse* and *providence*. The faithfulnesse is set

20 downe in *substance* vers: 11. and in *circumstance* vers. 12. The substance is declared by a double event. The First is <her> *The harte of her husbande trusteth in her*. 1. In respect of her *speech*. 2. of her *Deedes*. he may trust her for speech or silence if he tell her no *secrets* wch either go beyond her understanding as matter of state, or may drive her into suspision, greife,

4. "Jacob"—Genesis 29.17; "Booz"—Boaz married Ruth who "followedst not young men, whether rich or poor." Ruth 3.10.

7. 1 Kings 11.1—"But King Soloman loved many strange women (together with the daughter of Pharoah) women of the Moabites, Ammonites, Edomites, Zidomians and Hittites"; Genesis 6.2—"The sons of God saw the daughters of men, that they were fair, and they took them wives, of all which they chose."

10. "Berel"—Thomas Nicols states that a "*Beryll* in a spherick form hath the same power of begetting fire from the Sunne by its beams, that a Crystall glass hath." *A Lapidary: Or, The History of Pretious Stones*, p. 116; "Pyropus"—pyrope is a garnet whose name is derived from the Greek, meaning "fiery-eyed"; "Amathist"—amethyst, derived from the Greek, meaning "not drunken" and according to Pliny, "the Magicians, as vaine herein as in all other things, seem to beare us in hand that they have a speciall vertue to withstand drunkenness." *The Historie of the World, Commonly called, The Natural History of the World*, translated by Philemon Holland (1601), p. 621. "Bezoar"—supposedly found in the dung of a goatlike creature called a Param, it is referred to as an antidote to poison and infectious disease in Fioravanti, Burton, and also in several accounts of exploration such as Sir Richard Hawkins's *Voyage to the South Seas* (1622) and Nicolas Monardes's *Joyful Newes Out of the Newe Founde Worlde* (1577). Laslett records that Filmer's library, which remained intact at East Sutton Park until 1945, contained "the usual texts of the classics and works on recent European history, cosmography and exploration." "Sir Robert Filmer," p. 526. Whatever the specific source, this passage is another indication of the breadth of Filmer's interests and readings.

anger: or wherin she can give neither counsail nor helpe. The Jewes say
that Liah because of her silence the first night she lay wth Jacob was made
the mother// of Levi (gods principall secretary)[.]
   Againe for her deedes he may trust her three waies. 1. For her *Chastity.*
2. *Goverment.* 3. *Expences.* For her *Chastity* if she be free from adultery and   5
the reasonable suspition thereof; if [he] Deny her not due benevolence, if
he restraine her not of moderat libertie, pe[rmitting] that she visit not too
much the daughters of the lande Gen: 34.1. Nor wander like a busy pratler
1.Tim. 5.13. For goverment he may trust her first in regard of *Daughters*
and *maidservants*: Secondly even of sonnes when they be younge. *Lastly*   10
for expence wch is heere meant principally: if *prodigall pride* and *luxury*
wth *lust* and *vanitie* be not found to exceede he may trust her, and by
trusting make her trustye. The second event is he shall *have no neede of
spoile* the hebrew word signifieth *wealth* or *excellent thinges* so doth the
greeke worde Heb: 7.4. For *Abram payed tithes of his owne goods aswell as of*   15
the warlike spoyles. Againe theis wordes may be thus expounded. *As a*
victorious armie needes no bootehalinge: so the husband of a good woman needes
no needy shiftes to get his living. That theis things may be so, it is requisite,
First that <she> the woman be voyde of ignorance in *huswifrie*, secondly
of *ydlenesse*, thirdly of *bellychiere*, fourthly of *lust*, fifthly of *vanitie* in ap-   20
parell and building (wch frenzie doth possesse even some women also) of
all theis caterpillers the most daungerous are *ydlenesse* and *bellycheere.//*
Idlenesse are theis kindes. First *Nicenesse* when weoman will alwaies be
faineing themselves sicke (*this is a sumptuous sinne.*) The second is *care-*
lessnesse when things are spoyled for lacke of keepinge and attendance.   25
Thirdly sloathfullnesse when in labour there is neither *earilynesse*, *vehe-*
mency, *continuance*, nor *method*: sufficient *helpe*, or *allacritye*. Fourthly
fearefulnesse when theye will not *Chastise* their servants, beinge more
ready to change then amend them, whereas by the first lawe *servants should*
not alter under 7 yeares. Bellycheere hath theis partes, First *Daintynesse.*   30
Secondly *love of companie at home*, but especially abrode. he that [hath] a
wife wth theis viperous diseases shall have neede of spoyles. Thus much
the substance, the *circumstances of her faithfulnesse* are two. 1. *Entirenesse* 2.
Perseverance. Entirenesse in theis words: *She shall recompense him good and*
not evill: that is *she shal not shew him a cruel, bablinge, or lustful tricke.* Heere   35
observe, *a good woman may do her husband good*; First in his understanding,
if she teach him religion being more skilfull then hee; this must be done

2. "Liah"—Leah, Genesis 29.22–34.
   15. Hebrews 7.4—"Now consider how great this man was, unto even the patriarch Abraham gave the tenth of the spoils."
   22. "bootehalinge"—booty; "bellychiere"—luxurious self-indulgence; "building frenzy"—
perhaps a reference to one of Filmer's contemporaries, Anne, Countess of Pembroke.

modestly and secretly. Secondly in his affection, for she may sanctifie him
1.Cor: 7.15. In this kind she is most happy that can comfort her husband
against feare or greife: but this is a *black swan*: And yet we reade of
Hipsicratia ye wife// of *Mithridates* king of *Pontus* who accompanied her
5   husband [in] all his troubles and flightes. The next to her is she [who]
preserves her husband from anger. The last is she that *cures him of the
remedilesse disease of Jealousie*, this is also rather a thing to be wished then
hoped for. The *Perseverance* of her faithfulnesse in theis words, *All the daies
of her life*, being more fruitfull of good workes in her old age. Psal: 92.14.
10   whereof theis may be t[he] causes 1. If she have ledde her youth well, or
have repented of the sinnes of her youth, wch comonly are revenged wth
the sinnes of old age. 2. If she have used rather wisedome then vehemencie
in her love, for things violen[t] are not durable. 3. If she have praied
constantly for perseverance.
15   Thus much of her faithfulnesse, Now followes her *Providen[ce]* verse 13.
set downe in three things. 1. *In gettinge* 2. *In employinge* 3. *Preservinge*.
Getting is propounded verse 13. and expounded in the five next, It is
propounded in two things. For first she seeks *wooll* and *flaxe* as matter for
her labour. Secondly she labours wth the cheerefulnes or willingnes of her
20   handes upon this matter so purchased. Heere wee see the difference of
God, Nature, Arte. For God worketh wthout *matter*, creating the world of
nothinge; Nature of one substance frameth another. *Arte* onely// bringth
in new qualities: God having supplied all things to us if we can but use
them well. The laboure of a Mistres is more worth then yt of a servante
25   because it is wth more cheerfulnesse, not yssueinge from feare; but from
love of vertue, the family, and the master. Let servants then wch intende
heereafter to rule begin bytimes to put away eyeservice, and thinke themselves to be maisters not in surlynes of commanding but in cheerefulnesse
of working. Againe, let not ye husband kill the spirit of the wife wth bitter
30   lookes, wordes, deedes; wch make her of a rib to become an excrement.
      The providence in getting is expounded and that in regard of both
parts, before named, diligence in seeking, and labour. Seeking is set
downe verse 14. by a similitude of shippes, whereby bread or foode all
things are ment wch bring in foode or profit, as *wooll, flaxe* and the like.
35   In this seeking two thinges are to be remembered. 1. That she be a *house-*

2. 1 Corinthians 7.15—verse 14, "For the unbelieving husband is sanctified by the wife, and
the unbelieving wife is sanctified by the husband."
   4. "Hipsicratia"—one of the wives of Mithridates the Great (d. 63 B.C.), "who always
displayed a right manly spirit and extravagant daring . . . mounted and accoutred like a
Persian, she was neither exhausted by the long journeys, nor did she weary of caring for the
king's person and for his Horse." Plutarch, "Pompey," *Lives* 5.32 (Loeb).
   9. Psalms 92.14—"They shall still bring forth fruit in old age; they shall be fat and
flourishing."
   34. Proverbs 31.14—"She is like the merchants' ships; she bringeth food from afar."

keeper that is no gadder abroade, but a traviller for lawfull businesse wth
unsuspected company. *Tit*:2.5./ 2. She must seeke out such thinges as are
profitable for her country. for in some places it is more available to buy
cloath readymade then to make it. Use.1. wee see the excellency of laborious industry wch maketh even barren places to be fruitfull of all things,   5
though wooll be not meant had// <yet> yt may be fetcht from *Militus*;
for god hath made on[e] country neede another to take away self love.

    *Use.*2. Of all calings that of the merchant is the most daungerous, and
yet it is ymitable by a woman, though i[n] a weaker measure; so there is
no vertue in men so differen[t] wch weomen may not hope in some sort   10
to attaine, for e[ven] sayling and warre and goverment of kingdomes have
been often times well handled by weomen, *Queene Dido* may be example
for all, or rather *Q Elizabeth* in whose tim[e] theis things flourisht.

    *Use.*3. The woman must bee allowed by her husband, els how can she
employe missengers and money in theis matters; but in this allowanc[e]   15
love and discretion must meete. The second part of getting wch is Labour
is set out by three times, t[he] *Beginninge, Middle, Ende* of the day. In ye
beginning or morning she doth three things, *Riseth, Ordereth, meditateth*:
firstly verse 15. Use.1. Heere they are confuted who thinke the night to
serve onely for sleepe, for she riseth while it is yet night if it may stand wth   20
her health: besides the *moone* and *starres* were not made to sleepe by but to
worke by: neither indeede is the proportion betwen the times of the day
and night at some seasons of the yeare; that yt were straung[e] to sleepe 16
houres together, much more straunge to sleep[e] 6 monthes, all wch time
the night endureth in some <places> Countries. Use.2. Early rising is   25
commende[d] both heere and elsewhere as most naturall to man, and//
contrary to wild beasts Psal: 104. 22. 23. besides it is found to bring forth a
double commoditie, *Inward* and *Outward*. Inward threefould, It sharp-
neth the wit, lengtheneth the memory, cheereth the hart: For sleepe aris-
ing from cold and moisture keeping downe the spirits of the hart from   30
ascending into yt *wonderfull nette*, by coldnesse hurteth the wit, by moisture ye memory and by depressing the spirits shifteth the harts ioy. The
outward is threefould. First it keepeth a man from intemporat diet, seeing
he that riseth earely avoideth late meales a necessary ground of intemper-
ance, surfetting and fasting being ioyned together[.] Secondly it takes   35
away much occasion of impertinent company: for ydle persons come not

2. Titus 2.5—directs the behavior of women, ordering them to be "discreet, chaste, keepers
at home, good, obedient to their own husbands, that the word of God be not blasphemed."
   19. Proverbs 31.15—"She riseth also while it is yet night, and giveth meat to her household,
and a portion to her maidens."
   27. Psalms 104.22–23—"The sun ariseth, they gather themselves together, and lay them
down in their dens."

to a man in the morning; unlesse their be some who will confute St. Peter to be drunke before the third houer: but it is plaine that ordinarily *they that are drunke, are drunke at night*. So that he who goeth earely to bedd cuts of the possibility of much disorder. Thirdlye yt sets his businesse out
5 of the danger of the hazard if <he is> a man be not interrupted in the morneing, but if he sleepe in ye morning the least interruption cutts of all his time. Use.3. we must learne in spirituall things also to rise earely *Psalm*: 119. v: 147 and 148. *I prevented the morning light, and cried; for I waited on thy word, Mine eyes prevent the night watches to meditate on thy*
10 *word,//* The second worke of the morneing is to give foode or portion to our Household, this worde is used Psal: 111. vers: 3 Use.1. Order for meate and worke in families is most [need]full, examples of the first we have Exod: 16.18 and in 1 Kings. 4.22. allusions also to the same proverb: 30.8. Luke 12.42. Example of the second Gen: 39.23. Use. 2. Goverment of
15 maydes is to be permitted to ye w[ife] as ys plaine by the stories of *Abygail* and *Hester*. but it i[s] obiected that *Sara* dares not afflict *Hagar* wthout leave from Abram Gen: 16.6. Answer. *Hagar* was no[t] meerely a maid servant being a concubine: though indeed she were not mistres, heere of goods, nor perpetuall, as n[ot] being solemly marrid. Use.3. we must be
20 content wth y[e] portion that god gives, for the world is his family, so tha[t] we may not murmur to see fooles have full cups. Use.4. If the wife have such authority in the family concerninge things indifferent: why should we take away this power from the Church wch is the Lambes wife. The third worke of the morning is to meditate verse 16. werein we may
25 consider the act or deede, and the meanes. The deede, to purchase the

---

3. "St. Peter"—Peter refuted those who mocked the Apostles' speaking in tongues, "for these are not drunken, as ye suppose, seeing it is but the third hour of the day." Acts 2.13–15.

8. Psalms 119.147–48—"I prevented the dawning of the morning, and cried: I hoped in thy word. Mine eyes prevent the night watches, that I might meditate in thy word."

11. Psalms 111.3—verse 5 in the Geneva Bible has "he hath given a portion unto them that feare him," whereas the Authorized Version has "he hath given meat unto them that fear him."

13. Exodus 16.18—"And when they did mete it with an omer, he that gathered much had nothing over, and he that gathered little had no lack; they gathered every man according to his eating"; 1 Kings 4.22—"And Solomon's provision for one day was thirty measures of fine flour, and threescore measures of meal"; Proverbs 30.8—"Feed me with food convenient for me"; Luke 12.42—"And the Lord said, Who then is that faithful and wise steward, who his lord shall make ruler over his household, to give them their portion of meat in due season?"

14. Genesis 39.23—"The keeper of the prison looked not to any thing that was under his hand; because the Lord was with him, and that which he did, the Lord made it to prosper."

17. Genesis 16.6—"But Abram said unto Sarah, Behold, thy maid is in thy hand; do to her as it pleaseth thee. And when Sarah dealt hardly with her she fled from her fate."

24. Proverbs 31.16—"She considereth a field, and buyeth it: with the fruit of her hands she planteth a vineyard."

feild or vyneyard. the meanes are two. 1. wise consideration. 2. She pur-
chaseth yt wth money lawfully gotten. *Obiection. Sellinge of land is forbidden* Levit: 25.25. and theirfore buying. *Answ*: some buying is necessary,
some lawfull onely and indifferent; necessary when god commands either
in his lawe in general as when yssue faileth. *Ruth*.4.6. Or when yt is a   5
house in a walled towne not convenient for a mans use. *Levit*: 25.29. Or in
some special charge as yt of *Araunah* 2.*Sam*: 24.21. as the *younge man Mat*:
19.22. or ye disciples *Acts*. 4.35. because they were then to travail wth their
families, and to leave their country for ever; and the *Church* was in great
necessity as appears 2. *Cor*: 8.3. In theis cases selling was necessary   10
and so buying is lawful if not necessary also; as in some of the cases is
manifest. But in other cases the sale may be unlawfull, and yet the buying
lawfull enough, for *Jacob* might redeme his right from *Esau*, who yet was
most prophane in selling it. *Gen*: 25.30. neither is it unlawfull <for thee>
to redeeme thy brother from a pyrate who possessing him uniustly cannot   15
<iustly> wth *iustice* sell him. In like manner if a spendthrift sel his lande it
shall be lawfull for thee to buy it, neverthelesse *Naboth may not sell his
vineyard to Ahab*. 1. *Kings*: 21.3. *Obiect: Abram bought land. Gen*: 23.16. and
Joseph gen: 47.22. and *Jeremy Jer*: 32.7. *Answ: Abram* and *Jeremie* did it out
of speciall hope, for they were assured that their seede should possese the   20
land, The same was done by Jacob. *gen*: 33.19. *Joseph bought it for Pharao in
regard of domm[in]ion not of possession. Obiect: The law in Leviticus is
ceremoniall, beinge made for the distinction of tribes. Answ*: That End of the
law is not true: for had the lawe beene thus onely made *that they should not
sell it out of ye tribe//* this end had beene sufficiently observed, as for the   25

5. Ruth 4.6—"And the kinsman said, I cannot redeem it for myself, lest I mar mine own
inheritance: redeem thou my right to thyself; for I cannot redeem it."
6. Leviticus 25.29—"And if a man sell a dwelling house in a walled city, then he may
redeem it within a whole year after it is sold."
10. "Araunah"—sold lands to David on which to build an altar. 2 Samuel 24.21. Matthew
19.22—verse 21, "Jesus said unto him If thou wilt be perfect, go and sell that thou hast, and
give to the poor, and thou shalt have treasure in heaven"; Acts 4.35—verse 34, "for as many
were possessors of lands or houses sold them, and brought the prices of the things that sold
and laid them down at the apostles' feet"; 2 Corinthians 8.3—verse 2, "How that in a great
trial of affliction the abundance of their joy and their deep poverty abounded unto the riches
of their liberality."
14. "Jacob and Esau"—Genesis 25.29–34. "Naboth's vineyard"—"And Naboth said to
Ahab, The Lord forbid it me, that I should give the inheritance of my fathers unto thee." 1
Kings 21.3.
19. Genesis 23.16—Abraham's payment to Ephron; Genesis 47.22—"Only the land of the
priests bought he not; for the priests had a portion assigned them of Pharoah, and did eat
their portion which Pharoah gave them: wherefore they sold not their lands"; Jeremiah
32.7—"Behold, Hanameel the son of Shallum thine uncle shall come unto thee, saying Buy
thee my field that is in Anathorth: for the right of redemption is thine to buy it."

dist[inc]tion of families we hold it to be morrall and the breac[h] thereof to be *murther* and *theft*. Besides when the ten tribes were caried away into captivity, this lawe had little place by theis mens opinion<s>. Slips of this truth remaine in our law, for if a man dye intestate, t[he] eldest sonne by
5 the common law is heire to the land, if a man make an executor he is heire to the goods but not t[o] the land, so that howsoever things have beene corrupted by *tirannie* and *usurpation* yet the ordinary sale of land is not to be iustified. *Obiect*: sundry good deeds may be done by ye selling of land. *Answ*: The temple was built and sundry synagogues when this sale was
10 exhibit[ed] for in those daies sundry men did combyne ther revenewes for such publique workes. Heere then the good woman either buyeth a lease till the years of *Jubile*, or buyet[h] right out a house in a *City*, yet cutteth of no inheritan[ce] from a familie *Levit*: 25.24. Thus much of the morneing workes; *at Noone she guirdeth her loins* vers: 17. that is, she
15 sleepeth not at noone but armeth her self to labour: heere is a *similie* taken from ye *eastern* people who guirded up their garments when they went to labour. Use.1. hinderances of labour are to be avoided wch are 1. *lust*. 2. *surfettinge* and al *vuluptiousnesse*. 3. *leud companie* at home and abroad. 4. *disuse of labour* wherby many enfeeble their bodies and disable their
20 mindes. *Lastly at Night she puts not out her candle*. vers: 18.19. whereof the causes are renderd, *she feeleth that her// merchandise <are> is good*: she sits up late for profit not against health. Secondly by the effect, *she handles the wheele and spindle*. Examples we have in *Penelope Lucretia* and others. Use.1. *Example is of greate force*. The mistres example is a president for her
25 servants as *Ester* 4.16. Though she were a Courtier and lived among *pagans*, and fasting was a hard doctrine *Mat*. 9.16. yet she by her example moved her maids to do it. Thus we see gods example Exod: 20.11. and *Abimelecks Judges* 9.22 propounded for arguments. *Use.2.* By the wheele and spindle are ment all labour not onely of body but of mind: if any
30 woman excell in *Chirurgery*, *Phisick*, *goverment* of a commonwealth she

13. Leviticus 25.24—verse 23, "The land shall not be sold for ever: for the land is mine; for ye are strangers and sojourners with me."

16. Proverbs 31.17—"She girdeth her loins with strength, and strengtheneth her arms."

20. Proverbs 31.18–19—"She perceiveth that her merchandise is good: her candle goeth not out by night. She layeth her hands to the spindle, and her hands hold the distaff."

25. Esther 4.16—"Go, gather together all the Jews that are present in Shushan, and fast ye for me, and neither eat nor drink three days, night or day: I also and my maidens will fast likewise."

26. Matthew 9.16—verse 14, "Then came to him the disciples of John, saying, Why do we and the Pharisees fast oft, but thy disciples fast not?"

27. Exodus 20.11—declares that no work is to be done on the seventh day; "Abimelecks and Judges 9.22"—verse 48, Abimelech "said unto the people that were with him, What ye have seen me do, make haste and do as I have done."

shall be no more bound to the *wheele* then a prince is to ye *Plough*. Those
husbands therefore are to *froward* that hinder theis eminent graces in their
wives; provided alwaies yt the weomen neglect not huswifry nor be
bodshers [sic].

Thus much of her providence in getting, now foloweth that of *employ-*   5
ment vers: 20. wch is threefould for the matter, besides the manner. The 1.
matter is *Necessity*. 2. *of ornament*. 3. *of Profit*: of necessity twofold. First to
the *Poore*, vers: 20. Heere by the word *stretchinge* and *sendinge* is ment that
she helpes the poor fare of as well as neare; likewise by ye worde *poor* or
afflicted, and *needie* or *craving* is meant, that// she is aydeing aswel to   10
those that aske not, as to those that aske: wherefore it is said, that it is
religion to visi[t] *James* 1.27. that is rather to inquire out ye necessities of
men, then to be importuned by the clamours of the *wanderers*. *Use*. Hence
Husbands may learne to give first a generall then a speciall consent to
their wives upon triall in regard of liberality. The second necessity is in   15
respect of the family. *verse*. 21. where ye word *scarlet* is rather to be turned
doubles or changes of garments, not *double died scarlet* an attire not fit for
servants, howsoever the word be so taken commonly e[?] *Gen*: 38.25. *Use*.
Handsomnes is greatly commended in the changes of rayment: such as *Joseph*
gave to *Beniamin*, *Sampson to his freinds*, *Balthasar* to *Daniell* for filthinesse   20
in rayment is an argument of loosenesse in weomen[.] *Ornament* is twofold. First in herself, then in her husband. For herself she adornes the
familye and her person *vers*.22. for her house she makes *carpets*, for her
person she weares purple and silke: some translate it fine linnen or bom-
bast but yt cannot agree to the examples *gen*: 41.42. *Exd*: 25.4. It is more   25
likely to be of silke where of each thread is made of six strings yssueing
from ye worme; whereas they alledg that the worme was defiled, it is to be
considered that the worme is directly named *Exod*: 25.4. *Obiect*: Fine
apparell is condemned *Esay*. 3.18. 1.*Tim*: 2.9. 1.*Pet*: 3.3. *Answ*: This is done
in two cases. First// where the affliction of *Joseph* is not remembred, Amos.   30
6.6. wch is cruelty. Secondly in case of vanity when either ability is ex-
ceeded, or the degree of a mans calling *Use*. curious workes are allowable
both in private, as in the song of *Debora Judges*. 5.25. and in the Church as

---

6. Proverbs 31.20—"She stretcheth out her hand to the poor; yea, she reacheth forth her
hands to the needy."

12. James 1.27—"Pure religion and undefiled before God and the father is this, To visit the
fatherless and widows in their affliction, and to keep himself unspotted from the world."

16. Proverbs 31.21—"She is not afraid of the snow for her household: for all her household
are clothed with scarlet."

23. Proverbs 31.22—"She maketh herself coverings of tapestry: her clothing is silk and
purple."

29. "Esay. 3.18"—Isaiah 3.18.

appeered by *Bezaleell, Aholiab, Huram*. 2. *Chron*: 2.14. It is a sinne then to
let the house of god lye wast. Aggai. 1.4. Againe she adornes her husband
for he is *knowne in the gates sittinge wth the elders*, by the fine attire wch she
makes for him. Use. Garments are made not onely for covering of shame,
5 and health or safetie whether in peace or warre: but also for distinction of
orders, wch they yt breake doe also breake their workes like the gyants.
The *Profit* is set downe vers: 24. *shee makes and selles sheetes, and gives a
girdle to the merchant or Cannanite*: for the *Cannanites* were the cheifest
merchants, those were principally the *Phaenicians* that dwell in *Tyre* and
10 *Sidon* by the sea *Numb*: 13.30. the same is plaine by *Mat*: 15.21. and *Marke*:
7.26. *Use*.1. merchandise and trades are neither to be discommended, seeing they wer used by the men of *Juda*. *Ezek*: 27.33. neither yet (as being
used by the cursed Canaanites) to be folowed over eagerly: namely where
they cannot have free conscience, or wth the oppression of them wth
15 whome they deale. *Use*.2. Cheare must be had wth all even wth ye forraine
merchant. *The manner of her ymployment* is set downe verse 25. *She doth al
things in strenght,// honor and continewing ioye*; by strenght wee meane
ritches, by hence plaine and open dealing, honore follow[eth] ioye. the
word signifieth laughter; but thereby is men[t] ioye in olde age for youth
20 well spent. This is no[t] found in some aged weomen whose minds are full
of *male = contente morositie*.
    Hitherto of the providence of ymployment, their remain[eth] that of
Keepeinge. wch is twofould *spirituall* and *temporall*. The spirituall being
more noble & so first is in verse 26. *she openeth her mouth in wisedome, and
25 the lawe of pittye or mercy is under her tongue. Use*.1. Two things are required
of them that speake of *Religion*. First for the matter, that theye treate of
gods pitty to us, and our pitty to our neighbour, [or?] else religion is but
babling. Secondly for ye manner that they knowe the lawe, or *doctrinal
method* as the word ymports, not contenting themselves wth fragment[s]

    1. Judges 5.25—verse 30, "A prey of divers colours needlework, of divers colours of needle-
work on both sides, meet for the necks of them that take the spoil"; "Bezaleell"—Bezalel, the
chief architect of the Tabernacle who was directed by God "to devise cunning works, to work
in gold, and in silver, and in brass." Exodus 31.1–12. "Aholiab"— Oholiab, the chief helper to
Bezalel; "Huram and 2 Chronicles 2.14."—Huram, King of Tyre, sent a man to Solomon to
aid in building the temple who was "skillful to work in gold and silver."
    2. "Aggai 1.4."—Haggai, "Is it time for you Oye, to dwell in your cielded houses, and this
house lie in waste?"
    7. Proverbs 31.24—"She maketh fine linen, and selleth it; and delivereth girdles unto the
merchant."
    15. Ezekiel 27.33—"Thy wares went forth out of the seas, thou filledst many people; thou
didst enrich the kings of the earth with the multitudes of thy riches and of thy merchandise."
    18. Proverbs 31.25—"Strength and honour are her clothing; and she shall rejoice in time to
come."

of disyonted sentences. *Use*.2. knowledge of religion and artes pertaining to pitty: specially the arte of *Chirurgerie* and *Almes* are very convenient for weomen. The temporall meanes <for> of keeping are set down verse 27. wch are two 1. *overseeinge* 2. *labour*. namely overseeing that things be well done and in time, also that things be not spoyled nor spent in vaine. for   5
she overseeth the waies of her househould. *Labour*// likewise not so much for personal toyle as exemplarie cheerefulnesse, for she *eateth not the bread of ydleness*. *Use*. Heere gentlemen and gentleweomen are condemned who live by their lands in sloth, not in publique labour of profitable huswifry.

Hitherto of the workes now follows the *witnesses* verse 28. Theis are two,   10
First the *Children* who blesse her, secondly her *husband who praiseth her*. Blessing is either wth authoritye, or wth entreaty, and authority is either *absolute* as in *god*, or *delegate* as in *Ministers* and *Parents*: but thiere is blessinge wth entreaty, or rather a pronouncing of blessednes wth praise. *Use*.1. It is the mothers duty to bring up her children yt they may blesse   15
her: that is to give them good example, and love them wthout partiality, a sinne punished in *Jacob*, *Ely*, *David*, and why not in weomen? *Use*.2. Children must obey their mothers and be thankefull in their wants. *Use*.3. Husbandes must encourage their wives wth seasonable praise, and yet retaine their owne gravity for it is said her *Lord shall praise her*, His praise   20
is set downe by a *prosopopeia* or speech upon his death bedd to his sonnes, containing a *Narration* <or> and an *Exhortation*. The narration hath a double comparison, first of the unlike, verse 29. *Many daughters have done vertuously*,// some translate it (have gotten wealth) Ruth. 4.11. The word wch we turne wealth signifies *strenght*, not one[ly] because we place out   25
strenght in wealth *Pro:* 10.15. wth t[he] hornes whereof we push the needy: but cheifly for that wealth is a stronge organ of vertues, principally *Justic[e,] Clemencie, Liberalitye*. *Use*.1. Saints aswel dead as living may be praised though not worshipped. *Use*. 2 Some comparisons are not odious where they that ma[ke] them have authority of *guiftes* or *discretion*: and   30
where they are made betweene persons of *equall ranke* in matt[ers] of duty. the like is found *Philip:* 2.21. The second comparison is of the con-

3. Proverbs 31.27—"She looketh well to the ways of her household, and eateth not the bread of idleness."

10. Proverbs 31.28—"Her children rise up, and call her blessed; her husband also, and he praiseth her."

23. Proverbs 31.29—"Many daughters have done virtuously, but thou excellest them all."

24. Ruth 4.11—"The Lord make the woman that is come into thine house like Rachel and Leah, which two did build the house of Israel."

28. Proverbs 10.15—"The rich man's wealth is his strong city: the destruction of the poor is their poverty."

28. "Saints"—see also Filmer's reference to Julietta.

32. Philippians 2.21—"For all seek their own, not the things which are Jesus Christ."

trary verse 30. *favour is deceiptfull, and beautie is vanity*. The word favour
signifieth that wch *procureth favour* in regarde of mens carnall desires Gen:
4.22. and 6.2. *Ruth*. 1.20 It riseth principally from [pro (sic ? por)]ortions.
Beauty signifieth that *wch allureth* as *Gen*: 9.27. and consisteth not so
5 much <is> in *partes*, as in *mixture of coulors*. The word we translate *vanity*
was the name of *Abel* pretending the vanity and brittlenes of mans life.
The exhortatio[n] is in ver: 31. wch is double, First *give her of ye fruite of her
handes, my sonnes, what she hath gotten in my life time,* let her enioy a
convenient and honorable portion theireof after my death: though she
10 marrye againe grudge not at that wch she enioyes, And secondly let *her
workes praise her in the Gates*. If she be accused in the gates of *Judgement,*
either// for *witchcraft* or *whoredome,* or be molested in suites of lawe defend
her by declaring her former innocencye. Use.1. *Deedes doubtfull* are charita-
bly to be interpreted according to the former integritye Use.2. Children
15 must defend their parents in warre, and lawe, As heere, and *Psalme*. 127.5.

---

1. Proverbs 31.30—"Favour is deceitful; and beauty is vain: but a woman that feareth the
Lord, she shall be praised."

3. Genesis 6.2—"The sons of God saw the daughters of men, that they were fair, and they
took them wives, of all which they chose"; Ruth 1.20—"And she answered them, call me not
Naomi [beautiful], but call me Mara [bitter]: for the Almighty hath given me much bitterness." Genesis 4.22—the reason for Filmer's citation of this passage is unclear.

5. Genesis 9.27—the beauty of Leah and Rachel.

10. Proverbs 31.31—"Give her of the fruit of her hands; and let her own works praise her in
the gates."

15. Psalms 127.5—"Happy is the man that hath his quiver full of [children]: they shall not
be ashamed, but they speak with the enemies in the gate."

Mary More
"The Womans Right"

The Womans Right Or Her Power in a Greater Equality to her Husband
proved than is allowed or practised in England

From misunderstanding Some Scriptures, and false rendring others from
ye Originall, plainly shewing an equality in Man & Woman before ye
Fall, & not much difference after.

The Equality of their Souls is also proved in that Women have done
whatever is of Value that men have done, What hath been done may be
done.

Written by M.M.

THE PREFACE
To My little Daughter Elizabeth Waller[1]

At first veiw of this following discourse it may seem strange to thee that I
thy Mother of all Women should concern my self in a Subject of this
Nature, having never had any Reason as to my self to complain of the least
Ill Cariage of my Husbands to me, nor hath any occasion or action in my
whole life ever offered anything, wherein the Power and Will of my husband hath been disputed on mee, for we finding it our Interests to be
embarked in one bottom, and so must be guided and steered one way,
have (I hope I may say it without Vanity) so ordered our affairs and
actions to ye utmost of our Power and Skill, to tend to ye Comfort and
good liking of both.

So then that which made me more then ordinary to consider this Subject,
hath been from a trouble in me observing ye sad consequences & events
that have fallen on men and their Wives, through this mistake of mens

1. "Elizabeth Waller"—Mary More's daughter by her first marriage, born 1663, who married Charles Pitfield in 1680.

pertending a Power over their Wives, that neither God nor nature doe allow, and I dare be confident that if any unbiassed person observe it, they must conclude this to bee the first and great cause of most breaches between men and their Wives.//

If thou my Child shall live to years fitt, and thou purposes to marry

I. First I advise thee to seek God by earnest & frequent prayers, for direction and a blessing on this so great a work, as the choice of a Husband which is as ye hinges whereon hangs and turns all worldly Comfort to thee. And first in thy Choice (as far as is possible for thee to know) choose a man that fears and serveth God, tis usually the want of grace and ye not knowing the Scriptures, that is ye principall cause of the Ill carriage of men to their wives.

2. Secondly choose a wise and understanding Man, for as Solomon saith of a Foolish Wife, she is as rottenness in a mans bones which will soon destroy and ruine him I am sure may be truly said of a foolish Husband,[2] for the Laws of Our Country giving a Man after marriage a greater Power of their Estate than ye Wife, unless ye Wife take care before hand to prevent it (which I advise thee to doe) I say an unwise husband doth for the most part destroy and bring to nought what is in his power.

3. Thirdly (so far as thou canst discover it) choose one of a good naturall disposition & temper, I mean one that is free from that harshness & morosity that is sometimes naturally in men. Like Ishmael against all and all aginst him, a wife will find hard work and against the grain to live comfortably with such an Husband.//

4. Lastly choose a Person who thou dost love and affect and that loves thee, (for love hides a multitude of faults) but rather marry a man for his love to thee, than thine to him, for I seldome find the Wife fail on this part if the Husband love her.

But my Child if God shall see fitt to cross thee in all or any of these, in thy choice of a Husband, then I advise thee To a patient Submission to ye hand of God on thee, take up thy Cross and bear it for in Mariage you are joyned, as if were in a Yoke, and if either strive to get free, or loosed from their unruly yokefellow, they do but gall and tire themselves. Prudently hide it from the World, for I do not believe yt ever Husband or Wife yt complained of each other found comfort or releif in it, it being a complaint against ones self.

---

2. More reverses the opening text of Filmer's essay, Proverbs 12.4, to apply it equally to foolish husbands as well as wives.

Nor do thou ever study to requite him in his kind, if he be vicious be thou the more Virtuous, if he be a Spend-thrift, be thou ye more frugall. And remember to bear thee up, yt God will take thy part sooner or later: it being Gods usuall manner when we bear afflictions patiently (and leave him to revenge) to doe it for us and retaliate it on ye offender in some answerable punishment, we often reading ye Sin by ye Punishment.

That thou my Childe maist be blest with a Religious, Wise, good tempered & loving husband is the earnest & constant prayer of thy faithfull & affectionate Mother M:M://

THE WOMANS RIGHT
The Argument
It is one end (among others) in writing to doe something either as to ye thing or manner yt is new & not commonly known; of this I am sure not to miss in this little treatise, for the truth that I shall here endeavour, and doubt not to prove, is so unknown at this time in England that I find they do, as is said of ye Inventors of untruths, yt they tell them so long untill they bring themselves into ye belief of their truth; so it is grown between husbands & their Wifes in our time, by a long practising of Power towards Wives, (impowered to it by laws of their own making) I say they are by practise grown into a beleif of their Right to that, which I do not find allowed neither by ye Laws of God nor Nature.

That wch I shall principally aim at in this discourse shall be to prove a greater equality between Husbands and Wives then is allowed and practised in England.

And God said let us make man in our own Image after our likeness, & let them bear dominion over ye fish of ye Sea & over the fowl of ye Air, & over all ye Earth. So God created man in his own Image, in ye Image of God created him, male & female created he them.// *Gen. 1.* *v. 26* *v. 27*

And God blessed them and God said unto them, be fruitfull, & multiply, & replenish ye earth & subdueth & have dominion over the fish of ye Sea, & over ye fowl of ye Air, & over Every living thing yt moveth upon ye Earth. *v. 28*

Let us make man: ye word man here comprehend both sexes, or mankind, for in ye next verse we read God created him, male & female created he them. *v. 29*

And God blessed them and gave them dominion over all ye Creatures in ye earth, to subdue them from where I lay down this as a Truth, yt before *v. 30* ye fall Man and Woman, Adam and Eve had equally power over each other and over ye Creatures; finding noe difference onely Adams being created first in order of time, & his naming ye Creatures, and not Eve; neither of which seems to me to be a signe of superiority in Adam.

For first Adams being made before Eve, is but as beasts were made before Adam, for ye Evening and ye Morning were ye first day, none will from thence think ye night ye better, wch rather shows ye contrary for God in ye work of Creation went on gradually higher & higher, creating the choicest & the best last; so yt if I would be criticall I might say yt Eve was ye most curious peice of nature in ye whole creation being left till last, untill all things were fitted to receive & entertain her, besides she was made of ye most refined part of the Creation, Adam. Adam was made// of ye earth *1 Cor:* refined Eve of Adam. For ye man is not of ye Woman (but of ye earth) but *II v. 8* ye woman of ye Man; but all things of God.[3] So that doubtless Eve was, and all or most women ever since are of a finer mould and mettall yn most men are: nor do I see any Reason why we may not on good Grounds argue from thence; yt ye bodys of women being more fine; wch body is ye Organ yt Acts and declares ye soul, the souls of Women are acted mor[e] serene & agile then mens are: our common experience shewing us then when ever women < > give themselves to study etc. they prove as learned & good proficients, and with as much (or more) ease then men, but ye same hath been done by Women: What hath been done may be done is a rule in Philosophy.

2 Kings A Prophetess & a Scholar bred up in ye Colleges, Huldar & Eusebius *v. 22* quotes out of Philo, yt ye Women had their studys & conferences severally from the Men.[4]

A Schollar. Anna Maria a Shurman, & ye Lady Jane Gray both great Scholars.[5]

Jud: Valiant. Deborah, & Boadicea in England etc. Prudence to rule & Courage to maintain it: Queen Elizabeth of England who was also so expert in

---

3. "For man is not made of woman"—1 Corinthians 8.11.

4. "Huldar"—Josiah sends for "Huldar the prophetess, the wife of Shallum" who prophesies the destruction of Jerusalem. 2 Kings 22.14–20. "Eusebius and Philo"—In *Historia Ecclesiastica*, 2.17, Eusebius (c. A.D. 264) quotes Philo's account in *De vita comtemplativa* of the life of the ascetics in Egypt, the women of whom were called Therapeutrides. The Greek text of *Historia Ecclesiastica* was edited in Paris by Valesius in 1659 and was reprinted three times over the seventeenth century, but it appears that it was not available in either Latin or English.

5. "Anna Maria a Schurman"—Anna Maria van Schurman, author of *The Learned Maid* (1659) and pupil of Descartes.

Tongues & langauges, yt she heard & gave Answer to all Embassadours herself & had the Greek & Latine so// fluent that she frequently spake verses in those languages extempore.

As for ye Salique Law in France it is known to be made at first, onely as to a particular place Sala; for the faults of some dishonest Women who lived there, but after was falsly expounded to be for ye whole nation of France, onely to debar ye English Kings from ye claime of ye French Crowne, tho the French Kings themselves derive their Rights often from the heirs female.[6] By ye Law made by God ye Lawgiver the Daughters are to inherit their Fathers Inheritance alloted to them in ye tribe of Manasses, God telling them that if a man had noe Sons then ye Daughters should inherit, and if he hath no Daughters, then ye Inheritance should go to his Brethren.[7]

And Shesomes Daughter was sole heir to her fathers Patrimony tho she married an Egyptian, & her Posterity and their possessions among ye tribes of Judah to ye Captivity of Babylon.[8]

2 Cron: 2.54

The second seeming difference between Adam and Eve before the fall is that Adam named the Creatures, it appears to me that Adam named them before Eve was created (tho they were both created in one day) but if Adam did name the beasts when Eve was there Eve named her Children when Adam was there, and gave them as Significant names as Adam did her, or the rest// of the Creatures, it being ye practise of ye Women in ye Scriptures to name their Children significantly. Eve was made of Adams Rib, not his head, nor foot, but middle, his equall and meet helper, flesh of his flesh, and bone of his bone.

Gen. 2: 22

This equall and happy man and his Wife envied by ye Devil came in the Serpents shape, who was ye most subtle of all ye beasts, and assaulted Eve to break ye Command, yt God had newly enjoyned Adam & her, Thou in ye singular number includes both, for Eve tells ye Serpent, Wee may eat of ye fruit of the trees of ye Garden, but this God hath said yee shall not eat

Gen. 3:1

6. "Salique Law"—the Salic Law of Succession excluded women and men from the French throne whose descent from a former ruler was traced only through the female side. Made in the fourteenth century, it was, by the sixteenth, interpreted primarily as an expression of the theory of royal power. Charles II of Navarre claimed his right through Louis X's daughter Joan, as did Edward III of England.

7. Numbers 27.6–8—"and the Lord spake unto Moses saying, The daughters of Zelophehad speak right: thou shalt surely give them a possession of an inheritance among their father's brethren. . . . If a man die and have no sons then ye shall cause his inheritance to pass unto his daughters"; "tribe of Manasses"—Joshua 17.3–6.

8. "Shesomes Daughter"—1 Chronicles 2.34–35.

of etc. So then as they were equally partners in ye Power yt God first gave them so were they equally concerned in ye Command and in ye Penalty for ye breach of it, so I find ye 10 Commandments afterward given by God to Moses for ye People, are given in ye singular number, *Thou Shalt;* yet there God commands a man & his Wife equally, they being one as appears by ye 4th Command, *Thou & Thy Son and Thy Daughter;* not thou & thy wife, or thou & thy husband. By ye Devils assulting Eve & not Adam, it seems clear to me yt she had ye most high & strong soul, & so hardest to be overcome else would ye Devil (ye subtlest of the three) have fallen upon Adam, and not have left Adam ye stronger to have been tempted by Eve ye weaker, ye interests// of each others affections being (no doubt) of equall prevalence, Eve being as ready to have been persuiaded by Adam, As Adam was by Eve.

But unhappy were those her better parts, & yt she was first in the transgression, for she being first in ye Sin, was in some respect higher in ye punishmen[t] though I shall prove man & Woman more equall after the fall, then is beleived & practised. Eve being first tempted to Sin, & perswading her husband, Gods just hand of punishment (who is ever most just) took ye transgressours to task, according to their order in offending, first ye Serpent, then ye Woman, then ye Man.

Gen. 3: The Seed of ye Woman shall bruise ye serpents head, from whence I
15 observe, that before ye Woman had her Sentence of Sorrow, she hath a promise (ye greatest yt was ever made to mankind) to support her, where I cannot but take notice of ye high & unparalel Honour yt God hath done to Women above men: that Christ God-man should be born of a Woman without a man, Christ having no mans flesh.

Then comes Eves Sentence of Sorrow (though not till ye Support to bear
Gen. 3: her up) I will greatly multiply thy sorrows in conception, in sorrow shall
16 thou bring forth children, and thy desire shall be to thy Husband & he shall rule over thee,[9]// which words do shew something of a subjection to her husband after ye fall, tho not much, for I find the sence of these words mistaken by most readers, they being ye very Same in ye Originall, & are rendred in the very wordes in our Bibles; which God said to Cain when God saw Cains countenance fallen at his Brothers being better accepted
Gen. 4 than he. God comes to him as if were to expostulate ye case with Cain, if
v. 16 thou dost well shalt thou not be accepted,[10] and unto thee shall be his desire, and thou shalt Rule over him, which are the very same words that

---

9. "thy desire shall be to thy Husband"—Genesis 3.16.
10. "if thou dost well"—Genesis 3.16.

God said to ye Woman, so yt I make it (at most) but a superiority of Eldership, which God seems to tell Cain was his due, if he did well. So then tho there were no Superiority in Adam before the fall by being made first, yet after ye fall because Woman first Sind she lost that perfect equality.

Therefore ye Apostle (after ye fall) argues a difference betweene man and woman from his being first made.[11]

I Cor. 11
v. 7

The Man is ye glory of God, & ye Woman ye glory of ye man, which indeed is a Syllogysticall proof yt ye woman is ye Glory of God.

> Man is the Glory of God
> The Woman of ye Man
> Ergo The Woman is ye Glory of God.//

Wee find indeed after ye fall that when the thoughts of men grew altogether evil, they found out many inventions, as to take many Wives, and to abuse them for which hardness of their hearts Moses was forced to write them bill of divorce so to part them, but our Saviour saith from the beginning it was not soe:[12] I say we do find that ye most wicked thus sind yet ye good men and their Wives ruled equally. Which is plain in ye whole Story of ye Shunamite & divers others that were holy, and Solomons Mother tells us, ye good wife considereth a feild and buyeth it etc.[13] She perceiveth that her Merchandise is good, and we read Luke 8.v.3. that ye beleeving Women (when their Husbands were alive) ministred to Christ of their substances, the holy Ghost calling it theirs as well as their husbands, nor surely would Christ have taken it, had it not been their right to have disposed of it.

Gen. 6
v. 5

Prov. 31.
v. 11

And Joanna the Wife of Chuza Herods Steward, & Susanna, and many others which minstred to him of their Substance.

v. 3

Last of all God comes to Adam, and to make his curse the Greater, curseth the ground with barrenesse, that hereby he with the harder labour should make it bear fruit or else he must have non[e.]// In the sweat of thy face shalt thou eat bread, which reacheth to all men, plainly shewing it their Duty in some calling or employment yt they ought to labour, whereby to

---

11. "the Apostle"—Paul said, "For a man indeed ought not to cover his head, for as much as he is the image and glory of God: but the woman is the glory of the man." 1 Corinthians 11.7.

12. "bill of divorce"—Mark 10.4–5.

13. "Solomons Mother"—the song of Bathsheba, Proverbs 31.1–31, which formed the conclusion of Filmer's text as well as More's.

Cor. provide for their family, and is as really their duty, as it is ye womans to bear children, he being worse than an Infidell yt provideth not for his family. He in ye Masculine Gender, which cannot include the Woman.

Well then we find after ye fall, ye works different yt God hath laid out for men & Women, neither have cause to brag, nor I am sure to oppress each other, by adding that to either which I am sure God never intended, but to help & < > ease each others burdens: Therefore are they called Yokefellows from a Yoke of Oxen drawing equally through ye cloddy troubles of this life. The man carefully providing a maintenance for his Wife & family ye best he can leaving no Lawfull way untried, and with all tender affections comfort & cherish his wife. And ye wife on ye other part with all love & affection to her husband patiently Submitt to ye decree of God in her sorrowfull childbearing, and frugally use ye estate her husband so carefully gets, they both endeavouring ye promotion of Gods Glory & their own// Salvation, forsaking all other Persons & Interests. This I conceive is their whole duty.

And here I cannot but take notice of ye Practice of men in our time, who make it their business to raise themselves by estates with Wives, which seems to cross the command and curse of God laid on fallen man: whereas if men while they are young would take half ye pains and Industry in lawfull callings as they do [to] betray women (& children sometimes) to be their Wives, they would find it thrive better then now it doth: And sure our Laws are cruel to Women in this case (as many others more than in other Countrys)[14] it being lawfull in England for a girle of 12 years of age to marry, thereby giving her husband all her estates,[15] it being often very considerable, none can beleive any one marrys that child but for her Estate, nor can any Reason be given for that Law, but to empower ye Man & enslave the Woman.

To return to our happy man & wife each doing their Duty, which is ye true honourable mariage this is ye emblem of Christ & his Church, for whome he laid down his life. Christ hath but one wife, one spouse, which leads me to take notice of Polygamy:[16]// Marriage is ye indivisible conjunc-

14. "in other Countrys"—More is presumably referring to Scottish law, unusual in permitting divorce on grounds of adultery and desertion by either party.

15. Legal age of marriage—English marriage law followed the Roman, which set the age at fourteen for males and twelve for females; this was unchanged until the Age of Marriage Act in 1929.

16. Filmer, too, in "Touching Marriag and Adultery," shared More's concern over the existence of poligamy in the Old Testament and used it in his attempt to define the nature of domestic relationships in his own age.

tion of one man & woman onely, God created one man & one woman, And we find our Saviour tells his desciples, therefore must a man cleave to his wife, & they twaine shall be one flesh, not they 3 or they 4. And in this Christ makes no new Law, but revives ye first made by God, Poligamy doubtless was a Sin in ye Patriarchs yet not a known sin, because we do not read of their particular repentance for it. The World wanted replenishing, besides their great desire yt ye Messias might descend on their Line.

Lamech[17] was ye first that so Sind, Abram ye first holy man, but sure in Abram it was Sarahs fault tho her end was good, for she knowing ye promise was made to Abram, considered not yt tho yt promise was made to Abram alone, yt he then having a wife, it could not be fulfild but by being her Sonn too, ye Command & ye promises (as I proved before) being made to one, includes both. I say Sarah knowing ye promise not ye full meaning of God in it, thought yt if <Adam> Abram had a Son it was enough, so after she had waited till she was past children herselfe she propounds her maid: but this would not do, it must be Sarah & Abrams son yt must fulfill Gods promise made to Abraham.//

Let us now look into ye New Testament and see what that declares concerning Man & their Wives. First from our Saviour who when he was asked about this matter, makes no difference in ye Power of man and wife.

And he said unto them whosoever shall put away his wife & marrieth another committeth adultery and if a Woman shall put away her husband, & be married to another she committeth adultery;[18] now Christ using ye same words in ye Womans case as in ye mans sheweth their equal power over each other, nor do we read in any of ye Evangelists (who wrote of what Christ did & said) yt ever Christ commanded a Subiection from ye wife to ye Husband, or gave power to ye Husband over ye wife, but shewed them as much love & honoured them as high as he did men, both before he was crucified, and after he was risen he first appearing to Women etc.

Mark 20: 22

And it seems to me yt women did preach ye Gospell after Christs death. Saint Paul writing to ye Corinthians saith every man prophesiing or preaching ought not to have his head covered, & every woman prophesiing should be covered. Indeed I find ye same Apostle advises women to be in the Churches.//

2 Cor: 22
Rom. 16 v. 5

17. "Lamech"—the son of Methuselah. Genesis 5.25.
18. "whosoever shall put away his wife"—Mark 10.11–12.

When he sent his Epistles to ye Romans by Phebe he calls her his Assistant.[19]

Phil. 4. Saint Paul there speaks of ye Women yt laboured with him in the Gospell,
v. 13   whose names are in ye book of [life.][20]

Acts 18 We read of Priscilla yt she taught ye eloquent Apollos, & expounded ye ways of God to him more perfectly.[21]

And Anna ye Prophetess continued in ye Temple prophesing.[22]

I confess ye Apostles in their Epistles to ye severall Churches leave not any argument untryed to perswade ye holy Women to endeavour ye promotion of ye Gospell, pressing it hard on them to submitt to their husbands, to yt end.

The Apostle in ye first of Peter cap.2. urging men to a patient bearing with, and submitting to each other, saith it was thank worthy if a man for conscience <sake> towards God endured greif, suffering wrongfully instancing in Christ who did no sin, yet when he was reviled, reviled not again, etc.[23] The Apostle goes on in ye next verse (though it be divided into another chapter so to break ye sence) saith likewise ye wives be in subjection to your own husbands, yt if any obey not ye word they also without ye word may be wonn by ye conversation of ye wife which word *Likewise* ioyns the sence.[24]

So yt I find ye Apostle seeing more Women brought over to ye faith (and I beleive are now still) perswad[es] ye women (thereby to winn their husbands) to a greater subjection to them, then I find commanded by God in ye old Testament, or by our Saviour in ye new.

And here I cannot but take notice of our Translato[rs] who are not contented with our Apostles advice to women which is hard enough on them,

19. "Phebe"—Romans 16.1–2.
20. "Women yt laboured with him"—Romans 16.3–4.
21. "Priscilla"—"And a certain Jew named Apollos, born at Alexandria, an eloquent man, and mighty in the scriptures, came to Ephesus. And he began to speak boldly in the synagogue: whom when Aquila and Priscilla had heard, they took him unto them, and expounded unto him the way of God more perfectly." Acts 18.24–26.
22. "Anna"—Luke 2.36–38.
23. 1 Peter 2.19–25—verse 20 states, "For what glory is it, if when ye be buffetted for your faults, ye shall take it patiently: but if when ye do well, and suffer for it, ye take it patiently, this is acceptable with God."
24. "wives be in subjection"—1 Peter 3–7.

and (I doubt not) was endited by ye holy Ghost, I say our Translators do render severall places falsely.[25]

The Apostle there perswading ye beleiving husband to dwell with ye un- 2 Cor.
beleiving wife,[26] saith let him not put her away. and in ye next verse 22
perswading ye beleiving wife to dwell with ye unbeleiving husband, we read it let her not leave him, when ye word is ye same in both places in ye original viz ἀφιέτω, surely ye difference of putting away or leaving is very considerable, leaving implies leaving him in possession, put away to keep possession.

The 2d Titus 5 & 1 Cor.14.v.34 there we read it obedience speaking to ye Wives,[27] which is there false rendred ye word in ye original being ὑποτάτλω not ὑπακὅω, ye first signifing submission, ye last obedience, ye word ὑποτάτλω comes from ὑπο & τατλω certo <odd> ordine// subjicio: that is to be a degree lower and cannot be rendred to be obedient to a Command. The word ὑπακὅω comes from υπο & ακὅω audio to hear, & so to do what we hear is commanded us, wch word ye holy Ghost useth where ever this obedience is required as from children to parents, Servants to master etc. but is not any where used to wives thro out ye whole bible.

Objection ὑπακὅω & ὑποτάτλω will both bare a double interpretation, to obey, or to be subject, & we find them in Greek Authors so used.

I answer yt ye Holy Ghost God himself ye first & great Author of all Languages & Tongues hath thought fit to use ye word υπακόω wherever he requires ye greater duty as in obedience to himself and his commands, and of Children to Parents, & Servants to Masters. but ye word ὑποτάτλω in scripture we find still used when ye lesser duty is required as from ye younger to ye elder etc. and tho ye word ὑποτάτλω be often used to wives in scripture yet it is but twice rendred obey 1 Cor. 14.34. 2 Tit.5 and pray observe yt in 1 Cor. where ye word ὑποτάτλω they render to obey to ye Wife, in ye verse but one before that ye same word ὑποτάτλω is rendred subject or submit speaking of ye Prophets.[28]

25. "our Translators"—the Authorized Version.

26. "the beleiving husband"—1 Corinthians 7.12–13.

27. Titus 2.5—The old women are directed to teach the young, "to be discreet, chaste, keepers at home, good, obedient to their own husbands, that the word of God be not blasphemed."

28. 1 Corinthians 14.34—"Let your women keep silent in the churches . . . they are commanded to be under obedience, as also saith the law."

1 Pet. The Apostle there incouraging Women to an humility or submissiveness
v. 3 (still aiming at what I said before to draw their husbands to an holyness
like theirs) instancing in ye holy Women of Old,[29] as he calls them and in
particular Sarah, telling them that she obeyed Abram calling him Lord,
which saying of ye Apostle is an hyperbolical expression he well knowing
yt Sarahs calling him Lord was a small sign of her obedience, Lord being
Abrams title, as Sarah was Lady or Empress, being ye true signification of
both their names, after God had equally blest them, so yt we must beleeve
the expression of Saint Peter as an earnest desiring to have good Women
do more than their duty (as is plain in ye verses before it being thank
worthy) that so they may win their husbands to ye faith, nor <he> can he
mean in instancing in Sarahs obedience further then what he speaks, for in
a serious examination of ye Story we shall find that Abram obeyed Sarah
far higher than Sarah did Abram, she said turn out ye bond woman & her
Son, and tho the thing greived Abram, yet he did it with nothing but a
bottle and a bag.//

Luke Objection, it may be objected in Luke We read ye word ὑποτάτλω is there
rendred subject, and yet spoken of Christ to his Parents, & do you not
think Christ obeyed his Parents?[30]

Answer, Yes I beleive Christ obeyed his earthly Parents, else had he not
fulfilled ye whole Law, but because Christ Submitted to his Parents,
whom he also obeyed, must I therefore argue yt a wife who must submitt
must obey, arguing from ye lesser to ye greater here is incongruous, as for
example, I am commanded to obey God, I am commanded to love God, I
am also commanded to love my neighbour, shall I therefore argue, yt
because I am to love God & to love my neighbour, yt therefore I must
obey my neighbour[?]

Just so it is in ye case of ye Wife, I am commanded to obey my Parents, I
am also to submit to my Parents & I am also to submitt to my husband
shall I therefore argue, yt because I am to submitt to my Parents & to my
Husband yt therefore I must obey my husband?

Indeed had I been commanded to obey my husband I must have submitted, ye greater would have encluded ye less, but being onely to submit ye
less cannot include ye Greater, if I can carry one hundred pound, I can
carry one, but I may carry one & not one hundred.//

29. "incouraging Women to an humility"—1 Peter 3.1.
30. "Luke"—"And he went down with them, and came to Nazareth, and was subject unto
them." Luke 2.51.

Besides ye word which we read subject in Luke, speaking of Christ is ye same in ye Originall yt is used to Wives & to Wives is twice rendred obey, as if they would adventure to stretch ye sence to Wives, which they durst not do to Christ.

Pray observe yt ye Translation of ye Bible which was made by ye Protestants in Queen Marys days was done at ye City of Geneva by ye most holy & laborious divines of England, flying to yt city for Refuge, where they were labouring more then two whole year day & night to translate ye Bible into English, & it was not finished in ye Year 1560 and afterward presented to Queen Elizabeth & was received with ye approbation of her and her people, & that translation hath been printed by her & her rightfull Sucessors above thirty times. Now this translation done thus carefully & thus approved hath not translated ye word ὑποτάτλω obedient or obey, through the whole Bible, but rendred it to wives submitt, not obey, they not finding Gods Autority for it, but our modern Writers will have ye Geneva translation read with ye Spectacles of their Marginal notes, where they make yt which they render subject, to be obedient, & this onely to wives.

I shall conclude yt is ye want of learning, & ye same education in women, yt men have, which makes them loose their right. Men always held ye Parliament & have enacted their own wills, without hearing// them speak, & then how easy is it to conclude them <gul> guilty. Were this Errour in Parents amended in their not bringing up their Daughter[s] learned, then I doubt not but they would as much excel men in that as they do now in Virtue. And of bad Women, of whom I know but few, I say *Optima Corrupta, pessima.*

FINIS

DIVINITY MORALITY
HISTORY POETRY PHYSICK
SURGERY
Sturt sc:
The Excellent Woman
Printed for Joseph Watts

Frontispiece from The Excellent Woman Described by Her True Characters and Their Opposites, *translated by Theophilus Dorrington (1692). Courtesy of The Henry E. Huntington Library and Art Gallery*

Robert Whitehall
"The Womans Right Proved False"

The Womans Right Proved False
In which the True Right is easily discerned

To ye Reader
My intention is not to tell you a long story about a cock and a bull the
Meum and Teum of husbands and Wifes, or to envite you with a fair-
promising preface to read ye ensuing lines, nor yet to half-Proselyte your
Judgements to what is written, for it may be my Reason and Pen are of far
different Opinione: but onely to read my own Doom which I know Will
be attended with a Generall Amen, and to acquaint you with ye Cause of
this work.

It being an Age wherein ye Art of Courtship is infinitely refined, & advanced to that perfection yt every Rustick Swain will presume to accost &
court a Gentlewoman wth as gracefull deportment, eloquent Rhetorick,
and fine-spun Complements as the Greatest al a mode Courtier in ye
Primitive days of single and unfeigned affection: yea it being so devoted to honouring, serving, & adoring ye female Sex that whoever ranks
them in common discourse but one degree inferior to Goddesses or at
least Angels, is ready to be dubed an impenetrable & Stupid Stoick, enrolled in ye Catalogue of Clowns, and suspected as tainted with Geneva
Austerity. The very title therefore of my Book, I am confident, therefore will Create me an army of severest Censures and an hundred thousand Anathema's with bell, book & Candle: and in ye opinion of many
merit my excommunication from ye Smiles, favour, and affection of all
Ladies & Gentlewomen, wch is a Purgatory next door to Hell it self. I
know those that are not acquainted with ye Author will unanimously vote
him an Imperious, old, Doting Fop, one that hath been plagued with a
wife he was not able to please, and therefore prompted by Revenge hath
compiled this little Treatise to enthral our most delicate Sex into foreign
servitude and bondage: but to undeceive your Judgements in this particular be pleased to know ye Author as// yet lives in Batchelours Row at the
Sign of hope in ye land of Love.[1] And now I am certain I shall conjure up
a thousand conjectures as well as Interrogatories in your minds about it:

1. "the Sign of hope in ye land of Love"—Oxford slang during the Restoration.

an the generall query will be what motive should be so powerfull as to perswade an Amorous Batchelour to plead so strenuously for what grates so harshly on feminine ears much more on their Spirits, and the readist method to provoke them to entertaine him with frowns & contempt. To satisfie any inquisitive mind & yet make them no wiser then were before: perhaps ye Author has been crost in Love and so <was> being acted by malice has dipt his pen in Wormwood and Gall. perhaps his passion has been resented with a contrary fire which has fevered his blood & brains and made him write he knows not what himself. May be he is over-whelmed in Love he dares not reveal and was minded to obviate & re-move all suspicion by palliating it with a contrary guise. may be he hath a mind to encounter against the humour of the age, to court by Ironies and discover his passion in a Masquerade. perhaps he hath an Art to rail at Women with his tongue to their faces, and in the mean time assure them with his eyes he most passionately admires them, and that all his expres-sions are to be read in a contrary Dialect and are attended with a far greater tenderness of mind than all ye formalities and flattering comple-ments of the most acomplisht Parasite or eloquent Lover. may be twas onely to gratifie my own Phancy and see what I could say. Perhaps he had a mind to play the fool with ye rest of his Neighbours and say somewhat as well as they. perhaps was purely to provoke some ingenious feminine Pen to make a reply. perhaps was to find out ye temper of a particular Gentlewoman. perhaps was all these reasons in conspiracy & perhaps none. may be some what you may think of wch ye Author never did. and so adieu my paper not permitting me to say any more.[2]//

The Womans Right Proved False
in which the True Right is easily discerned.
Madam,
    If ye entire body of your Ingenious Discourse had been drawn with as apparent and legible Features of Truth, as your Argument, my Pen had never moved but in Justification of ye *Womans Right*. I must confess ye Virtue, Prudence, Ingenuity, Sweet disposition, Meekness, Affableness etc this Constellation of Perfections, characterized with Sun-beams in some of your Sex, force me to entertain so great an Honour, Service and Re-spect for them, that sometimes I dispute sharply with my self and others, whether ye Right Hand be theirs onely by Virtue of a Modish Comple-ment or due uncontrouable Right. Tis one Article of my Belief, that many Imperious Preists and Fathers in Ancient times made the Pulpit emitt a corrupt// and passionate Sound (especially when Women were the Sub-

2. "so adieu"—the writing here becomes smaller and smaller in order to fit in at the bottom of the sheet.

jects of their discourse) where by ye gratified Ears of their Auditt have bribed their Judgments to Inconsiderate Embracing [of] Painted Errour. I scorn that Baseness of Spirit, which prompts but to the least thought of robbing a *Woman of Her Right*, that acted by a Generous Principle, I could readily grant all your Ladiships Reasons and Ingenuity plead for, add some grains of Redundance to your Treatise, and increase ye Number of your Arguments to fortifie your Assertion. But beleeving my Opinion is single (tho I never met with strong Reason to oppose it) because most preach Contrary Doctrine, I chuse rather to abett an Ancient Faith, than introduce a New Creed. Moreover, suppose your Maxime not unsound, your Topick most proper, your Arguing not Sophisticall, yet if any Brave Virago will enter ye Feild, sound a Defiance, make ye first Assult to release the Womens Right prisoned by Ancient Tradition, let Her fight every Inch of Ground// she advances and by force of Arms deliver it out of the hands of *Usurping Autority*, that so regaining by strength of Reason, they may assure ye World they know how to manage it with highest Prudence: and that if the Victory after a sharp Contest be won by their hands, they may with Greatest Triumph wear a Crown of Immortal Praise on their Heads: Or that if this New Generation can keep still in their Possession *this Patrimony*, which their Fathers took with their Sword and with their Bow, with their Craft and their Cunning, and to which they are born Heirs; yet being convinced of Injustice in detaining what was got by Subtle Usurpation, tho conveyed by unquestioned Succession, may Gallantly restore ye Daughters of Zelophehad to their rightfull Inheritance to their content, and their own Honour, that Women may be constraind to beleeve, Every Age grows more Generous as well as Wise. Again because your treatise boasts of demonstrating// a *Truth New and not commonly known*, and Novelty is commonly pregnant with Errour, none can be reputed blame-worthy for bringing it to ye Test, weighing it in ye Balance of Discretion, and propounding his Objections, that these vanishing by an ADDITIONAL LIGHT, it may shine with such Meridian Splendour, that every one that runs may read it and acknowledge it Legitimate. These and some other Incentives not here nor now to be revealed, provoke me to resist your <your exist> Charge that so famous a Conquest may not be gained by one Single Stroke of a Womans Hand: and to play ye Defendant that the Plaintiff may not carry so momentous a Cause with a *Nemine contradicente.//*

What Power Husbands practice over their Wifes I am an Utter Alien to by experience, (having never practised any over mine own) therefore can form my Conception of it onely by Reason, Observation, and Report. That some of them exceed the Bounds of their Empire is undeniable; but where their Province terminates is rightly questionable: and He must be as famous in metaphisicks as those 7000 Archers, who could direct an Arrow to a hairs bredth, were in the Art of Shooting, who can exactly determine this Controversy, and prescribe ye Limits of ye Husbands oeconomy: for such an one must be sure to remember, it is dangerous to remove ANCIENT LANDMARKS: and that when EVIL SPIRITS have once got Possession its not every EXORCIST can cast them out.

That many Women are more than ready to snatch at ye Reins of Government, and surrogate a Power allowed neither by ye Laws of God or Nature, is so certain, that to prove it would be to suspect the Sun shines at Noon day; to whome Should an Inch be// given they would presently take more than an Ell, whose Brains being intoxicated with proud desire and ambition after Rule, were they admitted to co-equal sway in a Domestick Kingdome, would presently begin to aspire at Absolute monarchy, then to challenge an equall Autority in State, to make Laws, bear Offices, vote as Members in Parliament, and afterwards presume to sit in Moses his Chair pretending they have power to TEACH as well as RULE: and then what can we expect but to see those things which our Fathers dreaded to see, but saw not: and to hear those things which they dreaded to hear but heard not: viz to see all things post to Confusion, Princes {Men, Husbands} running on foot, Servants {Women, Wives} riding on Horseback, and to hear such Doctrines as never Heretick taught and so the last Errours and Age would be infinitely worse than *all the former*.

As for that Position you lay down as a Truth that before the Fall Man and Woman had equal Power and Autority over each other and the Creatures, I shall endeavour// to refute it with that contemptible Argument the order of the Creation, and proceed afterwards in answering your Treatise as it lies in order. The Order of Creation if we respect ye various species produced out of Nothing amounts not to a valid Argument for Superiority and Excellency of one thing above another, because then Bruits themselves would, and Inanimate Creatures might contend with Man for ye Dignity of Nature, and so consequently for ye Right of Government, than which Nothing more absurd. But as it regards ye Individualls of every Kind its like a three-fold Cord not easily broken, a firm Bases on which to build the Right of Rule and Government: for doubtless those Individuals first of all formed by the Almighty and Best of beings, were ye most perfect of that Kind, and therefore fitter to exercise Autority over others, and who is so blind with Ignorance as not to know Adam was first formed than Eve.

That she was made *out of Adam*, what Reason can be imagined for it (may a License be granted to guess at ye lower ends of Divine and Unsearchable

Wisdome) but to let her understand// she was not her own, not in her own power but the Mans, under his Absolute Autority as being His Own Bone and Flesh. that she was made as you affirm of dust refined. what Account can be alledged for it but this (*viz*) that Man being Lord of the entire Creation might not look on Her as an Animall too much Inferior to himself, but might be enamoured on Her knowing she was invested with such Excellencies as rendred her worthy of his highest Esteem and most loving Embraces, which perfections she drew from Himself every Atome of whome was most precious.

You argue the equality of the Female Sex by an Induction of a Few Particular Women who arrived to no small Pitch in masculine perfections, and strengthen your Argument by Two Philosophicall Maxims (that we may know Women can Philosophise) viz What hath been done may be done. The other Subjects receptive of ye same qualities are endowed with equall perfections and powers.

To this I reply

1. The last Maxim is true of things considered as cloathed onely with the endowments and gifts of Nature provide they be susceptive of tne most essentiall and in the same degree. but of things veiwed in a// Political Sphere its most erroneous. for then every one might challenge a Right to Dominion (the essentialls of all men being alike perfect and alike receptive naturally tho not perhaps accidently) and so every one would be a titular Lord, and none a real Moderatour or Governour there being none to be ruled but Bruits Insects etc. a Tenent horridly Whiggish and pernicious to all Kind, of Government, Monarchicall, Aristocraticall, Democraticall, Domesticall, Paternall, Despoticall etc.[3]

2. *What hath been done may be done* is true but not cogent here. Supposed Chronicles furnish us with Deborah we must not presently style her VAL-IANT, and arrogate Baraks due to Her out of meer Complement, for it was Barak went down Mount Tabor and ten thousand Men after him but no mention of her descent. Judg. 4.v.14. And when She celebrates ye Triumphant Victory with an Anthem of Praise cap. 5.v.14 she is so just as to ascribe no part of ye conquest to herself, but onely rouzes herself to sing ye Valour of Barak. Awake, Awake, Deborah, awake, awake, utter a Song. Arise Barak and lead thy captivity captive. Tho Barak refused to goe, unless she would accompany him// evidences no fear or Cowardice of spirit but Prudentiall increduality of mind not too easily beleeving Her (as most do Women now a days) that he might discover by her Constancy or

3. "Whiggish"—used in the second half of the seventeenth century to indicate any rebellion against authority.

Timerousness whether she did not prompt him to destruction with *Thus saith ye Lord*. And tho Priscilla of whom you glory instructed Eloquent Apollos, yet Scripture records (tho you overlook it) Aquila was both Present, and President when he was tutor'd. So that ye genuine consequence from your Induction is this; If Women arrive to any Admirable degree in any Excellencies above ye needle, it must be with the conjunction, tuition, or conduct of a Man.

3. What tho some Women have arrived to such heights of Perfection as with Aristotle and Des Cartes to stand on the Mountains of Metaphisicks and Philosophy and veiw of ye Glories of both; with Tully and Demosthemes have charmed the Ear with their ravishing Oratory, and with Kings and Potentates have swayed ye Scepter of Government.[4] yet have any attained to ye same pitch with Men? and whence drew they these Waters? out of their own Wells? no these are to shallow, therefore Rebeckah like they bring// their Pitchers to ye Wells ye men had dug. They learnt to Philosophise, to play ye Orator, to Govern in State by veiwing, reading, and observing ye Actions, Works, and politicks of Men. and is this such an Argument to be doted on[?] Cannot any Fop or Novice, yea or Parrot either speak as they are taught? do not the most Mimicall Creatures imitate some Actions of Men and must they therefore be presently dubd their Equals and Superiors to with a MAY BE or I MIGHT SAY.

The IMPOSITION OF NAMES is an Appendix onely to Autority & Superiority. none is empowered to bestow them but by Virtue of these, as might easily be evinct by Argument without alledging as Assembly of Divines and Commentators to justifie it. And yet behold Feminine insinuation to enfringe ye strength thereof, feminine evasion to escape the dint of its force and feminine Craft to wrest Womens equality with Men from that, which most certainly proves their Subjection and Inferiority? hath any man a rightfull Liberty to impose any Name what ever on anything but by virtue of his Right to it, or dominion over it?// Hence ye Supream Lord of Heaven and Earth named man (after he had created him) with his own lips, his being under the Dominion of none but Him who is God overall: and after he had substituted Adam his Vicegerent,[5] made him Prince of ye Lower <of ye> Creation, enstamped on Him ye Marks of Royalty, placed ye Crown on his head ye Scepter in his hand, and subjected all things under his Feet Gen.1 *Then and till then* Gen.2 he presents all Creatures before Him to receive their Names from him their Lord and

4. "Aristotle and Des Cartes"—this is probably a reference to Anna Maria van Schurman who was closely associated with Descartes in her early years. More also cites her.

5. "Vicegerent"—this was most commonly used to describe rulers and magistrates as representatives of God.

Owner, to signifie his Dominion over them, their Subjection and obligation to pay ye Tribute of Hommage & Obedience to him. Hence when
God had created ye Mother of all Living he brings Her also to Adam her
Earthly Lord to pay her Subjection to him, and acknowledge his Dominion over herself, by receiving Her Name from his mouth that he might
be Supream Monarch next under Him who subjected all things and all
Women in Eve to him *viz* Man, who discerning some Rays of more than
common Excellency about her presently knew his own *Bone* and *Flesh* and
therefore called her { אישה Isha} Woman because {מאיש} of Man. No
question but Adam was a little// surprised at first with ye lustre of her
Beauty, and ye Endowments of her mind visible in ye Liveliness of her Air,
but as soon as he seriously considered this amiable Object, he found it was
but a reflexion or rather a Particle {מאיש} somewhat of Man, wch leads
me to your Refutation of your next proof, onely I must first answer that
about Eves nameing her Children argued to enervate this Reason, tho it
doth nothing less. For if we consult ye History of ye best Historians as
Well ass Meekest of men, and do but open our eyes on 4 Gen. they will
instantly be enformed it was after ye deplorable Fall of our First Parents,
ere Mankind began to multiply, ye first born where of Eve < > Called
Cain, and his younger Brother Seth, SIGNIFICANT NAMES; indeed
but signifie nothing to ye matter in hand: for she having overwhelmed all
the Sons of Adam in a Gulf of misery, it comports best with Reason,
Scripture, and ye Analogy of faith to give this ensuing Account why Eve
not Adam named these their mentioned children: viz God and Adam
permitted her this priviledge, that men in future Generations might acknowledge a filial subjection & obedience// to their Mothers, and not
(being exasperated at her folly and indiscretion in listening to the Father
of lies) renounce their duty to them, but that not withstanding She was
ye Prime Cause of their Ruine, they should continue the Reverence,
Honour, Duty, and Affection of children, and that Mothers might have a
right to and Power to maintain their maternal Autority: which Right and
Power were granted to Eve (and all Women in her) by God and Adam
which License the Imposition of Names was a Witness of, that she might
not be upbraided as a Usurpress, and a token of due Subordination,
Homage, and obedience in those that received them, so that her giving
Names argues Superiority and Autority as well as Adams, onely with this
difference, His was more extensive and absolute, Hers can be interpreted
onely of Maternall, for to introduce any other Species would be to make
the text speak in a Paraphrase words but one degree better than nonsence
or very insignificant. from hence may probably arise the Custom of
Women changing their Names, when they enter a matrimoniall state, and
receiving their Husbands, acknowledging thereby they disclaim// all Power
over themselves, freely resign themselves up to the pleasure of their Hus-

bands, to be governed by them, be at their dispose, and to conform entirely to their Wills; they having nothing now they can properly stile their own, no not so much as themselves, who are known by no other names than that of their husbands.

As for Womens inheriting Land in sacred Writt its argumentative force is very weak, it being a dispensation peculiar to ye Jewish Nation, wch as it received numerous commands oblidging none but ye 12 Tribes of Israel and their Proselites, so they were honoured with a train of eminent Priviledges which none could challenge a Right to but themselves; among the number of which This is to be enrolled: now as many of their Precepts were not extensive as the Civil Law in their obligations but concerned the Jews onely embodied into a People, this with other rituall Institutions, Ceremonies, and Canons purely Judiack is fallen asleep ever since the abolition and death of the old Mosaick Law, wherein many things may be imitated tho they bind not. now are not Women very ambitious, yea do they not mightily long after Autority, who conjure up// Aged Moses buried many Centuries ago and make him like well fee'd Baristers or rather Common Barretors stretch the sence of his own Injunctions, and deduce such conclusions from his own <Principles> statutes which ye learnedst Civilian or acutest Logician could never have imagined?[6] What Artists in Sophistry but those that are next to the Serpent in subtilty would ever have attempted to deceive men into a belief of Womens equality with themselves, because the 5 Politick or Wise Sisters in Numbers pleaded earnestly for an Inheritance and co-habitation with men and obtained it to their great Joy, and Satisfaction being married presently into ye Families of the Sons of Manasseh. And now I less wonder than ever why Women pleade so ardently for inheritances for veiwing critically ye story of Zelophehads Daughters I find they do it onely to hasten their ripeness for felicity, and necessitate themselves to do what their inclinations prompt them to, and what many of them passionately desire to do *viz* marry, for its said expressly every daughter that hath an inheritance *shall be a wife*. Moreover these Daughters of Zelophehad obtained their inheritances not for their own sakes but the mens. <an> I would not therefore be thought to plead against// their Inheritance or Portions, but onely against ye equality of Power and Autority they would extort from them.

Your next Argument is formed out of that text Gen.2.22. Thus *Eve was made of Adams Rib, not his head, nor foot, but middle, His equal and meet helper*.

6. "Barretors"—a fradulent dealer. In law, a barrater is one who incites litigation for the sake of gain.

Here I cannot but observe that Equall is Apocryphall and not Authentick, not found in ye Originall or Translation and therefor may justly be rejected as fictious. Neither can Reason conclude (tho Feminine Subtilty may) because Woman was ordained a *Meet help* therefore a *Meet Helper*. Surely Logick is too strong for Feminine brains or else they would not thus conclude with Additions and Subtractions at their pleasure, with an Inference no nearer allied to the promises than East to West or black to white: as if Help and Helper were terms synonymous when any impartiall Eye, that looks not thro a deceitfull Optick, may see a vast disparity between the one and the other: for who knows not that *Help* is far inferiour to *Helper*. She was not made of his Head, nothing more certain, and therefore nothing more// presumptive than for a Crooked Rib to pretend equality to an Intelligent Head. nor of his Foot that she might not be so low in his Esteem, nor treated with such rigour as the bruits. But of his Rib, that part of Man under his Arm, intimating as he should protect and defend her from Evil and Dangers, so He should keep her in due Obedience to him. But *Middle*, This is ushered in Hercules like for what Reason I cannot imagine unless to tell ye World Women love ye Middle of a Man with a passionate and Superlative Affection.

As for the Commandments enforced in ye Singular number (*thou*), its not argumentative of any thing, but what weakens the weaker Vessel, Man and Wife being both one flesh, and that all the Husbands to, in a more eminent way than children are their Parents: and it being the universall Suffrage of all nations the masculine Gender is more worthy than the Feminine, there was no necessity the Precept should run in the Plural it being without all Controversy ye less is included in the Greater.//

As for the Devils assulting Eve first because she had the most high and strong Soul. Had a Man reasoned on this manner he would certainly have been ranked among ye Generations of Fools. I ever imagined Women to be better Politicians than to think ye Subtlelest of Creatures would set upon ye most Sagacious and Reasonable Being to foil ye weakest and most indiscreet. Certainly ye old Deceiver was a better Master of Arts then So, better skild in Politicks than to betray so little Craft in such a Grand Plot and design. and the Confirmation is as weak as ye Position is false, for suppose (at least for disputation sake) Eve not so perspicatious and acute as Adam, certainly ye Wisest and most probably effectuall Method hath been for Satan first to allure the woman by his Wiles as being Confident Adam, tho he might have suspected ye Serpents Oratory, yet he could never have imagined Guile, deceit, and a Snare in the perswasions of his Own Bone and Flesh.//

As for our Saviour being born of a Woman, it was an unparalel Honour to our Nature that he did assure it, an unparalel Honour to ye Woman, that ye Son of God should lodge in her Womb, and be teemed out into ye World by her. but Where was ye unparalel Honour to Woman more then Man? was it in taking ye nature common to both? or in being conceived in and born of Her? if this latter (for ye former it cannot be) how could it be other wise? when its impossible for men to bring forth? Supposing then the decree and Promise of a Messiah to be born, He must be born of a Woman or both must be frustrated. Now if this hypotheticall or conditionate necessity diminishes not somewhat of ye Honour that redounds to Women <by> more then Men, but our Saviours being born of a Woman, in opposition to being born of a Man let the Women judge? Moreover its but just and rationall that she, who travailed with and brought forth our Ruine, should travel with and bring forth ye Remedy of our Salvation, ye equity of which still obscures their Glory in this behalf, not to urge that Woman being ye Mother of ye former should suppress their insulting against and over the Men because Woman was the Mother of the latter.//

That *our Saviour had no Mans Flesh but Womans* is a proof as able to confirm what its brought for as parched Flax is to resist devouring Flames. to take away that Honour Women would extort from this by considering ye Ordination of Heaven about his Extraordinary Birth, that he might be free from Originall Guilt in the utmost latitude of it, would be to wade into ye Depths of Divinity and to spend a great deal of Time, Strength, & Study in pursuing, catching, and overcoming a fly or a Moth, which who would not vote most ridiculous? I must rather urge the Superabundant Excellency of a Man, because our Saviour was a Man & not a Woman; then Women might contend for a equality with men because our Saviour was born of ye Female not ye Male Sex: I say I might rather press this especially if we consider ye Womans flesh, which our Saviours Body was made of, was first converted, rarified, and Exalted into mans flesh before it could be meet for that Famous Design for which it was assumed, and was capable of being exalted to Honour and Dignity above all the Angels in Heaven.//

Thy desire to thy Husband. Your Pen assures us from these words that Husbands since ye Fall have onely the Superiority of Eldership. Are the Men then onely fallen an not ye Women? To give this sence (viz) (a Superiority of Eldership) of ye Words would seem in a Paraphrase most ridiculous. Her desire toward her husband: this is a Curse from ye Almighty upon her, therefore to be too criticall in comparing ye Phrase wth the like expression used concerning Abel His desire shall be toward thee, would make us beleeve that Abel was curst for offering a better Sacrifice than Cain. Strange Divinity indeed! or that Infinite Wisdom spake Words without sence. q.d. Abels desire shall be towards Cain i.e. Cain shall be ye Elder Brother because he was first born, and Abel ye younger because born latter of ye two: So man should be Elder because first made, and Woman the Younger because made after him. Is ye Anathema on ye Woman so light? Let not Wives think to escape ye Curse of Heaven by evading their Alleigance to their Husbands. To inspect ye words therefore a little more narrowly. Her desire towards her Husband. if by it be meant legitimate desire, its no Curse. if exorbitant lust after him,// your exposition is nothing to ye text. if it denotes Inferiority (as you concede) either Husbands must be all Ruling (tho perhaps some of them not sufficiently gifted) Elders whose discipline is severest of all; or it must be ye Subjection of Subjects to Magistrates, especially if what God hath joyned together we do not put asunder but take in ye immediate consequent clause, and H E S H A L L R U L E O V E R T H E E. The Hebrew word { משל masha} signifies not a Superiority by way of Eldership, but by way of Proper and formal Dominion and Government strictly taken, even such as Kings exercise over their Subjects in which Sence ye word is frequently used as Dut: 15.6. there God promiseth Israel he should reign over him.[7] The same word is used by Moses in both places, translated there *Rule*, in this place *Reign* ye more proper signification of the two, so that should we be criticall to argue from the significancy of words and their use, its such a ruling a Husband should exercise over his <Subjects> Wife, as equals ye Dominion and Reign of a King over his subjects, which should it be practised here in England the Women// many of them would have their Proper Right as some have in other Climates as Spain etc. and *if* this be ye Dominion here meant (which is most probably because ye word is so often used in this sence) the Inferiority specified in ye precedent words must be correspondent and not an *idle notion of Eldership* invented by a Spirit tainted with *Independency* and affecting a Grandeur more than is allowed or becomes it. And now is the Subordination of Wives to Husbands so small and Inconsiderable? What ever perfect equality might be imagined in Paradise, since the banishment thence there is Proper Subjection and obedience due from ye Woman to ye Man.

Now to compare your Logick and ye Apostles 1 Cor. 11.v.7 you assert ye Apostles argument is a Syllogisticall proof that ye Woman is ye glory of God and you mould it after this form.

7. Deuteronomy 15.6—"Thou shalt reign over many nations, but they shall not reign over thee."

> Man is ye Glory of God
> The Woman is ye Glory of Man
> Ergo The Woman is ye Glory of God.

which is not true Syllogism but a Sophism where in are four terms.[8] the subject of the Major changing its case in the Predicate of ye Minor// and so altering ye Sense, for its one thing to be a *Man* and another thing to be *but the Glory of a Man*, and one excels ye other as much as a Prince excels his Subjects who are ye Glory of a Prince. To supersede your Syllogism and come to ye Apostles reasoning. Paul about to prove Man should pray or prophesie with his head uncovered, Woman with hers covered, proceeds on this Medium Man being ye Glory of God, women ye Glory of ye Man. now if ye Apostle proves onely that Woman is ye Glory of God, why must man Pray with his head uncovered because ye Glory of God, & Woman with her head covered because ye Glory of God. Surely a Man, a Man instructed at ye Feet of Gamaliel,[9] an Apostle, an inspired Apostle never syllogised in this manner,

> Man is ye Glory of God
> Woman is ye Glory of ye Man
> Ergo Woman is ye Glory of God.

Ergo one must pray covered ye other uncovered because both are ye Glory of God. Had ye Apostles Pen been too nimble for his dictating understanding and wrote *Man* for *God*, surely upon a reflex veiw there of he would have corrected so considerable an Errour.// Let us substitute your words in ye room of ye Apostles and take a prospect of ye Sence. Man indeed ought to cover his head for as much as he is ye Glory of God, but Woman is the Glory of God. Arguing so profoundly by Rationall that ye sence and strength of it is past finding out.

That *some had many Wives, and ye most wicked thus erred* is to plain a truth to be excepted against yet that *Good men and their Wives ruled equally* is an assertion staggering for want of proof. tho *Good men* might wink at the aspiring ambition of such Wives, yet that such Wives should remain *Good* who affected an Equality with their heads Lords and Husbands is a Paradox I cannot understand: For a Proud Imperious Spirit, where Pride is ye predominant Humour, ye very complexion as it were of ye Soul, is certainly as many miles distant from ye true denomination of *good*, as an openly Profane and Debaucht, not withstanding may that creep

8. "1 Cor. ɪɪ.v.7"—See More's exposition of this text.
9. "Gamaliel"—a Pharisee, who was a member of the Sanhedrin noted for his teaching of the law. Acts. 22.3.

into Houses, and many Silly Women their Captives are of a Different Opinion.//

That *Beleeving Women ministred to Christ of their Substance*, and because ye Holy Ghost stile it *their substances*, therefore is equall Autority between Wives and their Husbands. this is your next Argument.

But who ever seriously meditates these following particulars will be induced to give a Bill of Divorce to this Sentiment and opinion.

1. To abridge them of all Power and Autority and that over small matters is to deal too rigidly with ye Weaker vessels, and yt wch ought not to be done, least they be swallowed up with too much greif.

2. That their Power is Co-extensive with their Husbands is as false as ye other is Severe. as if subjects who are Magistrates because they have a Right by ye Laws of Nature to govern their families which are under ye Power and Dominion of ye King, and another derived Power from their Prince ye Fountain of Autority ye lower Administrations of Publick Justice, should pretend an equality in ye Throne, and plead for as firm a Title to ye Sceptor as ye Hand that holds it. What is this but to affect ye Regalia, Treason and Rebellion in ye highest degree? and what is it but a Spice of that Crime which is as the Sin// of Witchcraft, when Women because they have a Subordinate and Inferior Power over many things imagine therefore, & plead for a Co-ordinate and collaterall over all things.

3. Its clear they have some kind of Dominion over their family, Servants, Goods, etc. but its by virtue of their Husbands, as Inferior Magistrates have a derived power from the Supream, by virtue of which they consult not always with them in their acting, tho they are obliged not to counteract their Placita's and Decrees, and may be summond to an account for all their good and mal-administrations. 4. Tis as clear from what hath been already said that ye Power of a Wife is limited and circumscribed by ye Autority of ye Husband her Lord and King, so that tho she enjoys a derived and communicated Power from him (wch many times she abuseth) yet His Empire is far larger then her Providence and ever in ye Throne He is or at least should be Greater than she.

5. Therefore to infer because Women by *Custom* and *an act of Kind Indulgence* from their Husbands have Power and liberty to order household affairs, and dispose of some small matters without ye// Pre-knowledge of

their husbands, and that by Virtue of their License empowering them thus to act, I say, therefore to conclude they are as absolute as their Husbands (unless it be in ye Kitchin) at first sight differs so much from a rational conclusion, that great Violence must be offered to ye premises to make them speak in a <Great> strange Language to gratifie an itching Humour after ye Domestick Crown and Sceptor.

6. Our Saviour and ye Apostles well understood what they did when they received their Administrations, and knew that either an explicit or implicit Leave from their Husbands did legitimate their donations and communications.

7. and lastly some of them its very probable were unmarried and Widows, and then ye Prime & ultimate Right of Possession was in their own hands others its undeniable were married, but who knows whether their kind and Indulgent Husbands did not onely provide things necessary and Decent for them but allow them over and above a Competency to dipose of at their own Pleasure; I say who knows whether it was not thus, and that then they ministered to Christ and his Apostles of *this their substance* by ungainsayed tho you see Derivative Right// Now let any unbyassed Judgment speak whether there be such argumentative force in that little Pronoun *their*, provided they put not on OLD WIVES SPECTACLES which are of ye nature of Magnifing glasses to help them in discerning it. Or whether Weakest Vessels had not much better rely on their Husbands Good nature, and be content with their allotment, than to lean on so short and broken a staff for Equality.

As for Adams curse I cant apprehend how the Woman can suck so great a blessing thence. he was doomd to hard toil and labour to eat ye bread of carefulness got by ye sweat of his brows: the Woman was sentenct to Subjection to her husband, to sharp agonies in child bearing wch sorrow was alleviated by a gracious unexpected promise: will this prove a parity? what tho neither have cause to boast, *brag or oppress each other*? hath ye Woman therefore any Reason to pretend to equality.//

To infringe your Argument from that topick *Yokefellow* I have these particulars to oppose.

1. Its Metaphorical therefore feeble and infirm for if Metaphors be leaned on too much they will prove so heavy that Woe indeed will be to the female Sex, and Matrimony will be as intollerable to them as it is pleasant.

2. Its as Rustick expression and savours too much of ye Clownishness of a Plow-jogger.

3. Its of Malignant Importance, if we strain ye first part of ye word *Yoke* as you do ye latter *Fellow* and seems to intimate a Matrimonial state is a state of Bondage.

4. Its a false Reddition of ye Authentick Copy. for σύγχ signifies onely *one joyned or coupled with an other*, not a *Yoke Fellow* especially if by fellow be meant *Equal* for many things may be coupled together which are neither *fellows* much less *Equalls*. and why then should it import an Equall in this Place? what reason can be produced but feminine Will? It must be so because they will have it so.

   Sic Volo, sic Jubeo, stat pro Ratione Voluntas[10]
As you cannot but take notice of ye practice of men in our times, *who make it their business to raise themselves by estates with Wifes.* so I cannot pass by your// observation without some small advertency. I cannot but commend those that seek to advance themselves by this method: for seeing you except ye Woman from work, and affirm ye Man onely was doomd to service and sweat, She onely to pleasure and to bring forth ye fruit thereof with a little Sorrow; and seeing ye Apostle expressly saith (and I know you will interpret it onely of Men) if any would not work neither should he eat: moreover because you press men with such zeal and Importunity to industry and diligence in their respective Callings: is it equitable ye Woman should eat, drink, and devour ye fruit of ye husbands pains, and bring nothing with her for a Compensation? must ye Man love her, cherish her, defend her, maintain her (and that Gentilely to or all the fat is in ye fire) work for her, sweat for her and all for her Person without a Portion? For a Man to make a Smithfield Bargain,[11] and aim principally at Riches argues gross avarice and meaness of soul, so to be regardless of her fortune while he dotes on her Beauty and endowments evidences puerile fondness not rational and Heroick affection, and may cause ye Woman justly to suspect ye weakness of such an ones Intellectuals: yea I could argue and I think prove to, it reflects an high affront, and pours// great contempt on ye Person courted and seemingly adored. I will be more Loyall than to repine at any Laws of Autority, and I should wonder you murmur (did not I know you are a Woman) at that Law that makes it Lawfull (to use your own words) *for a girl of 12 years old to marry*, when I

10. "Sic Volo"—"Hoc volo, sic iuebo, sit pro ratione voluntas," "Thus I will, thus I order, my will stands in place of my reason." Juvenal, *Satire* 6, "The Ways of Women."
11. "Smithfield Bargain"—a marriage made for financial reasons, so-called because of the Smithfield cattle market.

dare be confident there is not one Woman in a thousand but highly applaud and approve of that decree of the higher Powers, and would miserably repine at ye repeal of so gratefull an Act. Yea I beleeve should a Parliament of Women be assembled they would be so far from nullifing it, that in ye first place they would call for the Statute Book, and for *twelve* write down *Seven* or *eight*.

Your next Plea for equal Autority is grounded on Mark 10 where our Saviour speaking of Divorce saith, if a Man *putteth away* his Wife etc, and if a Woman *putteth away* her husband etc where because our Saviour useth ye same word you argue ye Same Autority belongs to both.

Here I might quarrel with ye Translators as you do else where. To *put away* seems to argue Autority but ye original word υπολύση ye word of our Saviour// doth not it signifie no more than to loose from: so that ye sense is if a man shall loose his wife from her conjugall obligations. i.e. signifie to her he will no longer discharge ye office of a Husband to her, and expects no more ye obedience or Submission of a Wife from her; or if a Woman shall loose her Husband from his conjugall obligations i.e. signifie to Him, She will no longer yeild ye obedience of a Wife to Him, & expects not he should perform ye office of a Husband to Her, then, He or She that thus looses ye other if they were married to another committed adultery. and what doth this amount to? will you say because a Master may signifie to his Servant he shall no longer be his servant, and ye Servant again may signifie to his Master he shall no longer be his Master, I say will you therefore affirm they are equall? further Consider this was a dispensation granted to ye Israelites onely, and that both to Israelitish Husbands and Wives not to equall them or empower them alike, but for the mutuall quiet of their lives onely, as is apparent by our Saviour v.5. where saith he for ye hardness of your heart, he {viz Moses} wrote// unto ye {viz ye Jews so called} this precept. The Jews were a kind of a Morose and churlish people (I speak in respect of both Sexes of them) very rebellious and frequently murmuring against Heaven and therefore probably not very obliging and courteous towards one another; so that for ye *hardness* of their *hearts* viz their cruel savage and morose dispositions, prone heinously to resent small offences, and very averse to forgett ye least injuries till Revenge was gratified; now that they might not embitter one anothers lives by this hardness of their hearts but might live comfortably, it was permitted them in some cases to loose ye bonds of Wedlock by which they were bound, and to oblige themselves with new ones, that their lives might not be filled with bitterness and vexation. And will you argue a Generall Equality of Husbands & Wives[,] Men and Women from an equal Indulgence granted to a particular People?

To proceed if *Christ himself did not command Wives to be subject to their Husbands*, yet if he Autorised his Apostles to do it, it binds with equal force and Autority.//

You say *it seems to you that Women did preach the Gospell after Christs death*. Did not I <find> tell you you would pretent to *teach* as well as to *rule*: must we have now a new Generation (I had almost said of Vipors) of *Gifted Brethren*. To defend which you might have alledged 1. Tim. c.2. v.10.11 Let ye Woman learn with *All Subjection*. But I suffer not a *Woman to teach* or usurp *Autority* over the man. or as it may be read to usurp ye *Autority of the man*. I say you might have as well produced this for a proof as made our Sister Phoebe Mount ye Pulpit and turn Evengelist; for you presently instance in Phoebe as an Assistant to Paul, whereas had you been Criticall here as about *obey*, you would never have put our Sister Phoebe thus to ye blush, Rom.16.v.1.2. I commend etc. and that in whatsoever business she hath need of you, for she hath been (not an Assistant, But) a προστάτις i.e. one that courteously received & entertained many Christians and myself also. In ye next place you acquaint us Paul speaks of *Women that laboured with him in the Gospell*. Phil. 4.3. You are for criticizing, and how much advantage do the Women gain by a narrow inspection into mens words? once more let// us see what a tribe of goodly She-Preachers we have crouded into one verse, for it runs in ye Plurall number Women. I entreat thee also true Yokefellow *help those Women which laboured with me in the Gospell*, συνήθλησάν μοι quae mihi colluctatae sunt, which strove together against me in ye Gospell (like those Women that did persecute Paul and Barnabas),[12] that did resist his preaching at first, but at last being converted Paul exhorts his Yokefellow to help them i.e. to strengthen, confirm, and comfort them; or else to succour and releive them: or to help them to receive and entertain Christians as Phoebe did. Let not ye Novelty of the interpretation offend, since you are of Athenian blood, principles, and practice delighted in hearing and spreading Tenents *New and not commonly Known*. Concerning Priscilla enough hath been said before. Your next Instance is Anna a Prophetess, who you say continued in ye Temple *prophesiing*. True the Scripture stiles her Prophetess, probably ye Surviving Wife of some deceased Prophet for she was a <Husband> Widdow, but my bible mentions nothing of Prophesiing, unless you will call fasting and praying so, for thus runs the entire story in my Book Luke 2. Your quoted place// and there was one Anna a Prophetess ye daughter of Phanuel of ye tribe of Aser, she was of great Age, and lived with an Husband 7 years from her Virginity, and she was a Widow of about 84

---

12. "Women that did persecute Paul and Barnabas"—the Jews incited "the devout and honourable women" of Antioch to rise up against the missionaries. Acts 13.50.

years, which departed not from ye Temple but served God with fasting and prayers night and day, and she coming at that instant gave thanks likewise unto ye Lord, and spake of him to all that looked for Redemption in Israel. where is Prophesiing now? is fasting and praying so? is serving God day and night prophesiing? is giving thanks prophesiing? is speaking of one prophesiing? then prophesiing as yet is not ceast, but there are troops of Prophetesses that are even an anon tatling of one <an> or other.

< > Your *Likewise* is like old wifes reasoning, as near to ye matter in hand as Heaven is to ye Center of ye Earth. Certainly women understand Conjunction better than division, and are more expert at ye former than the latter: for if the Analysis of Peters Epistle be drawn according to your method it will be drawn far otherwise then it should.

Your division of the 2d & 3d cap. at first blush demonstrates it was done by one that is accustomed to divide onely with a pair of scissors it being so undeniably plain, that the Apostle preaching to every one their duty exhorteth Subjects cap.2. from v. 12 to ye 18. quietly to obey their Magistrates: Then Servants to obey their Masters and that with the most powerfull Argument imaginable drawn from ye meek cariage of our Saviour Lord of Heaven & Earth; and this from v. 18 inclusively to ye end of the 2d cap. in ye beginning of ye 3d (for ye division need not be blamed) he commences a fresh subject whering it in with a Likewise viz as Subjects should Submitt to their Governours, and as servants should submitt to their Masters, so (hard words, I know you will say, and who can bear them) women should Likewise submitt to their own husbands viz yeild the same submission which is strict and formall obedience, as shall be shewed by and by, it being ye same word used concerning them all.

I cannot wonder what strange Doctrine ye Pulpits would bring forth had women power to teach, and what government there would be had they Power to rule in the Church: what wresting of scripture? what perverting of texts, what subverting of Reason & Faith,// what Anathema's, what censures, what excommunications would there be? seeing not onely ye Translators are censured by you, but ye Apostle to as an Egyptian Taskmaster imposing too heavy a burthen on your tender shoulders. for you say you cannot but take notice *our translators are not contented with the Apostles advise to Women, which is hard enough on them.* o peevish and perverse Generation!

As for ye word ἀφιέτω I will not justifie ye translation of it with two severall words that seem to import two different significations, the most

proper is, let him leave her, and let her leave him; concerning which
enough was said about the word ἀπολύσῃ rendred put away, to cut off all
hopes of Womens mounting to an Equality by putting away their Husbands.//

As I draw nearer the Conclusion I encounter with a (seeming) greater
force, a formidable Criticism that threatens Death and Destruction, that is
flourisht out two entire Pages, and renders all Objections speechless. But
they were accounted never Politick Exorcists who would conjure up a
Devil < > they could not lay: Therefore I highly commend you for
urging your objections no farther then you were able to Answer them.
What! could you Imagine men would be baffled with such Sophistry! no,
tho they cannot find out all the Cunning of Women, yet some they can
and subvert it to, which shall be done in these brief particulars.

1. I grant ὑπακούω comes from a word that signifies to hear, and so
denotes Obedience viz that is rational and comes by hearing, obedience
that is wrought by perswasion as when one man reasons another into ye
performance of a duty from the equity of necessity, conguity, Advantage
of it etc.

2. ὑποτάττω is a Compound and signifies certo ordine subjicio, which
whether you will permitt me to render obedience I matter not, this is ye
English of it, to subject or to bring things under// to their due order and
place. Logomachy belongs not to men but women. therefore call it submission or Subjection or what else you please, it denotes that those persons are or should be this Subject or Submissive are prone to be excen-
tricall and irregular, to run out of their place and way, therefore they
should ὑποτάονται be kept in subjection or order, be made not υπακοειν
to obey by perswasion (that you say ye word doth not signifie) but be
reduct by force (for there is no medium between these two) into their
proper place & order.

3. You affirm ὑπακούω is never spoken of ye Woman. What is ye Consequence then? they are not bound to obey? and pay that subjection which
is due from the less to the greater? no but rather this they were either so
senseless or stupid, that they could not hear or comprehend Reason, and
be perswaded to their duty by it, or so <selfish and w> self-wild and
perverse they would not, (either part of which dilemma is at their service)
which ye Apostles knowing always (according to your affirmation) use
ὑποτάττω when they frame any discourse either to them or of them from
hence.//

4. tis clear seeing ye word ὑποταττω and none else is used of them that they are most propense to be irregular and run out of their way and place, therefore it behoveth their husbands ὑποταττειν to keep them in subjection their due order & place: which how it can be done without force and compulsion seeing they know not or will not υπακοειν υπακοειν obey i.e. hearken to reason, let any evidence, et erit mihi magnus Apollo. Now let the Women boast at their pleasure that they are not ὑπακοειν to obey, but ὑποταυδαι to be subject to or in submission to their Husbands.

5. You affirm ye word ὑπακούω is always used whenever the greater duty is required viz Obedience, wch is from the less to the greater, and υποτατλω where the lesser duty viz. Submission is exacted which is the duty of the Younger to the Elder. Are Wives then obliged to submitt no more to their husbands than younger Brethern to the Elder, or younger Sisters to their Elder Sisters? surely those that plead for such *liberty of conscience* must needs be *great dissenters* from the truth. could you imagine none but your self had a Greek Testament? or that no eyes but your// own could read in it? Let any one turn to Pet.1. etc they will quickly be informed of the truth of your positive Assertion. the Apostle pressing Inferiours to their Respective duties saith cap.2.v.12. speaking to subject.[13] Submitted yourselves to every ordinance of ye Lords sake. ye originall word is ὑποταγητε v.18 exhorting servants to their duty saith ὑποτασσόμενοι be ye subject to your Masters. Now is it not proper and strict obedience not barely submission that is required from servants to their Masters and Subjects to their Magistrates? the affirmative is clear from your own words because required from ye less <from> to ye Greater. read on then v.1. cap. 3d Likewise ye Wives ὑποτασσόμενοι be ye in subjection to your own husbands. to omitt laying any force on the word *Likewise*, which might be thus urged *As* subjects should submitt to their Magistrates and servants to their Masters, *So* viz with the same Submission should Wives submitt or be subject to their husbands, wch submission would they be content to yeild, we would take away ye Scandalous word *obey*, and substitute *submitt*: giving them leave to call it by what name they will, so they do but perform ye thing.// I say omitting arguing from ye Particle, ye very word requires ye same kind of subjection an equall submission, it being your own way of Reasoning to infer an equality from ye same words. hence then Its a necessary and undeniable Consequence if Women must yeild subjection to their Husbands that Subjects do to their Magistrates, and Servants to their Masters, then the Husband is bound in duty to Exercise a corespondent Power, I mean such

13. "cap.2.v.12"—"Submit yourselves to every ordinance of man for the Lord's sake: whether it be to the King, as supreme; Or unto governors, as unto them that are sent by him for the punishment of evildoers, and for the praise of them that do well." 1 Peter 2.12–13.

Autority as Magistrates exercise over their Subjects and Masters over their Servants; which to tell in plain English would be to endanger my Eyes. now I beleeve you have criticized to purpose and would willingly barter ὑποκοειν to obey for ὑποτα < > to submitt.

Your last argument is wrapt up in a Latin dress as if you were either ashamed or afraid to present it in an English garb. *Corrupta optima, pessima* which nothing else but to tell the Women they *were the Best* because they *are now the Worst* optima consoltio! an excellent cordiall! the question is not what they were but what they are. the Devils themselves were once good. if they are// the worse as you tacitly concede, ye best because ye best are fitter to rule, tho the worst because ye worst are never the fitter to submitt. surely ye worst which is ye superlative in the lower degree can never pretend to equality with ye best <in> ye <highest de> superlative in ye highest degree, unless it be in this, as the best is certainly the best, so the worst is certainly ye worst. Token concedo.

To conclude for Wives to aspire after and plead for equall Autority with their Husbands is none of the best prudence, nor none of the most plausible medium to obtain it: rather let them learn to be meek, humble, loving, affable, Courteous, not to aspire after Principality, Power, and Dominion, but to win the affection of their Husbands, which is easily engrossed by an oblidging carriage and unfeigned kindness (unless their Fate <to> be to be wedded to churlish Nabals) and when once they have made themselves Empresses of their Husbands hearts, they may easily obtain what power, they can in reason desire, and may command as they please. so that by rendring to their husbands what is// their Husbands, they may gain as great an Ascendant over their Husbands themselves, and as ample and free dominion over all that is his, as they can in conscience desire. Thus both husband and wife, Man and Woman will have their *due right*, which is infinitely better then for one onely to have theirs.

FINIS

Notes

Abbreviations Used in Manuscript Citations

BOD   Bodleian Library, Oxford
BL   British Library, London
CAMB Cambridge University Library, Cambridge
CH   Henry E. Huntington Library, San Marino, California
DWL   Dr. Williams's Library, London
KCA   Kent County Archives, Maidstone
Laslett Private collection, Mr. Peter Laslett, Trinity College, Cambridge
RS   Royal Society Library, London

Introduction

1. Quoted in Acworth, *The New Matriarchy*, p. 128.
2. Fetterly, *The Resisting Reader*, p. viii.
3. Culler, *On Deconstruction*, p. 46.
4. Malekin, *Liberty and Love*, p. 140.
5. Locke, *Two Treatises of Government*, p. 140.
6. Higgins, "The Reactions of Women, with Special Reference to Women Petitioners," p. 178.
7. Nussbaum, *The Brink of All We Hate*, p. 12.
8. Wood, "The 'Female Eunuch,'" p. 44.
9. Higgins, "The Reactions of Women, with Special Reference to Women Petitioners," p. 222.
10. Morgan, *The Female Wits*, p. ix.
11. Gagen, *The New Woman*, p. 17.
12. Thompson, *Women in Stuart England and America*, p. 5.
13. Fraser, *The Weaker Vessel*, p. 464.
14. Bernikow, *The World Split Open*, p. 6.
15. Rogers, *Before Their Time*, p. vii.
16. Gilbert and Gubar, *The Norton Anthology of Literature by Women*, pp. 50–56.
17. Goulianos, *By a Woman Writt*, pp. xvii–xviii.
18. Showalter, "Feminist Criticism in the Wilderness," p. 186.
19. Engels, *The Origin of the Family, Private Property and the State*, p. 137.
20. Ibid., p. 141.
21. Showalter, "Feminist Criticism in the Wilderness," p. 183.
22. Kolodny, "Dancing Through the Minefield," pp. 1–2.

23. Showalter, "Feminist Criticism in the Wilderness," p. 180; Showalter, *A Literature of Their Own*, p. 11.

24. Kolodny, "Dancing Through the Minefield," p. 8.

Chapter One

1. Fraser, *The Weaker Vessel*, p. 121.

2. Nussbaum, *The Brink of All We Hate*, p. 9.

3. Brink, *Female Scholars*, p. 424.

4. See de Bruyn, "The Ideal Lady and the Rise of Feminism in Seventeenth-century England," p.23.

5. Fraser, *The Weaker Vessel*, p. 333.

6. Gardiner, *English Girlhood at School*, pp. 231–32.

7. Makin, *An Essay to Revive the Antient Education of Gentlewomen*, p. 4.

8. Fraser, *The Weaker Vessel*, p. 137.

9. Gardiner, *English Girlhood at School*, p. 209.

10. North, *The Lives of the Norths*, 1: 110.

11. Gardiner, *English Girlhood at School*, pp. 223–34.

12. Camm, "The Memoir of Anne Camm," p. 473.

13. Mollineux, *Fruits of Retirement*, Sig. A4r.

14. Quoted in Green, *Sarah, Duchess of Marlborough*, p. 23.

15. Fraser, *The Weaker Vessel*, p. 134.

16. Bell, "Medieval Women Book Owners: Arbiters of Lay Piety and Ambassadors of Culture," p. 767.

17. Brink, *Female Scholars*, p. 420.

18. Gardiner, *English Girlhood at School*, pp. 238–39.

19. Evelyn, *Diary*, 2: 36.

20. BL, Kings MSS 12.iii. and iv.

21. North, *Lives of the Norths*, 1: 46.

22. Ibid., 1: 7.

23. Gardiner, *English Girlhood at School*, p. 235.

24. Thoresby, *Ducatus Leodiensis*, pp. 499–500.

25. Cary, *The Returnes of Spiritual Comfort*, p. 148.

26. Ibid., p. 158.

27. Goodwin, *A Fair Prospect . . . Preached at the Funeral Sermon of the Honourable Lady Judith Barrington*, p. 63.

28. North, *Lives of the Norths*, 1: 18.

29. Ibid., 3: 29.

30. *Correspondence of the Family of Hatton 1601–1704*, 2: 237.

31. Smyth, *The Lives of the Berkeleys*, 2: 437–38.

32. Jackson, *The Life of Mrs. Elizabeth Rowe*, pp. 191–92.

33. Gifford, *Martha Lady Gifford: Her Life and Correspondence*, p. 213.

34. CH, EL 6495.

35. See Thompson, *Women in Stuart England and America*, chap. 2.

36. Elliott, "Single Women in the London Marriage Market," p. 90.

37. Ibid., p. 91; see also Kassmaul, *Servants in Husbandry in Early Modern England*, pp. 74–75.

38. Laslett, *The World We Have Lost*, p. 104.

39. Carlton, *The Court of Orphans*, p. 66.

40. KCA, Filmer MSS U120 T170, U120 T200/14.

41. North, *Lives of the Norths*, 1: 102.

42. BOD, Rawl. D. 398, f. 252v.

43. See Souden, "Migrants and the Population Structure" and "Pre-Industrial English Local Migration Fields."

44. Elliott, "Single Women in the London Marriage Market," p. 89.

45. *Barrington Family Letters, 1628–1632*, pp. 18–19.

46. Cavendish, *Natures Pictures Drawn by Fancies Pencil*, p. 374.

47. Dusinberre, *Shakespeare and the Nature of Women*, pp. 7–8.

48. *The Private Correspondence of Jane Lady Cornwallis 1613–1644*, pp. 213–14.

49. Ibid., p. 227.

50. Locke, *Correspondence*, 4: 658–59.

51. Ibid., pp. 341–42.

52. BOD, Tanner 22, f. 35v.

53. Randall, *Gentle Flame*, p. 48.

54. Russell, *Some Account*, pp. 213–14.

55. Ibid., p. 175n.

56. CH, HA 4834.

57. CH, HA 4840.

58. CH, HA 2333.

59. Smyth, *The Lives of the Berkeleys*, 2: 428.

60. CH, HA 4928.

61. North, *The Lives of the Norths*, 1: 104.

62. Russell, *Some Account*, p. 19.

63. Ibid., p. 217.

64. Russell, *Letters*, p. 329.

65. Russell, *Some Account*, pp. 82–83.

66. Russell, *Letters*, pp. 547–48.

67. Russell, *Some Account*, p. 116.

68. Laslett, *The World We Have Lost*, pp. 83–84.

69. Stone, *The Family, Sex and Marriage in England 1500–1800*, pp. 184–85.

70. BOD, Rawl. D. 78, f. 162.

71. See Craster, "Notes from a Delaval 'Diary,'" pp. 149–53, for further information about the family connections mentioned in the diary.

72. CH, HA 2516.

73. Laslett, *The World We Have Lost*, p. 101.

74. North, *A Forest of Varieties*, p. 45.
75. Quoted in Randall, *Gentle Flame*, p. 47.
76. *Barrington Family Letters, 1628–1632*, p. vii.
77. Weber, *Lucius Cary, Second Viscount Falkland*, pp. 24–25.
78. Clifford, *Diary*, pp. 24–25.
79. Lindsay, *A Memoir of Lady Anna Mackenzie, Countess of Balcarres*, pp. 11–12.
80. Burnet, *History of My Own Times* 3: 480.
81. Ibid., p. 492.
82. BOD, Rawl. D. 851, v. 95.
83. *Barrington Family Letters, 1628–1632*, p. 103.

Chapter Two

1. Smith, "Feminism and the Methodology of Women's History," p. 377.
2. Hull, *Chaste, Silent & Obedient*, p. 140.
3. Gibson, *A Womans Woorth*, p. 69.
4. Rich, *The Excellency of Good Women*, p. 2.
5. Newstead, *An Apology for Women*, p. 23. In her study of chapbooks, Margaret Spufford finds that 7 percent of the Pepys's collection was on the subject of courtship. The content of these books suggests strongly that "the concept of romantic love as a basis for marriage was very much present in seventeenth-century humble society." Spufford believes that the stress on sexual escapades found in many chapbooks is more likely to reflect the demographic situation, with its unusually high proportion of bachelors seeking compensation, rather than Roger Thompson's theory that it is "an anxious re-assertion of male dominance." Spufford, *Small Books and Pleasant Histories*, p. 157; Thompson, "Popular Reading and Humour in Restoration England," p. 667.
6. Hannay, *The Happy Husband*, p. 679.
7. Du Bosc, *The Compleat Woman*, Sig. B4r.
8. See Latt's "Praising Virtuous Ladies."
9. Saltonstall, "The Country Dame" in *Picturae Locquentes*, Sig. F11r.
10. Saltonstall, "The Fine Dame," Sig. F8r.
11. "The Properties of a Good Wife," BOD, Ash. 781, f. 157.
12. Heale, *An Apologie for Women*, p. 12.
13. Clifford, *A Sermon Preached at the Funeral of the Right Honorable Anne Countess of Pembroke, Dorset, and Montgomery*, p. 12.
14. Lewalski, "Milton on Women—Yet Once More," p. 7.
15. Brinsley, *A Looking-Glasse for Good Women*, pp. 38–39.
16. The indispensable nature of a wife's work in the family govenment is also suggested by the alacrity with which widowers remarried, particularly noticeable before 1650. Whether for financial or sexual reasons, wives seem to have been preferred to servants even when there were no small children in need of a mother.

The practice of the widowers of Colyton (see Wrigley and Schofield, *The Population History of England*), almost half of whom remarried within six months of the former wives' deaths, suggests that Filmer was not unique in believing that "the laboure of a mistress is more worth then yt of a servante because it is the more cheerfulness, not yssueinge from feare; but from love of vertue, the family, and the master."

17. CH, HM 116, f. 51.

18. Niccholes, *A Discourse of Marriage and Wiving*, p. 7.

19. Ibid., p. 5.

20. Wing, *The Crown Conjugall Or The Spouse Royall*, pp. 127–28.

21. CH, HM 116, ff. 43–44.

22. Overbury, *His Wife*, Sig. G5r. The affection Stuart readers had for Overbury's characters is reflected in the imitations of *His Wife* by Brathwaite, Hannay, and Sir John Davies among others, and the practice of using this character as the base for new collections.

23. Hannay, *The Happy Husband*, p. 690.

24. Shirley, *The Illustrious History of Women*, p. 155.

25. Heale, *An Apologie for Women*, p. 19.

26. Overbury, *His Wife*, Sig. G5r.

27. Powell, *A Very Good Wife*, p. 6.

28. Shirley, *The Illustrious History of Women*, p. 155.

29. For an account of Elizabethan writers' fascination with the Amazons, see Wright's "Amazons in Elizabethan Literature," pp. 433–56, and Shepherd's *Amazons and Warrior Women*.

30. Heywood, *Exemplary Lives and Memorable Acts*, Epistle Dedicatory.

31. Gerbier, *Elogium Heroinum*, Epistle Dedicatory.

32. Ibid., p. 41.

33. Ibid., p. 45.

34. LeMoyne, *The Gallery of Heroick Women*, p. 7.

35. Ibid., p. 74.

36. Shirley, *The Illustrious History of Women*, Sig. A2r.

37. Ibid., p. 123.

38. Rich, *The Excellency of Good Women*, p. 1.

39. CH, HM 116, f. 54.

40. Pyrrye, *The Praise and Dispraise of Women*, p. 5.

41. In her study of Elizabethan pamphlet literature, Sandra Clark notes, "If we did not know, for instance, that Alexander Niccholes' *A Discourse of Marriage and Wiving* derived its cynical attitude from a long tradition of anti-feminist satire and its structure from a medieval parody of a religious poem on the sorrows of the Virgin Mary, we might think Niccholes both more misogynistic as a man and more original as a writer than he deserves." *The Elizabethan Pamphleteers*, p. 38.

42. Stone, *The Family, Sex and Marriage in England 1500–1800*, p. 197; Gagen, *The New Woman*, p. 18.

43. Swetnam, *The Arraignment of Lewd, Idle, Froward, and Unconstant Women*, p. 16.

44. Ibid., p. 50.

45. Ibid., p. 6.

46. CH, HM 198, Part II, ff. 82b, 83b.

47. Tattlewell and Hit-Him-Home, *The Womens Sharpe Revenge*, p. 24.

48. CH, HM 116, f. 29.

49. Nussbaum, *The Brink of All We Hate*, pp. 26–35.

50. BL, Harl. 3918.

51. See Nussbaum, *The Brink of All We Hate*, chap. 2.

52. Taylor, *A Iuniper Tree Lecture*, pp. 28–29.

53. Tattlewell and Hit-Him-Home, *The Womens Sharpe Revenge*, p. 4.

54. Clapam, *A Treatise of the Nobilitie and Excellencye of Woman Kynde*, Sig. A4r.

55. Pyrrye, *The Praise and Dispraise of Women*, p. 14.

56. Care, *The Female Secretary*, p. 32.

57. Ibid., p. 39.

58. Anger, *Jane Anger her Protection for Women*, p. 1.

59. Tattlewell and Hit-Him-Home, *The Womens Sharpe Revenge*, p. 27.

60. Ibid., pp. 28–29.

61. For a discussion of Restoration satires that made actresses their targets and the counterattacks, see Nussbaum, *The Brink of All We Hate*, chaps. 2 and 4.

62. Tattlewell and Hit-Him-Home, *The Womens Sharpe Revenge*, pp. 37–38.

63. Newstead, *An Apology for Women*, p. 35.

64. Tattlewell and Hit-Him-Home, *The Womens Sharpe Revenge*, pp. 41–42.

65. Ibid., p. 42.

66. Du Bosc, *The Compleat Woman*, pp. 55–56.

67. Dorrington, *The Excellent Woman*, p. iv.

68. I.G., *An Apologie for Womenkinde*, Sig. A4r.

69. Davies, "Continuity and Change in Literary Advice on Marriage," pp. 58–80.

70. Dod, *A Plaine and Familiar Exposition of the Ten Commandments*, pp. 208–9.

71. Brathwaite, *The Good Wife*, Sig. B3r.

72. Brinsley, *A Looking-Glasse for Good Women*, p. 39.

73. Ibid.

74. Hindley, *The Roxburghe Ballads*, 1: 128.

75. Dod and Cleavor, *A Godly Forme of Household Government*, Sig. O6v.

76. Ibid., Sig. O7r–v.

77. Brathwaite, *Ar't Asleepe Husband*, pp. 3–4.

78. Gibson, *A Womans Woorth*, p. 61.

79. Rich, *The Excellency of Good Women*, p. 1.

80. Austin, *Haec Homo*, p. 12.

81. Milton, *Paradise Lost*, 11. 632–35, *Complete Poems*, p. 447.

82. I.G., *An Apologie for Womankinde*, Sig. B3v.

83. Brathwaite, *Ar't Asleepe Husband*, p. 5.
84. Heale, *An Apologie for Women*, p. 63.
85. Tattlewell and Hit-Him-Home, *The Womens Sharpe Revenge*, p. 77.
86. Care, *Female Pre-eminence*, p. 1.
87. Ibid., pp. 76, 77.
88. Ibid., p. 77.
89. Gerbier, *Elogium Heroinum*, p. 138.
90. BOD, Rawl. D. 1125.
91. Tuvill, *Assylum Veneris*, p. 96.
92. Ibid., p. 97.
93. I.G., *An Apologie for Womankinde*, Sig. B3v.
94. Ibid., Sig. B3v, B4r.
95. Wing, *The Crown Conjugall Or The Spouse Royall*, p. 128.
96. Ibid., p. 133.
97. Shirley, *The Illustrious History of Women*, Sig. A2r.
98. Ibid., p. 127.
99. Ibid., p. 128.
100. Dorrington, *The Excellent Woman*, p. 182.
101. E.F., *The Emblem of a Virtuous Woman*, p. 30.
102. Heale, *An Apologie for Women*, p. 49.
103. Milton, *Paradise Lost*, 5. 793–94, *Complete Poems*, p. 321.
104. Heale, *An Apologie for Women*, pp. 31–32.
105. Dod and Cleavor, *A Godly Forme of Household Government*, Sig. O2r.

Chapter Three

1. Sullivan, "Female Writing Beside the Rhetorical Tradition," pp. 143–60.
2. Goreau, *Reconstructing Aphra*, p. 149.
3. Ibid., pp. 153–54.
4. Bernikow, *The World Split Open*, p. 20. Fraser expresses a similar view, declaring that seventeenth-century women writers, "far from stepping forward in challenge, were inclined to retreat still further within the veilings of conventional female modesty, as though hoping to atone for the sheer flagrancy of their endeavours." *The Weaker Vessel*, pp. 335–36.
5. Nussbaum, *The Brink of All We Hate*, pp. 19–20.
6. Patricia Crawford has published a provisional checklist based on the Wing Short Title Catalogue with her essay "Women's Published Writings 1600–1700." A larger-scale project begun by David Latt is in progress at the Huntington Library to catalogue publications from 1500 to 1800. Neither of these projects includes manuscript pieces or correspondence in their assessments.
7. Vieth, *Attribution in Restoration Poetry*, p. 19.
8. BOD, North c.10, 17; Randall, *Gentle Flame*, pp. 100–101.

9. CAMB, Add. 32, iv. Part of Carrie's prophecy is also copied in the Somer's family commonplace book, CAMB D.d.14.25. (3).

10. BL, Stowe 940, title page.

11. BOD, Rawl. poet. 154, f. 50r.

12. BOD, Don.e.17, ff. 12–35v.

13. BL, Harl. 2311.

14. BOD, Rawl. D. 1308, ff. 1–221.

15. BOD, Rawl. 16.

16. CH, EL 8374 (35/c/16).

17. Gifford, *Martha Lady Gifford: Her Life and Correspondence*, p. 219.

18. BL, Add. 19,333.

19. BL, Harl. 3184.

20. DWL, Walton 186.18. (1).

21. BOD, Rawl. D. 1262; the drafts are found in Rawl. D. 1263 and Rawl. D. 1338.

22. More, *The Writings of Dame Gertrude More*, p. 23.

23. Ibid., p. 61.

24. Mollineux, *Fruits of Retirement*, Sig. A7v.

25. Monck, *Marinda*, Epistle Dedicatory.

26. Killigrew, *Poems*, p. 82.

27. Killigrew describes the transmission sequence of her manuscripts in this poem: "I writ, and the Judicious prais'd my Pen," and encouraged by this, she "to Fame I did commit, / (By some few hands) my most unlucky Wit." She attributes the attempted pirating of her poems to jealousy, noting that "Orinda" had gained great glory through her poetry, "Nor did her Sex at all obstruct her Fame" which has made others desire the same. "Upon the saying that my Verses were made by Another," *Poems*, pp. 44–47.

28. Jackson, *The Life of Mrs. Elizabeth Rowe*, p. 196.

29. Ibid., p. 241.

30. Ibid., p. 229.

31. BOD, Don.d.58, f. 21v; BOD, Rawl. poet. 160, f. 26.

32. BOD, Mus.b.I., f. 66; BOD, Rawl. poet. 153, f. 26v.

33. BOD, Rawl. poet. 84, f. 36; BOD, Rawl. D. 260, f. 35; see also BL, Add. 18220.

34. BOD, Rawl. poet. 84, ff. 2–4.

35. Ibid., 214, ff. 85–86.

36. Ibid., 173, f. 2v.

37. Ibid., 172, f. 110.

38. Ibid., 84, ff. 2–4.

39. *Tixall Poetry*.

40. *Tixall Letters*, 2: 133.

41. Ibid., 2: 132–33.

42. Quoted in LaBelle, "A True Love's Knot," p. 17.

43. CH, HM 904, 152–54.

44. Ibid., 158–60.

45. BOD, Eng.misc.e.4, f. 49.

46. Hickes, *A Second Collection of Controversial Letters*, p. ix.

47. Ibid.

48. BOD, Ballard 43, f. 147v.

49. BOD, Eng.lett.c.28, f. 78.

50. BOD, Rawl. D. 198, ff. 91–99.

51. Cockburn, *Works*, 1: xliv.

52. Astell and Norris, *Letters Concerning the Love of God*, p. 3.

53. Ibid., p. 52.

54. Ibid., pp. 52–53.

55. Ward, *The Life of . . . Dr. Henry More*, pp. 192–209; see also Finch, *Conway Letters*.

56. Locke, *Correspondence*, vol. 2.

57. Hickes, *A Second Collection of Controversial Letters*, p. x.

58. Ibid., p. xi.

59. Hopton, *A Collection of Meditations and Devotions*, preface.

60. BOD, Bod.154 and BOD, Ms.e.mus.169.

61. A complete account of the controversy is found in Ballard's *Memoirs of Several Ladies*, p. 326; see also Pakington's entry in Reynolds's *The Learned Lady*, p. 27.

62. BOD, Ballard 43, f. 85r.

63. CH, HA 9465.

64. CH, RB 102354.

65. Locke, *Correspondence*, 3: 430–31.

66. Russell, *Letters*, p. 308.

67. DWL, Baxter, letters.4, 121.

68. DWL, Baxter, letters.2, 216.

69. Ibid., 215.

70. DWL, Stillingfleet letterbook, 201.38, f. 5.

71. Ibid., f. 6.

72. Van Schurman, *Opuscula*, pp. 164–65, 195.

73. "Pylades to Corinna" in *Whartoniana*, 2: appendix, p. 30.

74. *Whartoniana*, 2: 108.

75. Locke, *Correspondence*, 7: 638–39, 650–51, 702.

76. Smith, *Mary Astell*, pp. 10–11.

77. Bury, *An Account of the Life and Death of Mrs. Elizabeth Bury*, Sig. R3v.

78. See Ballard, *Memoirs of Several Ladies*, p. 298, and *Whartoniana*.

79. Crawford, "Women's Published Writings 1600–1700," appendix I.

80. Ibid., p. 211; see Gilbert and Gubar's introduction for Chudleigh for an example of this problem, *The Norton Anthology of Literature by Women*, p. 95.

81. Gosse, *Catherine Trotter*, p. 27.

82. Woolley, *The Gentlewoman's Companion*, p. 10.

83. Leigh, *The Mother's Blessing*, pp. 3–4.

84. Quoted in Gifford, *Martha Lady Gifford: Her Life and Correspondence*, p. 41; Goreau, *Reconstructing Aphra*, p. 310n.

85. Souers, *The Matchless Orinda*, p. 168.

86. Ibid., pp. 168–76.

87. Philips, *Letters from Orinda to Poliarchus*, p. 95.

88. Quoted in Gifford, *Martha Lady Gifford: Her Life and Correspondence*, p. 41.

89. Woolley, *The Gentlewoman's Companion*, p. 10.

90. Bathurst, *Truth's Vindication*, Sig. A2.

91. James, *Mrs. James Vindication of the Church of England*, title page.

92. Jackson, *The Life of Mrs. Elizabeth Rowe*, p. 195.

93. Chudleigh, *Essays Upon Several Subjects*, Sig. A5v.

94. Thomas, "Women and the Civil War Sects," p. 339.

95. Flowres, *Severall Queries Concerning the Church of Jesus Christ upon Earth*, Sig. A2r.

96. Reyner, *Orders from the Lord of Hostes for Regulating the Hostes of the Lord*, Sig. A2r.

97. T.M., *A Box of Spikenard Newly Broken*, Sig. A2r–v.

98. Ferrars, *The Worth of Women*, Sig A3v.

99. Brookes, *The Unseasonable Riches of Christ*, Epistle Dedicatory.

100. BL, Add. 29, 300, f. 40.

101. Leigh, *The Mother's Blessing*, Sig. A5r.

102. BL, Add. 19, 333, f. 2v.

103. Crawford, "Women's Published Writings 1600–1700," Table 7.3.

104. Higgins, "The Reactions of Women, with Special Reference to Women Petitioners," p. 214.

105. *A True Copy of the Petition of the Gentlewomen and Tradesmens Wives*, p. 269.

106. Quoted in McArthur, "Women Petitioners and the Long Parliament," p. 708.

107. Quoted in Higgins, "The Reactions of Women, with Special Reference to Women Petitioners," p. 202.

108. Ibid., p. 204.

109. Forster, *These Several Papers Was Sent to the Parliament*, "To the Reader."

110. Ibid., p. 53.

111. Russell, *Some Account*, p. 208.

112. Shaw, *A Plaine Relation of my Sufferings*, Sig. A2r–v.

113. Hindle, *A Bibliography of . . . Lady Eleanor Douglas*; Spencer, "The History of an Unfortunate Lady," pp. 43–59.

114. Hindle, *A Bibliography of . . . Lady Eleanor Douglas*, p. 98.

115. BOD, Rawl. D. 833, f. 82.

116. Ibid., 832, f. 47.

117. DWL, Walton 186.48.(1), f. 1v.

118. BOD, Rawl. D. 833, f. 56.

119. Crawford, "Women's Published Writings 1600–1700," Table 7.3; see also Brailsford, *Quaker Women 1650–1690*, p. 287.

120. Brailsford, *Quaker Women 1650–1690*, pp. 48–50; see also Ross, *Margaret Fell, Mother of Quakerism.*

121. James, *Mrs. James Vindication of the Church of England*, title page.

122. Locke, *Correspondence*, 7: 650–51.

123. Ibid., 7: 730–31.

124. Cockburn, *Works*, 1: xxxv–vi.

125. Fage, *Fames Roule*, "Certain Rules for the True Discovery of Perfect Anagrams."

126. Mary Oxlie, "To William Drummond of Hawthornden," in Drummond, *Poems.*

127. Philips, *Advice to His Grace.*

128. Palomo, "A Woman Writer and the Scholars: A Review of Mary Manley's Reputation," pp. 34–46; see also Richetti, *Popular Fiction Before Richardson.*

129. See Morgan, *The Female Wits.*

130. Boothby, *Marcelia*, "Prologue," Sig. A3v.

131. Ibid., "Epilogue."

132. See Shepherd, *Amazons and Warrior Women*, p. 204.

133. Fige, *The Female Advocate*, p. 24.

134. Crawford, "Women's Published Writings 1600–1700," p. 214; Showalter, "Feminist Criticism in the Wilderness."

Chapter Four

1. Upham, "English *Femmes Savantes* at the End of the Seventeenth Century," p. 262.

2. "Directions for Damosels" in *Roxburghe Ballads*, 4: 72.

3. *Roxburghe Ballads*, 7: 147.

4. "A Good Husband, " CH, HM 93, f. 24.

5. *Roxburghe Ballads*, 7: 148.

6. BOD, Rawl. D. 398, f. 252v.

7. *Roxburghe Ballads*, 7: 148.

8. Leigh, *The Mother's Blessing*, p. 54.

9. CH, HM 116, ff. 55–56.

10. *Tixall Poetry*, p. 86.

11. Quoted in *Biographium Faemineum: The Female Worthies*, 2: 135.

12. Bradstreet, "A Letter to My Husband, Absent Upon Public Employment," in *A Woman's Inner World*, p. 25.

13. Finch, *The Poems of Anne Countess of Winchilsea*, pp. 19–20.

14. Lady Katherine Dyer, "Sir William Dyer, Knight," in Broadbent, *Poets of the Seventeenth Century*, 2: 341–42.

15. BOD, Rawl. D. 682, f. 10.

16. BL, Add. 4457, f. 61.

17. Halkett, *The Memoirs of Anne, Lady Halkett and Ann, Lady Fanshawe*, p. 103.

18. Behn, "Love Arm'd," in *Poems Upon Several Occasions* in *The Works of Aphra Behn*, 6: 163–64.

19. Quoted in Frank, *Hobbled Pegasus*, p. 400.

20. *Roxburghe Ballads*, 4: 77.

21. BOD, Firth, c.15, f. 335.

22. Barker, *Poetical Recreations*, p. 102.

23. *Roxburghe Ballads*, 4: 77.

24. Barker, *Poetical Recreations*, p. 103.

25. Chudleigh, *Poems*, p. 40.

26. BOD, Firth, c.15, f. 336.

27. [Philips], *Female Poems on Several Occasions*, p. 98.

28. Douglas, *The Star to the Wise*, p. 12. For a discussion of such sentiments in the context of radical sects, see Thomas, "Women and the Civil War Sects."

29. Fell, *Womens Speaking Justified*, p. 13.

30. Ibid., p. 17.

31. Ibid., p. 13.

32. Bathurst, *The Sayings of Women*, p. 23.

33. Blackborow, *The Just and Equall Ballance Discovered*, p. 14.

34. Pope, *A Treatise of Magistracy*, Sig. C2r.

35. James, *Mrs. James Vindication of the Church of England*, p. 3.

36. Ginnor, *The Womans Almanack*, Sig. A2r.

37. Cavendish, *Sociable Letters*, pp. 14–15.

38. Fraser, *The Weaker Vessel*, pp. 30–31.

39. Cary, *The Returnes of Spiritual Comfort*, p. 158.

40. Ibid., p. 191.

41. Van Schurman, *The Learned Maid*, pp. 27–28.

42. Makin, *An Essay to Revive the Antient Education of Gentlewomen*, p. 4.

43. For further analysis of Makin's strategy, see Paula L. Barbour's introduction to Makin's text in the Augustan Reprint Society edition no. 202 (1980); Barbour sees Makin as "the most sincere, imaginative, and systematic proponent for the education of women in the late seventeenth century" (p. x).

44. Drake, *An Essay in Defence of the Female Sex*, p. 21.

45. Astell, *A Serious Proposal to the Ladies*, p. 20.

46. Kinnaird, "Mary Astell: Inspired by Ideas," p. 37.

47. Astell, *A Serious Proposal to the Ladies*, p. 109.

48. Ibid., p. 19.

49. Perry, "The Veil of Chastity: Mary Astell's Feminism," p. 38.

50. Crawford, "Women's Published Writings 1600–1700," p. 220.

51. Chudleigh, *Essays Upon Several Subjects*, Sig. A4r.

52. BL, Add. 4457, ff. 163–64.
53. [Philips], *Female Poems On Several Occasions*, pp. 72–73.
54. CH, HM 904, f. 158.
55. Ibid, ff. 159–60.
56. *Tixall Letters*, 2: 108.
57. Ibid., p. 122.
58. Ibid., p. 109.
59. Saintsbury, *Minor Poets of the Caroline Period*, 1: 552.
60. Ibid., "To Mrs. M.A. at Parting," 1: 550.
61. Philips, *Familiar Letters*, pp. 57–58.
62. Saintsbury, *Minor Poets of the Caroline Period*, 1: 550.
63. Mollineux, *Fruits of Retirement*, p. 161.
64. CH, HM 183.
65. Killigrew, *Poems*, p. 55.
66. Chudleigh, *Poems*, p. 35.
67. CH, EL 35/B/62.

Chapter Five

1. Stone, *The Family, Sex and Marriage in England 1500–1800*, p. 152; Malekin, *Liberty and Love*, chap. 4.
2. Laslett, "Sir Robert Filmer," p. 526.
3. Laslett's article remains the best biographical source on Filmer. See also Laslett's article "The Gentry of Kent in 1640," pp. 148–64.
4. Filmer, *Patriarcha*, p.21. For further discussion of Filmer's political ideas in their historical context, see also Laslett, "The Gentry of Kent in 1640," pp. 160–61; Schochet, *Patriarchalism and Political Thought*; and Daly, *Sir Robert Filmer and English Political Thought*.
5. Schochet, "Sir Robert Filmer: Some New Bibliographical Discoveries," pp. 135–60.
6. Ibid., p. 151.
7. Ibid., p. 147.
8. Laslett, "Sir Robert Filmer," p. 537.
9. Ford, "The Filmer Manuscripts: A Handlist," pp. 814–25.
10. Filmer, "In Praise of the Vertuous Wife," Laslett MSS 13, 3v.
11. Filmer, "Theology or Divinity," Laslett MSS 4, chap. 14.
12. Heale, *An Apologie for Women*.
13. Filmer, "Theology or Divinity," chap. 13.
14. Filmer, "Touching Marriag and Adultery," BL, Harl. 6866, ff. 514r–522r (515r).
15. Foster, *London Marriage Licenses 1521–1869*, p. 484.

16. See entries under "Filmer" in Burke, *Memorials of St. Margaret's Church, Westminster*.

17. See the letter from Thomas King, York Herald, to Sir Edmund Filmer concerning the Filmer genealogy. KCA, Filmer MSS U120, F7.

18. Ibid., U120, T171.

19. Ibid., T200.

20. Ibid., T200/14.

21. Ibid., T200.

22. Walne, "Henry Filmer of Mulbery Island, Gentleman," p. 423.

23. Oyler, "East Sutton Church," lvi.

24. KCA, Filmer MSS U120, C4/1–5.

25. Ibid., C12/2.

26. Ibid., C12/4.

27. Ibid., C12/3.

28. Ibid., C12/2.

29. Ibid., C12/6.

30. Ibid., C12/4.

31. See the title page to Heale's *An Apologie for Women*.

32. Thompson, *Women in Stuart England and America*, p. 13.

33. Walpole, *Anecdotes of Painting in England*, 3: 135–36.

34. Clayton, *English Female Artists*, 1: 38–39. The same information can be found in Ellet, *Women Artists in All Ages and Countries*, p. 100, and Greer, *The Obstacle Race*, pp. 70, 257.

35. Foster, *London Marriage Licenses 1521–1869*, p. 1065.

36. Ezell, "Richard Waller, S.R.S.," pp. 215–17.

37. RS, MS W.3.70; *Le Neve's Pedigrees of Knights*, p. 262; RS, MS D.1.55.

38. Stephens, *John Aubrey on Education*, p. 27.

39. The will of Richard Waller, P.C.C. 11, 546, fagg 104 (May 1715), Public Record House.

40. Ezell, "Richard Waller, S.R.S.," p. 217.

41. Ibid, p. 216.

42. Richard Waller to Sir Hans Sloane, RS, W.3.70, and BL, Sloane 4036, f. 194.

43. William Derham to Richard Waller, RS, D.1.60.

44. Evelyn, *Diary*, 5: 176.

45. Thoresby, *The Diary of Ralph Thoresby*, 1: 8.

46. Greer, *The Obstacle Race*, p. 70.

47. BL, Add. 27347.

48. Whitehall appears fleetingly in several biographies of Rochester, including Pinto, *Enthusiast in Wit*, and Williams, *Rochester*, p. 26.

49. Whitehall, *To the No Less Virtuous Than Ingenious Mris Mary More*.

50. BOD, Rawl. D. 912, f. 197.

51. "A Reproof to R.W. ffor his late addresse to Mrs. Mary More," Univ. of Nottingham, Portland MS PwV, 504.

52. Ibid.

53. Wood, *Athenaes Oxonienses*, 4: 176–78 (p. 177).

54. Whitehall, "A Poem to Rochester, 1666/7" in Needham, *A Collection of Poems by Several Hands*, pp. 44–45.

55. Birch, *Anna Maria van Schurman*, pp. 83–84, 101.

Bibliography

Manuscript Collections

Bodleian Library, Oxford
British Library, London
Cambridge University Library, Cambridge
Dr. Williams's Library, London
Friends' Library, London
Guildhall Library, London
Huntington Library, San Marino, California
Kent County Archives, Maidstone, Kent
Mr. Peter Laslett, Trinity College, Cambridge
University of Nottingham, Nottingham
Royal Society of London

Printed Materials

PRIMARY SOURCES

Unless otherwise indicated, London is the place of publication.

A., I. *The Good Woman's Champion: Or, A Defense for the Weaker Vessell.* 1650.
An Address of Thanks on Behalf of the Church of England to Mris. James for Her Worthy Vindication of that Church. 1687.
Alexander, Helen. "A Short Account of the Lord's Dealing with Helen Alexander." In *A Voice from the Desert*, ed. Robert Simpson. Edinburgh: 1861.
Ames, Richard. *The Folly of Love.* 1691.
The Anatomy of a Woman's Tongue. In *The Harleian Miscellany.* 4 (1809): 267–85.
Anderdon, Mary. *A Word to the World.* 1662.
Anger, Jane. *Jane Anger her Protection for Women To Defend Them Against the Scandalous Reportes of a Late Surfeiting Louer.* 1589.
Astell, Mary, and John Norris. *Letters Concerning the Love of God.* 1695.
————. *A Serious Proposal to the Ladies for the Advancement of their True and Greatest Interest.* 2d ed. 1695.
————. *Some Reflections Upon Marriage, Occasion'd by the Duke and Dutchess of Mazarine's Case.* 1700.
Austin, William. *Haec Homo, Wherein the Excellency of the Creation of Woman is Described.* 1637.

Avery, Elizabeth. *Scripture Prophecies Opened . . . In Several Letters Written to Christian Friends.* 1647.

Baker, Augustine. *The Inner Life of Dame Gertrude More.* Ed. Dom Benedict Weld-Blundell. R. T. Washbourne, 1937.

Ballard, George, ed. *Memoirs of Several Ladies of Great Britain, who have been Celebrated for their Writings or Skill in the Learned Languages, Art, and Sciences.* Oxford: 1752.

Barker, Jane. *Poetical Recreations.* 1688.

Barrington Family Letters, 1628–1632. Ed. Arthur Searle. Camden Society, 4th series, 28 (1983).

Bathurst, Elizabeth. *The Sayings of Women.* 1683.

―――. *Truth's Vindication, Or a Gentle Stroke to Wipe Off the Foul Aspersions, False Accusations and Misrepresentations, Cast upon the People of God, Called Quakers.* 1679.

Behn, Aphra. *Miscellany, Being a Collection of Poems by Several Hands.* 1685.

―――. *The Novels of Mrs. Aphra Behn.* Routledge, 1905.

―――. *The Works of Aphra Behn.* Ed. Montagu Summers. 6 vols. William Heinemann, 1915.

Bercher, William. *The Nobility of Women.* 1559.

Biographium Faemineum: The Female Worthies: Or, Memoirs of the Most Illustrious Ladies. 2 vols. 1766.

Blackborow, Sarah. *The Just and Equall Ballance Discovered.* 1660.

―――. *A Word Unto You Rulers, Justice of Peace, Constables, and other Officers.* 1659.

Blundell, William. *Cavalier: Letters of William Blundell to his Friends, 1620–1698.* Ed. Margaret Blundell. New York: Longmans, 1933.

Boothby, Frances. *Marcelia: Or the Treacherous Friend.* 1670.

Bradstreet, Anne. *A Woman's Inner World: Selected Poetry and Prose of Anne Bradstreet.* Ed. Adelaide P. Amore. Washington, D.C.: University Press of America, 1982.

Braithwaite, Elizabeth. *A Brief Relation of the Life and Death of Elizabeth Braithwaite.* 1684.

Brathwaite, Richard. *Ar't Asleepe Husband: A Boulster Lecture.* 1640.

―――. *The English Gentlewoman.* 1631.

―――. *The Good Wife, Or a Rare One Amongst Women.* 1618.

Brinsley, John. *A Looking-Glasse for Good Women.* 1645.

Broadbent, John, ed. *Poets of the Seventeenth Century.* 2 vols. New York: New American Library, 1974.

Brookes, Thomas. *The Unseasonable Riches of Christ.* 1655.

Burnet, Elizabeth. *A Method of Devotion.* 1709.

Burnet, Gilbert. *History of My Own Time.* Ed. H. C. Foxcroft. 3 vols. Oxford: Clarendon Press, 1897–1902.

Burnet, Margaret. *Letters From Lady Margaret Burnet to John, Duke of Lauderdale.* Edinburgh: 1828.

Bury, Elizabeth. *An Account of the Life and Death of Mrs. Elizabeth Bury . . . together with her Funeral Sermon.* Ed. Samuel Bury. 1720.

Camm, Anne. "The Memoir of Anne Camm." In *The Friends' Library,* ed. William and Thomas Evans. Philadelphia: 1837, 1: 473–79.

Capella, G. F. *Della Eccellenza et Dignita delle Donne.* 1524.

Care, Henry, trans. *Female Pre-eminence: Or the Dignity and Excellency of that Sex, about the Male.* 1670.

———. *The Female Secretary.* 1671.

Cary, Elizabeth, Viscountess of Falkland. *The Tragedie of Mariam, The Faire Queen of Jewry.* 1613.

Cary, Lettice, Viscountess of Falkland. *The Returnes of Spiritual Comfort and Grief in a Devout Soul.* 1648.

Cavendish, Margaret, Duchess of Newcastle. *Letters and Poems in Honour of the Incomparable Princess, Margaret Duchess of Newcastle.* Savoy: 1676.

———. *The Life of the Duke of Newcastle and Other Writings.* J. M. Dent & Sons, n.d.

———. *Natures Pictures Drawn by Fancies Pencil.* 1656.

———. *Plays.* 1662.

———. *Sociable Letters.* 1664.

Cellier, Elizabeth. "A Scheme for the Foundation of a Royall Hospital." In *The Harleian Miscellany* 9 (1810): 191–98.

———. *Malice Defeated.* 1680.

Chamberlayne, Edward. *An Academy or Colledge: Wherein Young Ladies and Gentlewomen may . . . be duly Instructed.* 1671.

Chudleigh, Lady Mary. *Essays Upon Several Subjects in Prose and Verse.* 1710.

———. *The Ladies Defence: Or, The Bride-Woman's Counsellor Answer'd.* 1701.

———. *Poems.* 1700.

———. *Poems on Several Occasions.* 1703.

Clapam, David, trans. *A Treatise of the Nobilitie and Excellencye of Woman Kynde.* 1534.

Clifford, Lady Anne, Countess of Pembroke. *Diary.* Intro. V. Sackville-West. William Heinemann, 1923.

———. *A Sermon Preached at the Funeral of the Right Honourable Anne Countess of Pembroke, Dorset, and Montgomery.* 1677.

Cockburn, Catherine. *The Works of . . . with an Account of the Life of the Author.* Ed. Thomas Birch. 2 vols. 1751.

A Collection of Poems by Several Hands. 1693.

Collings, John. *Par Nobiles Two Treatises, the One Concerning The Excellent Woman . . . With the Narratives of the Holy Lives and Deaths of those two noble Sisters.* 1669.

Collins, Anne. *Divine Songs and Meditations*. Augustan Reprint Society 94 (1961).

Colville of Culross, Lady Elizabeth. *A Godlie Dream*. Edinburgh: 1606.

Correspondence of the Family of Hatton 1601–1704. 2 vols. Ed. Edward Maunde Thompson. Camden Society, new series 22 (1878).

D'Anvers, Alicia. *Academia: Or, The Humours of the University of Oxford in Burlesque Verse*. 1691.

———. *The Oxford Act: A Poem*. 1693.

———. *A Poem on His Sacred Majesty, his Voyage for Holland*. 1690.

Darcie, Abraham. *The Honour of Ladies: Or, A True Description of their Noble Perfections*. 1622.

A Discourse of Women, Shewing their Imperfections Alphabetically. 2d ed. 1673.

Dod, John. *A Plaine and Familiar Exposition of the Ten Commandments*. 18th ed. 1632.

Dod, John, and Robert Cleavor, eds. *A Godly Forme of Household Government*. 1630.

Domenichi, L. *La Nobilta delle Donne*. 1549.

Dorrington, Theophilus, trans. *The Excellent Woman Described by Her True Characters and their Opposites*. 1692, 1695.

Douglas, Anne, Countess of Morton. *The Countess of Morton's Daily Exercises: Or, A Book of Prayers and Rules*. 1666.

Douglas, Lady Eleanor. *The Star to the Wise*. 1643.

———. *Strange and Wonderful Prophecies*. 1649.

———. *The Word of God*. 1644.

Drake, Judith. *An Essay in Defence of the Female Sex*. 1696.

Drummond, William. *Poems*. 1656.

Du Bosc, Jacques. *The Compleat Woman*. Trans. N.N. 1639.

Dunton, John. *Lady Lettice Vi-Countess Falkland*. Ed. M. F. Howard. John Murray, 1908.

Engels, Frederick. *The Origin of the Family, Private Property and the State*. 1942. New York: International Publishers, 1972.

Eugenia. *The Female Preacher*. 1699.

Evelyn, John. *Diary*. Ed. E. S. de Beer. 6 vols. Oxford: Clarendon Press, 1955.

———. *The Life of Mrs. Godolphin*. Ed. Harriet Sampson. Oxford Univ. Press, 1939.

———. *Numismata: A Discourse of Medals, Antient and Modern*. 1697.

———. *Tyrannus or the Mode*. 1661.

Evelyn, Mary. *Mundus Muliebris: Or, the Ladies Dressing Room Unlock'd and her Toilette Spread in Burlesque*. 1690.

Examen Miscellaneum. 1702.

F., E. *The Emblem of a Virtuous Woman*. 1650.

Fage, Mary. *Fames Roule: Or, The Names of our Dread Soveraigne . . . Anagrammatiz'd and Expressed by Acrosticke Lines on their Names*. 1637.

Fell, Margaret. *A Brief Collection of Remarkable Passages and Occurrences Relating* to the Birth, Education, Life, Conversion, Travels, Services, and Deep Sufferings. 1710.

―――. Womens Speaking Justified. Augustan Reprint Society 194 (1979).

Female Excellence: Or, Woman Display'd in Several Satyrick Poems. 1679.

Ferrers, Richard. The Worth of Women. 1622.

Fields, Nathaniel. Amends for Ladies. 1618.

Fige, Sarah. The Female Advocate. Augustan Reprint Society 180 (1976).

Filmer, Sir Robert. An Advertisement to Jury-men of England Touching Witches. 1653.

―――. Patriarcha and Other Political Writings. Ed. Peter Laslett. Blackwell, 1949.

Finch, Anne, Viscountess Conway. Conway Letters: The Correspondence of Anne, Viscountess Conway, Henry More, and their Friends 1642–1684. Ed. Marjorie Hope Nicolson. Oxford Univ. Press, 1930.

Finch, Anne, Countess of Winchilsea. The Poems of Anne Countess of Winchilsea. Ed. Myra Reynolds. Chicago: Univ. of Chicago Press, 1903.

Fleetwood, Edward, trans. The Glory of Women: Or, A Treatise Declaring the Excellency and Preheminence of Women Above Men. 1651.

Flowres, John. Severall Queries Concerning the Church of Jesus Christ upon Earth, Briefly Explained and Resolved. 1658.

Forster, Mary. These Several Papers Was Sent to the Parliament. 1659.

G., I. An Apologie for Womenkinde. 1605.

Gamon, Hanniball. The Praise of a Godly Woman. 1627.

Gataker, Thomas. A Good Wife Gods Gift and A Wife Indeed: Two Marriage Sermons. 1623.

Gerbier, Charles. Elogium Heroinum: Or, The Praise of Worthy Women. 1651.

Gethin, Lady Grace. Misery's Virtues Whet-stone: Reliquiae Gethinianae. 1699.

Gibson, Anthony. A Womans Woorth, Defended Against All the Men in the World. 1599.

Gifford, Lady Martha. Martha Lady Gifford: Her Life and Correspondence (1664– 1722). Ed. Julia G. Longe. George Allen & Sons, 1911.

Ginnor, Sarah. The Womans Almanack. 1659.

Goodwin, Thomas. A Fair Prospect . . . Preached at the Funeral of the Honourable Lady Judith Barrington. 1658.

Gould, Robert. Love Given O're. Augustan Reprint Society 180 (1976).

Grey, Elizabeth, Countess of Kent. A Choice Manuall, or Rare and Select Secrets in Physick and Chyrugery. 2d ed. 1653.

Grimston, Elizabeth. Miscelanea, Meditations. Memoratives. 1604.

H., M. The Vision of the Lord of Hosts. 1662.

Halkett, Lady Anne. Instructions for Youth. Edinburgh: 1701.

―――. The Memoirs of Anne, Lady Halkett and Ann, Lady Fanshawe. Ed. John Loftis. Oxford: Clarendon Press, 1979.

Hannay, Patrick. The Nightingale, Sheretine, and Mariana . . . The Happy Husband. 1622. In Saintsbury, ed., 1: 614–726.

Heale, William. *An Apologie for Women.* Oxford: 1609.

Heywood, Thomas. *The Exemplary Lives and Memorable Acts of Nine of the Most Worthy Women in the World.* 1640.

———. *The Generall Historie of Women.* 1657.

———. Γυναικειον: *Or, Nine Books of Various History Concerning Women.* 1624.

Hickes, George. *A Second Collection of Controversial Letters Relating to the Church of England and the Church of Rome, As They Passed Between an Honourable Lady, and Dr. George Hickes. To which is Added a Letter Written by a Gentlewoman of Quality to a Romish Priest.* 1710.

Hindley, Charles, ed. *The Roxburghe Ballads.* 2 vols. 1873–74.

Hooke, Robert. *The Diary of . . . 1672–1680.* Ed. Henry W. Robinson and Walter Adams. Taylor and Francis, 1935.

Hopton, Susanna. *A Collection of Meditations and Devotions.* 1717.

———. *Devotions in the Antient Way of Offices.* 1700.

Hoskens, Jane. "The Life of Jane Hoskens." In *The Friends' Library*, ed. William and Thomas Evans. Philadelphia: 1837, 1: 460–73.

Hume, Anna. *The Triumph of Love: Chastitie: Death: Translated out of Petrarch.* Edinburgh, 1644.

Hutchinson, Lucy. *Memoirs of the Life of Colonel Hutchinson.* Oxford Univ. Press, 1973.

Jackson, Thomas, ed. *The Life of Mrs. Elizabeth Rowe.* Library of Christian Biography 10 (1839): 185–275.

James, Elinor. *Advise to the Citizens of London.* 1688.

———. *The Case Between a Father and his Children.* 1682.

———. *Letter to the King.* 1685.

———. *Mrs. James Advice to the Citizens of London.* 1688.

———. *Mrs. James Vindication of the Church of England.* 1687.

———. *Speech to the Honourable Convention.* 1688.

Jevon, Rachel. *Carmen Θριαμβευτικον: Regiae Majestati Caroli II.* 1660.

———. *Exultationis Carmen: To the Kings Most Excellent Majesty Upon His Most Desired Return.* 1660.

Jocelin, Elizabeth. *The Mother's Legacie to her Unborne Childe.* 1625.

Killigrew, Anne. *Poems.* 1686.

The Lawes Resolutions of Women's Rights: Or, The Lawes Provision for Women. 1632.

Leigh, Dorothy. *The Mother's Blessing: Or, The Godly Counsell of a Gentlewoman, not long since deceased left behind for her Children.* 1636.

LeMoyne, Peter. *The Gallery of Heroick Women.* Trans. Marquise of Winchester. 1652.

Lindsay, Alexander. *A Memoir of Lady Anna Mackenzie, Countess of Balcarres and Afterwards of Argyall 1621–1706.* Edinburgh: 1868.

Livingston, Eleanor, Countess of Linlithgow. *The Confession and Conversion of the Right Honourable, Most Illustrious. . . .* Edinburgh: 1629.

Locke, John. *Correspondence*. Ed. E. S. de Beer. 8 vols. Oxford: Clarendon Press, 1982.

——. *Two Treatises of Government*. Ed. Peter Laslett. 2d ed. Cambridge: Cambridge Univ. Press, 1976.

M., T. *A Box of Spikenard Newly Broken*. 1622.

Makin, Bathsua. *An Essay to Revive the Antient Education of Gentlewomen*. 1673. Augustan Reprint Society 202 (1980).

Markham, Gervase. *The English House-Wife, Containing the Inward and Outward Vertues which ought to be in a Compleat Woman*. 9th ed. 1683.

Milton, John. *Complete Poems and Major Prose*. Ed. Merritt Y. Hughes. Indianapolis: Odyssey Press, 1957.

Mollineux, Mary. *Fruits of Retirement: Or, Miscellaneous Poems, Moral and Divine*. 1702.

Monardes, Nicolas. *Joyful Newes Out of the Newe Founde Worlde*. 1577.

Monck, Mary. *Marinda. Poems and Translations Upon Several Occasions*. 1716.

Montague, Walter, trans. *The Accomplished Woman*. 1656.

More, Edward. *The Defence of Women*. 1560.

More, Dame Gertrude. *The Writings of. . . .* Ed. Dom Benedict Weld-Blundell. R. & T. Washbourne, 1937.

Needham, Francis, ed. *A Collection of Poems by Several Hands*. Welbeck Miscellany 2 (1934).

Newstead, Christopher. *An Apology for Women: Or, Women's Defence*. 1620.

Niccholes, Alexander. *A Discourse of Marriage and Wiving*. 1615.

Nicols, Thomas. *A Lapidary: Or, The History of Pretious Stones*. Cambridge: 1652.

North, Dudley, third Lord North. *A Forest of Varieties*. 1645.

North, Roger. *The Lives of the Norths*. Ed. A. Jessop. 3 vols. 1890.

Osborne, Dorothy. *The Letters of Dorothy Osborne to William Temple*. Ed. G. C. Moore Smith. Oxford: Clarendon Press, 1928.

Overbury, Sir Thomas. *His Wife with Additions of New Characters*. 16th ed. 1638.

The Petitions of the Widows, in and about London and Westminster for a Redress of their Grievances. 1693.

Philips, Joan. *Advice to His Grace*. 1681.

——. *Female Poems On Several Occasions*. 1679.

Philips, Katherine. *Familiar Letters*. 1697.

——. *Letters from Orinda to Poliarchus*. 1705.

——. *Poems*. 1678. In Saintsbury, ed., 1: 485–612.

Piccolomini, A. *Della Bella Creanza delle Donne*. 1539.

Poems by Eminent Ladies. 2 vols. 1755.

Pomfret, Thomas. *The Life of the Right Honourable and Religious Lady Christian, Late Countess Dowager of Devonshire*. 1685.

Pope, Mary. *A Treatise of Magistracy*. 1647.

Powell, George. *A Very Good Wife*. 1693.

Primrose, Diana. *A Chaine of Pearle. Or, A Memoriall of the Peerless and Heroick Vertues of Queene Elizabeth*. 1630.

The Private Correspondence of Jane Lady Cornwallis 1613–1644. 1842.

Pyrrye, Christopher. *The Praise and Dispraise of Women*. 1569.

Reyner, Edward. *Orders from the Lord of Hostes for Regulating the Hostes of the Lord*. 1646.

Rich, Barnaby. *The Excellency of Good Women*. 1613.

Richardson, Elizabeth, Baroness Crammond. *A Ladies Legacie to her Daughters*. 1645.

Rowton, Frederic. *Cyclopedia of Female Poets*. Philadelphia: 1939.

The Roxburghe Ballads. 7 vols. 1881. New York: AMS Press, 1981.

Russell, Lady Rachel. *Letters of Lady Rachel Russell*. 4th ed. 1792.

———. *Some Account of the Life of Rachael Wriothesley Lady Russell*. 3d ed. 1820.

Saintsbury, George, ed. *Minor Poets of the Caroline Period*. 3 vols. Oxford: Clarendon Press, 1905.

Saltonstall, Wye. *Picturae Loquentes*. 2d ed. 1635.

Schurman, Anna Maria van. *The Learned Maid: Or, Whether a Maid May be a Scholar*. 1659.

———. *Opuscula*. 1648.

Seymar, William. *Conjugium Conjurium: Or, Some Serious Considerations on Marriage*. 1675.

Shaw, Hester. *Mrs. Shaws Innocency Restored, and Mr. Glendons Calumny Retorted*. 1653.

———. *A Plaine Relation of my Sufferings*. 1653.

Shirley, John. *The Illustrious History of Women, Or a Compendium of the Many Virtues that Adorn the Fair Sex*. 1686.

Smyth, John. *The Lives of the Berkeleys*. Ed. Sir John Maclean. Gloucester: 1883–85.

Sprint, John. *The Bride-Woman's Counsellor*. 1699.

Stafford, Anthony. *The Female Glory*. 1635.

Sutcliffe, Alice. *Meditations of Man's Mortalitie. Or A Way to True Blessedness*. 1634.

Swetnam, Joseph. *The Arraignment of Lewd, Idle, Froward, and Unconstant Women*. 1628.

Swetnam, the Woman-Hater, Arraigned by Women. 1620.

Tattlewell, Mary, and Ioan Hit-Him-Home. *The Womens Sharpe Revenge*. 1640.

Taylor, John. *A Iuniper Tree Lecture. With the Description of all Sorts of Women, Good and Bad*. 2d ed. 1635.

Thoresby, Ralph. *The Diary of Ralph Thoresby*. Ed. Joseph Hunter. 2 vols. 1830.

———. *Ducatus Leodiensis: Or, The Topography of the Antient and Populous Town and parish of Leedes*. 1740.

Tixall Letters: Or, the Correspondence of the Aston Family and their Friends during the 17th Century. Ed. Arthur Clifford. 2 vols. 1815.

Tixall Poetry. Ed. Arthur Clifford. 1813.

Trapnel, Anna. *The Cry of a Stone: Or a Relation of Something spoken in Whitehall.* 1654.

A True Copy of the Petition of the Gentlewomen and Tradesmens Wives. 1642. In *The Harleian Miscellany* 5 (1810): 268–72.

Tuvill, Daniel. *Assylum Veneris, Or a Sanctuary for Ladies.* 1616.

Waite, Mary. *A Warning to All Friends.* 1679. Augustan Reprint Society 194 (1979).

Walsh, William. *A Dialogue Concerning Women, Being a Defence of the Sex.* 1691.

_____. *Letters and Poems, Amorous and Gallant.* 1692.

Ward, Richard. *The Life of the Learned and Pious Dr. Henry More.* 1710.

Wharton, Anne. *The Temple of Death.* 1695.

Whartoniana: Or Miscellanies in Verse and Prose by The Wharton Family. 2 vols. 1727.

White, Dorothy. *An Alarm Sounded to Englands Inhabitants.* 1661.

_____. *A Call from God out of Egypt.* 1662.

_____. *An Epistle of Love, and of Consolation.* 1661.

_____. *A Trumpet of the Lord of Hosts Blown Unto the City of London.* 1662.

_____. *Unto All Gods Host in England.* 1660.

_____. *Upon the 22 Day of the 8th Month, 1659.* 1659.

_____. *A Visitation of Heavenly Love Unto the Seed of Jacob yet in Captivity.* 1660.

Whitehall, Robert. *To the No Less Virtuous Than Ingenious Mris Mary More.* 1674.

Wing, John. *The Crown Conjugall Or The Spouse Royall.* 1620.

With, Elizabeth. *Elizabeth Fools Warning.* 1659.

The Women's Petition. 1651.

Wood, Anthony à. *Athenaes Oxonienses.* Ed. Philip Bliss. 4 vols. 1813–20.

Woolley, Hannah. *The Gentlewoman's Companion: Or, a Guide to the Female Sex.* 1675.

Young, Edward. *The Idea of Christian Love . . . To which are Added Some Copies of Verses from that Excellent Poetess Mrs. Wharton with others to her.* 1688.

Zins-Pennick, Judith. *Some Worthy Proverbs Left Behind by Judith Zins-Pennick, To be Read in the Congregation.* 1663.

SECONDARY SOURCES

Acworth, Evelyn. *The New Matriarchy.* Victor Gollancz, 1965.

Ariès, Philippe, and André Béjin, eds. *Western Sexuality: Practice and Precept in Past and Present Times.* Trans. Anthony Forster. Oxford: Basil Blackwell, 1985.

Armitage, Evelyn Noble. *The Quaker Poets of Great Britain and Ireland.* 1896.

Barker, Arthur. "Christian Liberty in Milton's Divorce Pamphlets." *Modern Language Review* 35 (1940): 153–61.

Barker, Francis, et al. *1642: Literature and Power in the Seventeenth Century*. Colchester: Univ. of Essex Press, 1981.

Bell, Susan Groag. "Medieval Women Book Owners: Arbiters of Lay Piety and Ambassadors of Culture." *Signs* 7 (1982): 742–67.

Bernikow, Louise, ed. *The World Split Open: Women Poets 1552–1950*. Women's Press, 1979.

Betham, Matilda. *A Biographical Dictionary of the Celebrated Women of Every Age and Country*. 1804.

Bettey, J. H. "Marriages of Convenience by Copyholders in Dorset during the Seventeenth Century." *Dorset Natural History and Archaeological Proceedings* 98 (1976).

Birch, Una. *Anna Maria van Schurman*. Longmans, 1909.

Boucé, Paul-Gabriel, ed. *Sexuality in Eighteenth-Century Britain*. Manchester: Manchester Univ. Press, 1982.

Bouten, Jacob. *Mary Wollstonecraft and the Beginnings of Female Emancipation in France and England*. Philadelphia: Porcupine Press, 1975.

Bower, Reuben A. "Lady Winchilsea and the Poetic Tradition of the Seventeenth Century." *Studies in Philology* 42 (Jan. 1945): 61–80.

Brailsford, Mabel Richmond. *Quaker Women 1650–1690*. Duckworth, 1915.

Brink, J. R. "Bathsua Makin: Scholar and Educator of the Seventeenth Century." *International Journal of Women's Studies* 1 (1978): 417–26.

————. *Female Scholars: A Tradition of Learned Women Before 1800*. Montreal: Eden Press, 1980.

Bullough, Vern L., and Bonnie Bullough. *The Subordinate Sex: A History of Attitudes Towards Women*. Urbana: Univ. of Illinois Press, 1973.

Burke, A. M. *Memorials of St. Margaret's Church, Westminster*. Eyre & Spottiswoode, 1914.

Buyze, Jean, ed. *The Tenth Muse: Women Poets Before 1806*. Berkeley, Calif.: Shameless Hussy Press, 1980.

Carlton, Charles. *The Court of Orphans*. Leicester: Leicester Univ. Press, 1974.

Carroll, Berenice A., ed. *Liberating Women's History*. Urbana: Univ. of Illinois Press, 1976.

Case, Arthur E. *A Bibliography of English Poetical Miscellanies 1521–1750*. Oxford: Bibliographical Society, 1935.

Clark, Alice. *The Working Life of Women in the Seventeenth Century*. George Routledge & Sons, 1919.

Clark Peter, ed. *The Transformation of English Provincial Towns 1600–1800*. Hutchinson, 1984.

Clark, Sandra. *The Elizabethan Pamphleteers: Popular Moralistic Pamphlets 1580–1640*. Rutherford, N.J.: Fairleigh Dickinson Univ. Press, 1983.

Clayton, Ellen. *English Female Artists*. 2 vols. 1876.

Craster, H. H. "Notes from a Delaval 'Diary.'" *Proceedings of the Society of Antiquarians of Newcastle-Upon-Tyne* 3d series, 1 (1905), 149–53.

Crawford, Patricia. "Women's Published Writings 1600–1700." In Prior, ed., pp. 211–82.

Culler, Jonathan. *On Deconstruction: Theory and Criticism.* Ithaca, N.Y.: Cornell Univ. Press, 1982.

Daly, James. *Sir Robert Filmer and English Political Thought.* Toronto: Univ. of Toronto Press, 1979.

————. "Some Problems in the Authorship of Sir Robert Filmer's Works." *English Historical Review* 98 (Oct. 1983): 737–62.

Davies, Kathleen M. "Continuity and Change in Literary Advice on Marriage." In Outhwaite, ed., pp. 58–80.

Day, Robert Adams. "Muses in the Mud: The Female Wits Anthropologically Considered." *Women's Studies* 7 (1980): 61–74.

de Bruyn, Jan. "The Ideal Lady and the Rise of Feminism in Seventeenth-Century England." *Mosaic* 17 (Winter 1984): 19–28.

Dupâquiet, J., et al., eds. *Marriage and Remarriage in Populations of the Past.* Academic Press, 1981.

Dusinberre, Juliet. *Shakespeare and the Nature of Women.* Macmillan, 1975.

Ellet, Elizabeth Fries. *Women Artists in All Ages and Countries.* 1859.

Elliott, Vivien Brodsky. "Single Women in the London Marriage Market: Age, Status and Mobility, 1598–1619." In Outhwaite, ed., pp. 81–100.

Ezell, Margaret J. M. "Richard Waller, S.R.S.: 'In the Pursuit of Nature.'" *Notes and Records of the Royal Society of London* 38 (1984): 215–33.

Fetterley, Judith. *The Resisting Reader: A Feminist Approach to American Fiction.* Bloomington: Indiana Univ. Press, 1978.

Figes, Eva. *Patriarchal Attitudes: Women in Society.* Faber & Faber, 1970.

Finlay, Roger. *Population and Metropolis: The Demography of London 1580–1650.* Cambridge: Cambridge Univ. Press, 1981.

Ford, Robert. "The Filmer Manuscripts: A Handlist." *Notes* 34 (1978): 814–25.

Foster, Joseph. *London Marriage Licenses 1521–1869.* 1887.

Frank, Joseph. *Hobbled Pegasus: A Descriptive Bibliography of Minor English Poetry 1641–1660.* Albuquerque: Univ. of New Mexico Press, 1968.

Fraser, Antonia. *The Weaker Vessel: Women's Lot in Seventeenth-century England.* Weidenfeld & Nicolson, 1984.

Gagen, Jean. *The New Woman: Her Emergence in English Drama 1600–1730.* New York: Twayne Publishers, 1954.

Gardiner, Dorothy. *English Girlhood at School.* Oxford Univ. Press, 1929.

Gilbert, Sandra M., and Susan Gubar, eds. *The Norton Anthology of Literature by Women.* New York: W. W. Norton, 1985.

Glass, D. V. *London Inhabitants Within the Walls.* London: Record Society, 1966.

Godfrey, Elizabeth [pseud.]. *Home Life Under the Stuarts 1603–1649.* Stanley Paul & Co., 1925.

Goldberg, Steven. *The Inevitability of Patriarchy.* New York: William Morrow, 1973.

Goreau, Angeline. *Reconstructing Aphra: A Social Biography of Aphra Behn*. Oxford Univ. Press, 1980.

———. "Two English Women in the Seventeenth Century: Notes for an Anatomy of Feminine Desire." In Ariès and Béjin, eds., pp. 103–13.

Gosse, Edmund. "Catherine Trotter, The Precursor of the Blue-Stockings." *Transactions of the Royal Society of Literature* 34 (1916).

Goulianos, Joan, ed. *By a Woman Writt: Literature from Six Centuries by and about Women*. Baltimore: Penguin Books, 1973.

Green, David. *Sarah, Duchess of Marlborough*. New York: Charles Scribner's Sons, 1967.

Greer, Germaine. *The Obstacle Race*. Secker & Warburg, 1979.

Greg, W. W. *Some Aspects and Problems of London Publishing between 1550 and 1650*. Oxford: Clarendon Press, 1956.

Higgins, Patricia. "The Reactions of Women, with Special Reference to Women Petitioners." In Manning, ed., pp. 178–222.

Hindle, C. J. *A Bibliography of the Printed Pamphlets and Broadsides of Lady Eleanor Douglas, the Seventeenth-century Prophetess*. Edinburgh: Edinburgh Bibliographical Society, 1936.

Hindley, Charles, ed. *The Roxburghe Ballads*. 2 vols. 1873–74.

Hinton, R. W. H. "Husbands, Fathers and Conquerors." *Political Studies* 15 (1967): 291–300.

Hole, Christina. *The English Housewife in the Seventeenth Century*. Chatto and Windus, 1953.

Hull, Suzanne W. *Chaste, Silent & Obedient: English Books for Women 1475–1640*. San Marino, Calif.: Huntington Library, 1982.

Jaggar, Alison. "Political Philosophies of Women's Liberation." In *Feminism and Philosophy*, ed. Mary Vetterling-Braggin, Frederick A. Ellison, Jane English. Totowa, N.J.: Littlefield, Adams, 1978, pp. 5–21.

Jenkins, Philip. "Mary Wharton and the Rise of the 'New Woman.'" *National Library of Wales Journal* 22 (Winter 1981): 170–86.

Johnson, James T. "The Covenant Idea and the Puritan View of Marriage." *Journal of the History of Ideas* 32 (Jan./March 1971): 107–18.

Kassmaul, Ann. *Servants in Husbandry in Early Modern England*. Cambridge: Cambridge Univ. Press, 1981.

Kinnaird, Joan. "Mary Astell: Inspired by Ideas." In *Feminist Theorists*, ed. Dale Spender, pp. 28–39. New York: Random House, 1983.

Kolodny, Annette. "Dancing Through the Minefield: Some Observations on the Theory, Practice and Politics of a Feminist Literary Criticism." *Feminist Studies* 6 (Spring 1980): 1–25.

Konigsberg, Ira, ed. *American Criticism in the Poststructuralist Age*. Ann Arbor: Michigan Studies in the Humanities. 1981.

LaBelle, Jenijoy. "A True Love's Knot: The Letters of Constance Fowler and the

Poems of Herbert Aston." *Journal of English and Germanic Philology* 79 (Jan. 1980): 13–31.

Laslett, Peter, ed. "The Gentry of Kent in 1640." *Cambridge Historical Journal* 25 (1948): 148–64.

———. *Household and Family in Past Time.* Cambridge: Cambridge Univ. Press, 1978.

———. "Sir Robert Filmer: The Man Versus the Whig Myth." *William and Mary Quarterly* 3d series, 5 (Oct. 1948): 523–46.

———. *The World We Have Lost—Further Explored.* Methuen, 1983.

———. "The Wrong Way through the Telescope: A Note on Literary Evidence in Sociology and in Historical Sociology." *British Journal of Sociology* 27 (Sept. 1976): 319–42.

Latt, David J. "Praising Virtuous Ladies: The Literary Image and Historical Reality of Women in Seventeenth-Century England." In Springer, ed., pp. 39–63.

Le Neve's Pedigrees of Knights. Ed. George W. Marshall. Harleian Society, 1873.

Leites, Edmund. "The Duty to Desire: Love, Friendship and Sexuality in some Puritan Theories of Marriage." *Comparative Civilizations Review* 3 (Fall 1979): 40–82.

Lewalski, Barbara. "Milton on Women—Yet Once More." *Milton Studies* 6 (1974): 3–20.

McArthur, Ellen A. "Women Petitioners and the Long Parliament." *English Historical Review* 24 (1909): 698–709.

McColley, Diane Kelsey. *Milton's Eve.* Urbana: Univ. of Illinois Press, 1983.

Mahl, Mary R., and Helene Koon, eds. *The Female Spectator: English Women Writers Before 1800.* Bloomington: Indiana Univ. Press, 1977.

Malekin, Peter. *Liberty and Love: English Literature and Society 1640–88.* Hutchinson, 1981.

Manners, Emily. *Elizabeth Hooton: First Quaker Woman Preacher (1600–1672).* Headley Brothers, 1914.

Manning, Brian, ed. *Politics, Religion and the English Civil War.* New York: St. Martin's Press, 1973.

Marshall, Rosalind K. *Virgins and Viragos: A History of Women in Scotland from 1080–1980.* Collins, 1983.

Meyer, Gerald Dennis. *The Scientific Lady in England 1650–1760.* Berkeley and Los Angeles: Univ. of California Press, 1955.

Morgan, Fidelis, ed. *The Female Wits: Women Playwrights of the Restoration.* Virago Press, 1981.

Notestein, Wallace. "The English Woman 1580 to 1650." *Studies in Social History: A Tribute to G. M. Trevelyan.* Longmans, 1955, pp. 71–107.

Nussbaum, Felicity. *The Brink of All We Hate: English Satire on Women, 1660–1750.* Lexington: Univ. Press of Kentucky, 1984.

Outhwaite, R. B. "Age at Marriage in England from the Late Seventeenth to the Nineteenth Century." *Journal of the Royal Historical Society* 5th series, 23 (1973): 55–70.

———, ed. *Marriage and Society: Studies in the Social History of Marriage*. Europa Publications, 1981.

Oyler, T. G. "East Sutton Church." *Archaelogia Cantiana* 25 (1902): lvi.

Palomo, Dolores. "A Woman Writer and the Scholars: A Review of Mary Manley's Reputation." *Women and Literature* 6 (1978): 34–46.

Perry, Ruth. "The Veil of Chastity: Mary Astell's Feminism." *Studies in Eighteenth-Century Culture* 9 (1979): 25–43.

Pinto, Vivian de Sola. *Enthusiast in Wit*. Rev. ed. Routledge & Kegan Paul, 1962.

Prior, Mary, ed. *Women in English Society 1500–1800*. Methuen, 1985.

Quaife, G. R. *Wanton Wenches and Wayward Wives: Peasants and Illicit Sex in Early Seventeenth Century England*. Croom Helm, 1979.

Randall, Dale B. J. *Gentle Flame: The Life and Verse of Dudley, Fourth Lord North (1602–1677)*. Durham, N.C.: Duke Univ. Press, 1983.

The Register of the Parish of Addington. Ed. William Bradbrook. Bucks Parish Register Society, 1916.

Reynolds, Myra. *The Learned Lady in England 1650–1760*. Boston: Houghton Mifflin, 1920.

Richetti, John. *Popular Fiction Before Richardson: Narrative Patterns 1700–1739*. Oxford: Clarendon Press, 1969.

Rogers, Katherine, ed. *Before Their Times: Six Women Writers of the Eighteenth Century*. New York: Frederick Ungar, 1979.

Ross, Isabel. *Margaret Fell, Mother of Quakerism*. Longmans, 1949.

Rowbotham, Sheila. *Hidden from History: Three Hundred Years of Women's Oppression and the Fight Against It*. Pluto Press, 1973.

Saunders, J. W. *The Profession of English Letters*. Routledge & Kegan Paul, 1964.

———. "The Stigma of Print: A Note on the Social Bases of Tudor Poetry." *Essays in Criticism* 1 (April 1951): 139–64.

Schochet, Gordon J. *Patriarchalism and Political Thought*. New York: Basic Books, 1975.

———. "Sir Robert Filmer: Some New Bibliographical Discoveries." *The Library* (June 1971): 136–60.

Sheavyn, Phoebe. *The Literary Profession in the Elizabethan Age*. 2d ed. rev. New York: Barnes & Noble, 1967.

Shepherd, Simon. *Amazons and Warrior Women: Varieties of Feminism in Seventeenth-Century Drama*. New York: St. Martin's Press, 1981.

Showalter, Elaine. "Feminist Criticism in the Wilderness." *Critical Inquiry* (Winter 1981): 179–205.

———. *A Literature of Their Own: British Women Novelists from Brontë to Lessing*. Princeton: Princeton Univ. Press, 1977.

Smith, Charlotte Fell. *Mary Rich, Countess of Warwick (1625–78) Her Family and Friends*. New York: Longmans, 1901.

Smith, Florence M. *Mary Astell*. New York: Columbia Univ. Press, 1916.

Smith, Hilda. "Feminism and the Methodology of Women's History." In Carroll, ed., pp. 368–84.

————. *Reason's Disciples: Seventeenth-Century English Feminists*. Urbana: Univ. of Illinois Press, 1982.

Souden, David. "Migrants and the Population Structure of Seventeenth-Century Provincial Cities and Market Towns." In Clark, ed., *The Transformation of English Provincial Towns*, pp. 133–68.

————. "Pre-Industrial English Local Migration Fields." Ph.D. diss., Cambridge Univ., 1981.

Souers, Philip Webster. *The Matchless Orinda*. Cambridge: Harvard Univ. Press, 1931.

Spencer, Thomas. "The History of an Unfortunate Lady." *Harvard Studies and Notes in Philology and Literature* 20 (1938): 43–59.

Spivak, Gayatri Chakravorty. "Finding Feminist Readings: Dante-Yeats." In Konigsberg, ed., pp. 42–65.

Springer, Marlene, ed. *What Manner of Woman*. Blackwell, 1977.

Spufford, Margaret. *Constrasting Communities: English Villagers in the Sixteenth and Seventeenth Century*. Cambridge: Cambridge Univ. Press, 1974.

————. *Small Books and Pleasant Histories: Popular Fiction and its Readership in Seventeenth-Century England*. Athens: Univ. of Georgia Press, 1981.

Stanglmaier, Karl. *Mrs. Jane Barker: Ein Beitrag zur Englischen Literaturgeschichte*. Berlin: Druck von E. Ebering, 1906.

Stecher, Henry F. *Elizabeth Singer Rowe, The Poetess of Frome: A Study in Eighteenth-Century Pietism*. European University Papers, series 14, vol. 5. Bern: Herbert Lange, 1973.

Stenton, Doris Mary. *The English Woman in History*. George Allen & Unwin, 1957.

Stephens, J. S., ed. *John Aubrey on Education*. Routledge & Kegan Paul, 1972.

Stone, Lawrence. *The Family, Sex and Marriage in England 1500–1800*. Weidenfeld and Nicolson, 1977.

Strong, Roy. "Holbein in England." *Burlington Magazine* 111 (May 1967): 276–81.

Sullivan, Patricia A. "Female Writing Beside the Rhetorical Tradition: Seventeenth-century British Biography and a Female Tradition in Rhetoric." *International Journal of Women's Studies* 3 (1980): 143–60.

Thomas, Keith. "The Double Standard." *Journal of the History of Ideas* 20 (April 1959): 195–216.

————. "Women and the Civil War Sects." In *Crisis in Europe 1560–1660*, ed. Trevor Aston. Routledge & Kegan Paul, 1965, pp. 332–40.

Thompson, Roger. "Popular Reading and Humour in Restoration England."

Journal of Popular Culture 9 (Winter 1975): 653–71.

———. *Women in Stuart England and America*. Routledge & Kegan Paul, 1974.

Upham, A. H. "English *Femmes Savantes* at the End of the Seventeenth Century." *Journal of English and German Philology* 12 (1913): 262–76.

Vieth, David. *Attribution in Restoration Poetry*. New Haven: Yale Univ. Press, 1963.

Walne, Peter. ed. "Henry Filmer of Mulbery Island, Gentleman: A Collection of his Letters from Virginia 1653–1671." *Virginia Magazine of History and Biography* 68 (1960): 148–64.

Walpole, Horace. *Anecdotes of Painting in England*. 3 vols. Strawberry Hill, 1762–63.

Weber, Kurt. *Lucius Cary, Second Viscount Falkland*. New York: Columbia Univ. Press, 1940.

Williams, Charles. *Rochester*. Arthur Baker, 1935.

Williams, E. M. "Women Preachers in the Civil War." *Journal of Modern History* 1 (1929): 561–69.

Wood, John A. "The 'Female Eunuch': An Eighteenth-Century Ideal." *McNeese Review* 26 (1979–80): 40–46.

Woodbridge, Linda. *Women and the English Renaissance: Literature and the Nature of Womankind, 1540–1620*. Chicago: Univ. of Chicago Press, 1984.

Wright, Celeste Turner. "Amazons in Elizabethan Literature." *Studies in Philology* 37 (July 1940): 433–56.

Wrigley, E. A. and R. S. Schofield. *The Population History of England 1541–1871: A Reconstruction*. Edward Arnold, 1981.

Index